Men Talk

Men Talk

Stories in the Making of Masculinities

Jennifer Coates

Blackwell
Publishing

P
120
,M45
C6
2003

350 Main Street, Malden, MA 02148-5018, USA
108 Cowley Road, Oxford OX4 1JF, UK
550 Swanston Street, Carlton South, Melbourne, Victoria 3053, Australia
Kurfürstendamm 57, 10707 Berlin, Germany

First published 2003 by Blackwell Publishing Ltd

Library of Congress Cataloging-in-Publication Data

Coates, Jennifer.
Men talk : stories in the making of masculinities / Jennifer Coates.
    p. cm.
  Includes bibliographical references and index. ISBN 0-631-22045-3
  (hardcover : alk. paper) – ISBN 0-631-22046-1 (pbk. : alk. paper)
  1. Men – Language.   2. Discourse analysis, Narrative.   I. Title.

P120.M45 C6   2003
401'.41'081–dc21

2002004262

A catalogue record for this title is available from the British Library.

Set in 10/12.5 pt Meridien
by Graphicraft Limited, Hong Kong
Printed and bound in the United Kingdom
by MPG Books Ltd, Bodmin, Cornwall

For further information on
Blackwell Publishing, visit our website:
http://www.blackwellpublishing.com

Contents

Acknowledgements

I have been working on this book for many years, in the sense that I started collecting recordings of single-sex conversation in the 1980s. These recordings, in particular those of all-male friendship groups, have been at the centre of my research for this book, and my chief debt is unquestionably to the men and boys who agreed to co-operate in the research and to allow their talk to be used in the book. I'm also grateful to the men and their friends and families who allowed their conversation in mixed groups to be recorded for this project.

Some of the recordings I have made use of were made initially by other researchers, including students taking my Conversational Narrative course at the University of Surrey Roehampton. I would like to put on record my gratitude to the following for giving me access to their recordings and/or for acting as intermediaries: Alex Bean, Keith Brown, Robert Clark, Joanne Fieldhouse, Noni Geleit, Elinor Green, Kate Harrington, Jacqueline Huett, Emma Ogden-Hooper, Sarah Pascall, Sarah Prince, Janis Pringle, Andrew Rosta, Julia Stevens, Karl Stuart, Alexandra Thorogood, Amanda Vanstone, Simon Vivian, Jonathan Waldron, Mark Wildsmith and John Wilson.

In chapter 5, where I make comparisons between all-male talk and all-female talk, I drew on the corpus of all-female conversations which I used in *Women Talk*. I would like once again to express my gratitude to all the women and girls who participated in this earlier research and who have allowed their talk to be used in this chapter. I'm particularly grateful to Christine Cheepen for giving me access to all-female conversations she'd recorded.

This book would never have seen the light of day if it hadn't been for the stirling efforts of Louise Aldrich, Mark Aldrich, Julia Stevens and Jacqueline Huett, who helped with transcribing the audio-tapes of the all-male and mixed conversations, and with making notes on these conversations. I am extremely grateful to them for their help.

I would like to acknowledge the support of the following grant-giving bodies who made my research into men's talk and men's narratives possible: the British Academy (small grant, 1997–8); the Arts and Humanities Research Board (Research Leave, 1999); the University of Canterbury, Christchurch, New Zealand (Erskine Fellowship, 1999). The Linguistics Department at the University of Canterbury deserves a special note: they made me very welcome as an Erskine Fellow, and provided a very supportive and stimulating environment. It was in Christchurch that I started to write the book. I'd also like to thank Janet Holmes for inviting me to give a Plenary Lecture at the Language and Gender Symposium held at Victoria University, Wellington, in October 1999: this galvanized me into action and provided me with the core of chapter 3. (I would also like to thank the British Council, who funded the trip to North Island.)

I would also like to pay tribute to the support I have had from my own institution, the University of Surrey Roehampton. The Research Committee awarded me a grant in tandem with the British Academy award which allowed me to buy myself out of some teaching and pay for help with transcription, among other things. The School of English and Modern Languages granted me a semester's Study Leave in 1999–2000 to work on the book, for which I am very grateful. Colleagues in the English Language and Linguistics programme have been unfailingly supportive and have tolerated my obsession with narrative, men and masculinities with great fortitude. I'd like to thank them all, past and present: Frances, Ishtla, Jean, Jo, Judith, Linda and Tope.

Last but definitely not least, many thanks go to those who have read and commented on earlier drafts of individual chapters: Michael Bamberg, Wallace Chafe, Jenny Cheshire, Elizabeth Gordon, Margaret Gottschalk, Alison Kuiper, Dick Leith, Mary Porter, Joanna Thornborrow, John Tosh and Mark Turner. I'm also indebted to people who gave me feedback after papers I presented. Many of these were strangers, so I cannot name them here, but their questions and comments have influenced my thinking so I would like to acknowledge their contribution to the book by listing the events concerned: the Symposium on Language and Gender, Victoria University, Wellington, 1999; seminars and public lectures organized by the Linguistics Department at the University of Canterbury, 1999; the Symposium on Narrative and Identity organized by Michael Bamberg at Clark University, Worcester, Massachusetts, USA, in March 2000; Sociolinguistics

Symposium, University of the West of England, April 2000; the BAAL Annual Conference, Cambridge, September 2000; Cardiff University Round Table on Narrative, Gregynogg, 2001. I should also mention the support I have had from everyone at Blackwell, particularly from Philip Carpenter, who believed in the book from the beginning and who gave me invaluable feedback, and from Margaret Aherne, a star copy-editor.

Finally, very particular thanks go to Margaret Gottschalk who has read every chapter more than once, who asked provocative questions and made challenging comments, and who has always believed in the book. I'm enormously grateful for her support (and for the fact that she didn't let me starve when I was in the throes of completing the final manuscript).

The imperfections of the book are of course my own.

Jennifer Coates
London, January 2002

Transcription Conventions

The transcription conventions used for the conversational data are as follows:

- Capital letters are used for words/syllables uttered with emphasis, e.g.

  they're BASTARDS honest

- A hyphen indicates an incomplete word or utterance, e.g.

  I must admit-
  is that the one with all the loa- lots of different things on it?
  y- y- your paint?

- Short pauses (less than 0.5 second) are indicated by a full stop with space on either side, e.g.

  well . he was quite frightened

  Longer pauses are given in round brackets, and timed to the nearest second, e.g.

  I'm just trying to think what I've done lately (6.0)

- An equals sign at the end of one speaker's utterance and at the start of the next utterance indicates the absence of a discernible gap, e.g.

  Geoff: oh that are- that are about that big=
  Chris: =it's tiny . with WAP services

- The symbol .hh indicates that the speaker takes a sharp intake of breath, e.g.

  so then I- .hh I had a look at the fuses

Transcription Conventions

- The symbol % encloses words or phrases that are spoken very quietly, e.g.

  %fuck it%

- The symbol → indicates that the line to the right of the arrow is the one to pay attention to.

- The symbol [. . .] indicates that material has been omitted.

- Angled brackets give additional information, e.g.

  John: <LAUGHS>

- Angled brackets also add clarificatory information about underlined words, e.g.

  <u>can I have some pot noodles please Kevin</u> <SILLY VOICE>

- Double round parentheses indicates that there is doubt about the accuracy of the transcription, e.g.

  ((hurt himself))

- Where speech is impossible to make out, it is represented as ((1 syll)) or ((xxx)), e.g.

  ((xx)) name
  it's ((2 sylls))

- A question mark indicates the end of a chunk of talk which I am analysing as a question, e.g.

  did he have to sit down and stuff?

- A slash (/) indicates the end of a tone group or chunk of talk, e.g.:

  it nearly had him out/

- Words in italics in square brackets give listener's responses, e.g.

  and now the fucker won't start [*oh no*]

- Words appearing between asterisks on adjacent lines were spoken at the same time, e.g.

  Henry: but I really couldn't **climb into your bed in the morning**
  Julian: **yeah that- that was fairly-** that was unfortunate

- A broken line marks the beginning of a stave and indicates that the lines of text enclosed by the lines are to be read simultaneously (like a musical score), e.g.

```
Alan:   it nearly had him out/ <LAUGHS> he come out all white/
Chris:                          <LAUGHS>
Kevin:                             <LAUGHS>
```

- An extended square bracket indicates the start of overlap between utterances, e.g.

```
Alan:   he was quite frightened ⌈actually/
John:                           ⌊I know/
```

For Margaret

1

'We Was Playing Naked Football the Other Night': Introduction

What is men's talk like? If the stereotypes are to be believed, men either don't talk much (strong and silent) or talk compulsively and competitively about sport, cars and drinking exploits. Are these stereotypes accurate? Do they apply to men's talk in all contexts or just to all-male talk? In other words, do men talk differently when they are with other men rather than in mixed company? And does all-male talk differ from all-female talk? These are some of the questions that will be explored in this book.

Everyone will have their own views on men's talk, but we can only find out what men's talk is like by examining examples of real conversation. Here is an extract from a conversation involving four men, Dave, Chaz, Ewan and George:

George: we was playing naked football the other night, like it was only about half eleven, er-

Chaz: play that often, do you?

George: well I was- in our pants like, we were only kicking it about back I live off

Chaz: what, in your duds or wi' fuck all?

George: duds, and boots like [. . .] fucking next-door neighbour comes out like that fucking Gareth or whatever he's called from-

Dave: is that what he's called?

George: 'I'm from Wales' <MOCK WELSH ACCENT> fucking

Dave: 'hello I'm from Wales' <MOCK WELSH ACCENT> <LAUGHTER>

George: and he comes out and says-

Dave: fucking opening line

George: 'don't you think you're being a bit unreasonable playing football at this time on a Monday night?' I says 'Fuck off <LAUGHTER> yer bunch of knobheads, go on fuck off back inside' <LAUGHTER> full of beer, funny.[1]

Anyone who lives in Britain or in any country in the Western industrialized world will recognize this as authentic men's talk. Even if the transcript did not give the names of the speakers, we would be in no doubt about their gender, and could also guess that they are younger rather than older men. What is it about this talk that we recognize as masculine? Is it the fact that the extract starts with a boast (*we was playing naked football the other night*)? Is it the topic (football)? Is it the swearing (*fucking, fuck off, knobheads*)?

Boasting, swearing and topics such as football are characteristic of men's talk, as I hope to show. But there are other points to notice about the extract that are revealing about men's talk and about masculinity. First, when Chaz queries the idea of naked football (line 4), George reveals that he and his friends had actually been wearing underpants as well as football boots. This suggests that the boasting persona he begins with is not as robust as might appear, and that there is some ambivalence about the idea of male nakedness. Another point to notice is the work George and Dave do as a joint effort to construct the neighbour, Gareth, as 'other'. They make fun of his Welshness by mimicking his accent and they pretend not to be sure of his name. In so doing they construct themselves as the 'in-group', people who understand that having a game of football at half-past eleven at night in your underpants is a cool thing to do.

Even in this short stretch of talk, the four men are collaborating in making claims about who they are and who they are not. This is George's story, but through their appreciative acceptance of the story (shown in particular through laughter) his three friends signal their concurrence with the position it marks out. They are men who enjoy a drink and a game of football; they are not people who worry about whether eleven-thirty is a 'reasonable' time to be outside playing football. They present themselves as laddish rebels against convention. It is also salient that they present themselves as not Welsh. Identity work of this kind is one of the key functions of talk among friends. In talk with close friends, we can explore who we are in a more relaxed way than in other, more formal, contexts. The reason that we get such pleasure from friendly interaction is that it has the potential for 'the exchange of recognition'. This phrase was coined by the psycho-analyst Jessica Benjamin to describe the ideal relationship between two people where each acknowledges the real-ness of the other. 'Recognition is that response from the other which makes meaningful the feelings, intentions and actions of the self.'[2] In this book one of my aims is to explore the way talk can perform the work of recognition, and to look at the links between talk and identity. At the same time, I want to avoid sweeping generalizations and simplistic stereotypes about men and about men's talk.

'Drinking a Quadruple Jack Daniels': Men and Masculinity

Until recently it has been women, not men, who have been the object of scrutiny in gender-orientated research, but since the 1990s the whole issue of men and masculinity has been problematized. In the past, the concepts 'man' and 'person' were often indistinguishable, while 'woman' remained a marked term. However, the elision of male person with person is now being dismantled, and the new focus on men has been accompanied by a huge outpouring of books with titles such as *Masculinity and Power*; *Men, Masculinity and the Media*; *Men, Masculinities and Social Theory*; *Young Masculinities*.[3] These books are the result of work in a wide range of disciplines: sociology, anthropology, psychology, media studies, literary criticism. But whatever their disciplinary framework, all of them provide evidence that the idea that maleness was somehow unmarked is no longer accepted. 'Scholars have begun to examine men's lives and experiences, not simply as normative assumptions, but as gendered and socially and historically variable.'[4]

A case in point is the conversational extract involving George and his friends. It comes from an article published in *The Sociological Review* entitled 'The beer talking: four lads, a carry out and the reproduction of masculinities'. The article was written after one of the two co-authors invited his friends to his flat for a beer and a 'carry out' and recorded the evening's conversation. The authors' aim was 'a detailed exploration of one all-male gathering and the ways in which four young white heterosexual men [. . .] negotiate and reproduce a range of masculinities whilst drinking alcohol'.[5] This aim illustrates the shift in men's view of themselves – a shift from seeing themselves as unmarked representatives of the human race to focusing on themselves *as men*. The two male authors of this article reflect on their everyday lives as men, and explore the ways in which drinking and talking in all-male groups serves to construct and maintain norms of masculinity.

Work in sociolinguistics has followed the same trend, with a shift from male speakers as unmarked to male speakers in focus. One of the most important sociolinguistic works of the 1970s was an account of the language of Black male adolescents and pre-adolescents entitled *Language in the Inner City*. The title ignores the fact that the language analysed in the book is *male* language. By contrast, a collection of articles on the language use of male speakers in the 1990s is entitled simply *Language and Masculinity*. This latter book was the first to focus explicitly on men and language.[6]

So we are now beginning to build up a picture of men's talk, but what we know is skewed to young men and adolescents and to non-domestic contexts such as the street, the pub and the sports changing room. We know, for example, about the linguistic behaviour of Black male adolescents in Harlem; of white adolescent boys in Reading; of rugby players in New Zealand; of college athletes in Ohio, USA; of unemployed men in the English West Midlands; of young working-class men in Barcelona; and of male university students in many parts of the world (South Africa, the USA, Britain).[7]

In this book, I shall build on these earlier accounts to give a broader account of men's talk at the turn of the twenty-first century. I shall attempt to show how masculinity is constructed in talk, and to show how men's talk sustains and perpetuates 'hegemonic' masculinity,[8] that is, ' "approved" ways of being male'.[9] Inevitably, dominant or hegemonic modes of masculinity come into conflict with other, alternative, masculinities. At any moment in time there is a range of masculinities extant in a culture, masculinities which differ in terms of class, sexual orientation, ethnicity, age, and so on. And these masculinities intersect in complex ways. So although I shall some-times use the term 'masculinity' as a convenience, rather than the plural form 'masculinities', that does not mean that I subscribe to a notion of some essential masculinity that can be treated as con-stant across time and space.[10] Moreover, masculinity cannot be under-stood on its own: the concept is essentially relational. In other words, masculinity is meaningful only when it is understood in relation to femininity.[11]

I shall draw on a data-base of spontaneous conversation among men friends which includes men from all social classes and a wide range of ages. I shall focus on male friendship groups with the aim of investigating men's talk at its most relaxed and informal. I shall look at male conversation in general, but will concentrate on the narratives produced within these conversations.

'A Funny Thing Happened Today': Story-telling in Conversation

We all take part in a multiplicity of conversations every day of our lives, but we spend little or no time thinking about what exactly conversation is or what it does. Conversations can be analysed in terms of two main components: discussion and narrative.[12] Discussion refers to those parts of conversation where a topic is established and conversational participants exchange views on that topic, whether it be Manchester United's chances of winning the League or the growing of genetically modified foods in Britain. Narrative refers to those parts of conversation where an individual tells a story about something they have done recently or that has happened to them in the past. One of the reasons that friends meet is to catch up, and this is usually done by exchanging stories. Story-telling is the way we present to each other what has been happening in our lives.

The discussion parts of conversation tend to involve all participants, who make brief contributions to the topic in hand. When you listen to conversation, there is a general noisiness about discussion sections which results from everybody's involvement. When somebody starts to tell a story, however, other participants listen in a different, more attentive way, at least initially. In other words, telling a story gives a conversational participant special rights to the floor. This doesn't mean that other participants remain silent – they will often chip in with comments – but there is an understanding that a story is being told and that the narrator will hold the floor until the story is finished.

Most conversations are full of stories. The example at the beginning of this chapter involves George telling a story to the others about himself. It is easier to identify it as a story if the comments from other participants are omitted:

1   we was playing naked football the other night,
2   like it was only about half eleven, er-
3   [. . .]
4   fucking next-door neighbour comes out like that fucking Gareth or whatever he's called from-
5   'I'm from Wales' <MOCK WELSH ACCENT> fucking-
6   and he comes out and says,
7   'don't you think you're being a bit unreasonable playing football at this time on a Monday night?'

8   I says 'Fuck off <LAUGHTER> yer bunch of knobheads,
9   go on fuck off back inside' <LAUGHTER>
10   full of beer,
11   funny.

This is a typical conversational narrative. It describes an event in George's recent past ('the other night') when he came into conflict with a neighbour. The neighbour represents mainstream values ('don't you think you're being a bit unreasonable playing football at this time on a Monday night?') while George and his mates represent laddish values. Men's stories often focus on conflict, as we shall see in later chapters. Story-tellers also use dialogue or reported speech to dramatize events and animate characters. George presents the clash between the neighbour's values and his own through what they say to each other: the neighbour's words represent him as a calm adult who appeals to reason, while George presents himself as intransigent, as not open to reason, and talking with a Manchester accent. Another typical feature of this story is its ending. George's final comment 'funny' tells his audience what he feels about the story and shows them how it is meant to be evaluated. Adjectives such as 'funny', 'weird', 'incredible', are common at the end of stories. A full account of the way stories are structured will be given in the next chapter.

So why are most conversations full of stories? We couldn't function *without* telling stories, but we tend to be unaware of their significance in our lives. Every culture provides its members with what Jerome Bruner calls a 'tool kit' for constructing narratives: a set of canonical characters (heroes, villains, tricksters, etc.) and canonical plots.[13] As fully fledged members of our culture, we use tools from the tool kit to make sense of our lives, to establish some order and to explain why things happened the way they did. These tools allow us to establish our continuity over place and time, and to give our lives shape and meaning. Try to imagine what it would feel like if daily experience was perceived as 'a series of discrete, endlessly juxtaposed moments'.[14] In fact, an individual's life *could* be described as a series of discrete, endlessly juxtaposed moments, but human beings seem to need to interpret this series of moments as coherent and goal-directed. We do this by giving our experience a narrative framework. In other words, our thinking and understanding is fundamentally narrative in character.

This means that narrative has a crucial role to play in our construction of our identities, in our construction of the 'self'. Just as we use narrative modes of thinking to make sense of what we call our 'life', so we present ourselves to others by means of narratives, shaping and selecting events to create particular versions of the self.[15] And because the narrative tool box of any given culture is particular to that culture, then the stories we tell also play a key role in our locating of ourselves in a social and cultural world.[16] Without narrative order, our lives would lack a sense of meaning and direction.[17]

Every aspect of story-telling contributes to our presentation of self: it is not only first-person accounts of our lives which do this. The characters we construct in our story-telling and their relationships with each other, our attitudes as narrators to the characters in our stories and their actions, the voices we use to animate characters in chunks of direct speech, all combine to express who we are.

'The Scary Fact of Hearing Yourself on a Tape': Collecting the Data

The focus of this book is men's talk and the stories occurring within that talk. The analysis and commentary presented here depend on data collected over several years in the form of audio-recorded talk. These spontaneously occurring conversations were recorded with the men's agreement[18] and were subsequently transcribed for this project.

Thirty-two all-male conversations were collected as part of a wider research project exploring gender differences in language use. The data-base resulting from this project includes all-female and mixed conversation as well as all-male conversations. (Analysis of the all-female conversations has already been published as a book – Women Talk.) Participants in all cases were friends (or close family in the case of some of the mixed conversations): in other words, recordings were made of groups or pairs of people who had a well-established relationship. The choice of pre-existing friendship groups as informants was determined by the need to obtain large amounts of spontaneous speech and to guarantee that such speech was relaxed and informal.[19]

The methodology employed in this research is an innovative form of participant observation: after contact was made with a group, they were asked to take responsibility for recording their conversations.[20] My contact with the groups was often via an intermediary, whose relationship to the group – or to one individual in the group – might be that of friend, colleague, girlfriend, sister, or even housemaster in the case of a group of public school boys. (Of course, these intermediaries were not present when the groups met to talk.) The assumption was made that any self-consciousness induced by the presence of the tape-recorder would be overcome by the strong normative pressure which such groups exert over their members. Participants were simply asked to record themselves when they were with their friends.

Even this aspect of the research produced marked gender differentiation. The women who took part in my research almost invariably recorded themselves in the home. The men, by contrast, recorded themselves in a wide range of settings: in their homes, in pubs, in a restaurant, in a university office after hours, in a youth club, even in a garden shed in the case of one group of dope-smoking adolescent boys. And because male participants in my study seemed to be more sophisticated than female in their use of such gadgets as lapel microphones, they also recorded themselves in unexpected places like men's lavatories and walking along the street to the chip shop. The pub was, however, by far the most popular setting for all-male talk, a finding which is not surprising, given that 'the pub seems to be a pivotal site for both the expression and reinforcement of traditional masculinities and gendered consumption'.[21]

This initial stage of data collection produced a large number of recordings, with some groups proving enthusiastic participants. This data-base was reduced on the principle that no one group should contribute more than five conversations to the corpus. In all, twelve separate groups are represented in the final corpus of thirty-two conversations, though this figure may be misleading, as the groups tended to vary from one recording to the next. In other words, the total of twelve groups disguises the variety of male voices involved here.[22] But it would be equally false to say that there were thirty-two groups (one for each conversation) since the groups tended to have a stable core, consisting of one, two or three speakers, one of whom was always the member of the group who was liaising with the research project and who took responsibility for carrying out recording. An example of fluctuation in group composition is given by the youngest group participating, 15- and 16-year-old boys at a public school. There was a core group of three boys, but one conversation involves only two of them, while another includes a fourth boy. Among older males a similar pattern is found: one group who met in a pub after work consisted of six adult education lecturers, but there were never more than four present on any one occasion, and membership of the group varied on every occasion. This fluidity in the composition of male friendship groups contrasts with the all-female groups involved in this research, which were much more consistent in terms of membership.

'1 Hope This Professor Isn't an Ardent Feminist': Research Dilemmas

Writing this book has not been a straightforward process. I began collecting the data many years ago but was not sure initially if I wanted to use it to write a book. My observations of my own sons and the sons of friends made me curious about men's conversational norms and concerned to come to an understanding of contemporary masculinities. But I was uncomfortable with the position the research put me in. Same-sex talk is by definition exclusive of the opposite sex, so only men participate in all-male talk, just as only women participate in all-female talk. Yet I, a woman, was the person who ended up with the audio-tapes, and in order to transcribe and analyse the conversations, I had to listen to – that is, vicariously participate in – talk which involved only men and which was designed for an all-male group. This made me uncomfortable at first; it made me feel like a voyeur.

But the evidence of the conversations themselves is that participants were not worried about the involvement of a female researcher. For example, two men, Chris and Geoff, start their conversation by discussing the recording process. They have agreed to record themselves over lunch in an Italian restaurant for Chris's girlfriend, Kate, and their talk demonstrates that this is unproblematic as far as they are concerned:

Chris: Kate was telling me apparently the best thing to do is to start
         off with just talking about the fact that you're recording=
Geoff: =well yeah obviously
Chris: which is what makes you then forget that it's on the table
Geoff: that's right well I mean the- although to be honest I'm
         quite used to it because of the- as I said in my e-mail the
         disciplinaries . that I've done
Chris: yeah
Geoff: which all get recorded and the scary-
Chris: that's very scary=
Geoff: =fact of hearing yourself on a tape they a- they actually have
         to translate it all into written as well=

9

Chris: =yeah
Geoff: s- she should actually have some of those because <LAUGH>
Chris: probably
Geoff: they're quite entertaining as long as she sort of scrubbed out
          the names

This opening fragment from their conversation shows quite a sophisticated understanding of what is involved in conversational research: they understand that initially the presence of a tape-recorder may make them self-conscious, they understand that recordings have to be transcribed ('translated into written') and that participants' names have to be changed or 'scrubbed out'. Their use of the name 'Kate' and the pronoun 'she' also demonstrate their understanding that the tape is destined to be heard by a woman.

Younger participants also make occasional comments which make clear that they are aware that the tape will be heard by a female researcher. In fact, the public schoolboys often have fun directing remarks at me. This joking exploitation of the recording situation seems to be a feature of the talk of young people; it occurred in my recordings of all-female talk and has been remarked on by John Wilson in his research on adolescent talk.[23] Their first tape starts with a discussion about the process of being taped and self-consciousness. Their talk *is* initially self-conscious, to the extent that one of them drawls 'must be bloody boring for this poor woman'. Later, the conversation develops into a competition about who drinks most, and about who has 'scored' with members of the opposite sex. (The conversation is by now relaxed and uninhibited.) Robert mentions Julie Smith:[24]

Julian: she is such a slag
Robert: so what – she's an attractive slag
Julian: I hope this professor isn't an ardent feminist, she'll be very
           annoyed

In a conversation recorded nearly eighteen months later, by which time the recording process has become routine, reference to the researcher only happens at rare moments such as the following:

[Arguing about whether or not a fellow student speaks French]
Julian: but the boy speaks French
Henry: he does not . do you want this knife embedded in your face?
Julian: do you want that tape-recorder inserted up your rectum?

Henry: <LAUGHING> she'd get some pretty interesting sounds then
Julian: yeah she would actually

In both these examples, the boys' choice of reference terms ('this poor woman', 'ardent feminist') and their use of the pronoun 'she' demonstrate their understanding that their (all-male) talk will eventually be listened to by a female.

Despite this, I still found listening to the audio-tapes an uncomfortable experience at the beginning. The men's conversations were so unlike conversations I was accustomed to as a female speaker. They struck me initially as either vulgar and aggressive, or extraordinarily tedious in their attention to (technical) detail.

I persisted with the research for a variety of reasons. First, it struck me that male researchers had for centuries studied and analysed women's cultural practices, and that I could at least bring to my study of male cultural practices a feminist sensitivity about the issues raised by cross-gender research of this kind. As a member of the marked category 'woman', I could contribute to the deconstruction of men's unmarked status and could help to bring masculinity into focus. Second, I realized that logically there was no way out of the position I found myself in: if one single researcher was to do comparative work on same-sex talk, then that researcher would inevitably feel like an intruder when it came to the conversations of the other sex. Any solution that involved, say, two researchers, one male and one female, would still have the problem that no real comparative work could be done unless both researchers listened to all the data.

My final reason for sticking with the all-male tapes and carrying out an analysis of these conversations was that, as time went by, I became more comfortable with the recordings as the all-male talk became more familiar to my ears. More importantly, my reading in the growing literature on men and masculinity, and my observations of my sons and the sons of friends growing up in the late twentieth century, made me more aware of the complexities of masculinity and more concerned to develop a better understanding of what it means to be a man in our culture today.

The Structure of the Book

My aim in this book is to use stories told by men as a way in to the basic cultural ideas which lie behind men's lives and masculine identities at the turn of the century in Britain.[25] The focus of the book will be stories told by male speakers to each other in the course of everyday conversation. Previous studies of male narrative have focused on story-telling as performance, a speech event set apart from ordinary talk.[26] The performance narrative is a quintessentially masculine speech event: it can be described as 'a ludic exercise in dominance, control and display'.[27] By contrast, the narratives that are the subject of this book are the kind that every one of us produces every day of our lives, regardless of gender. They occur spontaneously as part of relaxed informal conversation involving friends or family. Such narratives are less self-conscious than performance narratives and are crucially concerned with the self and relationship, though dominance and display may sometimes be themes that are relevant to an understanding of men's stories.

The thirty-two all-male conversations I collected contain a total of 203 stories. These 203 stories range from very short (minimal narratives) to very long. They deal with incidents ranging from the trivial to the life-changing. In some of the stories, the narrator presents himself as the protagonist; in others, the protagonist is a non-present third person. Stories may be set in the distant past – they may be about childhood, about wartime experiences, about what happened in the 1960s; or they may be set in the recent past – what happened yesterday or this morning. The events narrated take place in a wide range of contexts – in the workplace, in the pub, on the sports field, on motorways, up mountains. There are stories of success and also stories of failure. There are stories on stereotypically masculine topics – cars, sport, drink, violence; and stories involving topics that are less obviously masculine – about appendicitis, probability theory, getting planning permission, buying a fridge-freezer.

In the next chapter (chapter 2) I shall analyse the structure of conversational narrative, with the aim of demonstrating what the key constituents of a story are. Chapter 3 will explore the claim that narrative plays a key role in the construction of masculinity, and will examine the range of masculinities expressed in the stories. Chapter 4 will focus on sequences of stories and will ask whether telling stories in sequence allows men to express connection with each other. Chapter 5 will explore gender differences in narrative. Chapter 6 will examine male story-telling in conversations involving women as well as men, focusing on the peer group and the family. Chapter 7 will focus on stories co-narrated by men with a heterosexual partner, and will explore the role of collaborative narrative in mixed talk. The book will close with an overview of men's talk and of the ways in which narrative constructs and maintains the prevailing norms of masculinity.

Notes

1 This extract is taken from the conversational data presented in Brendan Gough and Gareth Edwards, 'The beer talking: four lads, a carry out and the reproduction of masculinities'. Spelling has in places been regularized.
2 Jessica Benjamin, *The Bonds of Love*, p. 12.
3 The books referred to are (in the order mentioned in the text): Arthur Brittan, *Masculinity and Power* (Oxford: Blackwell, 1989); Steve Craig (ed.), *Men, Masculinity and the Media* (London: Sage, 1992); Jeff Hearn and David Morgan (eds), *Men, Masculinities and Social Theory* (London: Unwin Hyman, 1990); Stephen Frosh, Ann Phoenix and Rob Pattman, *Young Masculinities* (London: Palgrave, 2002).
4 Michael Kimmel, 'Rethinking "masculinity"', p. 7.
5 Gough and Edwards, 'The beer talking', p. 411.
6 The two books referred to here are: William Labov, *Language in the Inner City*; Sally Johnson and Ulrike Hanna Meinhof (eds), *Language and Masculinity* (Oxford: Blackwell, 1997).
7 The research referred to here can be found in: Labov, *Language in the Inner City*; Jenny Cheshire, *Variation in an English Dialect*; Koenraad Kuiper, 'Sporting formulae in New Zealand English'; Timothy Curry, 'Fraternal bonding in the locker room'; Sara Willott and Christine Griffin, '"Wham bam, am I a man?": unemployed men talk about masculinities'; Joan Pujolar i Cos, 'Masculinities in a multilingual setting'; Debra Kaminer and John Dixon, 'The reproduction of masculinity: a discourse analysis of men's drinking talk'; Deborah Cameron, 'Performing gender identity: young men's talk and the construction of heterosexual masculinity'; Gough and Edwards, 'The beer talking'.
8 The concept of hegemonic masculinity was developed by Robert Connell and his colleagues working in feminist sociology. According to Connell, in order to carry off 'being a man' in everyday life, men have to engage with hegemonic masculinity. Hegemonic masculinity maintains, legitimates and naturalizes the interests of powerful men while subordinating the interests of others, notably those of women and gay men. See in particular R. W. Connell, *Masculinities*.
9 Frosh, Phoenix and Pattman, *Young Masculinities*, p. 3.
10 For more on the plurality of gender, see Michael Kimmel, *The Gendered Society*, pp. 10–11.
11 Connell, *Masculinities*, p. 68; Kimmel, 'Rethinking "masculinity"', p. 12; Michael Roper and John Tosh, 'Introduction' to *Manful Assertions: Masculinities in Britain since 1800*, p. 2.

12 See Christine Cheepen, *The Predictability of Informal Conversation*; Jennifer Coates, *Women Talk*.

13 Jerome Bruner, 'Life as narrative', p. 15.

14 Kenneth J. Gergen and Mary M. Gergen, 'Narrative and the self as relationship', p. 19.

15 Anthony Kerby, *Narrative and the Self*; Charlotte Linde, *Life Stories: The Creation of Coherence*.

16 Jerome Bruner, 'Autobiography as self'; Wallace Chafe, *Discourse, Consciousness and Time: The Flow and Displacement of Conscious Experience in Speaking and Writing*.

17 Bruno Bettelheim, *The Uses of Enchantment*.

18 I am enormously grateful to all the men and boys who agreed to allow their conversations to be used in this project. Some of the recordings were made initially by other researchers, including students taking my Conversational Narrative course at the University of Surrey Roehampton. I would like to put on record my gratitude to the following for giving me access to these recordings: Alex Bean, Keith Brown, Noni Geleit, Jacqueline Huett, Emma Ogden-Hooper, Janis Pringle, Andrew Rosta, Karl Stuart, Simon Vivian, Mark Wildsmith, John Wilson.

19 See Lesley Milroy, *Observing and Analysing Natural Language*, p. 35.

20 I started using this methodology in 1985. Other sociolinguists who have collected conversational data using a similar approach are John Wilson, *On the Boundaries of Conversation*, and Ben Rampton, *Crossing*.

21 Willott and Griffin, ' "Wham bam, am I a man?" ', p. 115.

22 Fifty-one male speakers were involved in total.

23 Coates, *Women Talk*, pp. 7–8; John Wilson, 'The sociolinguistic paradox'.

24 All names in the transcripts have been changed.

25 See Livia Polanyi: 'story materials [can be used] as an entry into the cluster of basic interwoven ideas which lies behind and supports our daily lives' (*Telling the American Story*, p. 112).

26 For example, Roger Abrahams, *The Man-of-Words in the West Indies: Performance and the Emergence of Creole Culture*; Richard Bauman, *Story, Performance, and Event*; Labov, *Language in the Inner City*.

27 Bauman, *Story, Performance, and Event*, p. 36.

2

'Good Story!': The Formal Characteristics of Male Narrative

What do we mean when we use the word 'story'? This chapter will explore what a story is; it will also act as an introduction to men's talk and men's stories. Inevitably, the focus on men's stories rather than on stories in general raises the question, are stories gendered? In other words, is it the case that a story is a story is a story? Or do men's and women's stories differ? This question will be addressed later in the chapter.

In order to establish how a typical story is structured, and to develop some terms to use about story structure, let's look at two stories from the men's conversations. The first, 'Jonesy and the Lion', is a typical third-person narrative, that is, a narrative in which the narrator is not the chief protagonist. It comes from a conversation involving three male friends in their twenties or early thirties: Eddie, Geoff and Simon. They are talking in Simon's flat about a man who Eddie and Geoff used to know. Eddie is the narrator (Geoff's comments are in italics; Simon's are in italic capitals).[1] The arrow indicates the start of the story proper.

(1) Jonesy and the Lion
    1   God that reminds me talking of lion cages d'you remember Jonesy?
    2   *oh yeah Jonesy yeah*
    3   well he lost his job at the um-
    4   he worked at an army camp but lost his job there
    5   [. . .]
→ 6   but the one I was thinking of was when he was at er- he worked at the zoo

  7 [. . .]

  8 and somebody said that they needed some electrical sockets in the lion's cage

  9 and they said that that would be his next task to put some electrical sockets in the- in the lion's cage

10 but- <LAUGHS> but then <LAUGHS> what he did

11 he just went and picked up the keys from the office one day

12 and he went IN to the lion's cage <LAUGHS>

13 [*G laughs*]

14 and started drilling

15 and this lion . became sort of <LAUGHS> quite aroused by the er- by this drilling

16 *OH NO* <LAUGHING>

17 and he ended up being chased around the cage by the- by the lion

18 *OH NO*

19 and then the-

20 and well by this time there was quite a commotion in the zoo generally

21 *THERE WOULD BE* <LAUGHING>

22 so the um head or- the head keeper discovered what was going on

23 so he was outside the cage you know

24 doing um whatever er lion um tamers do to keep the lion away from this guy

25 and eventually they managed to get him out of the cage

26 so um-

27 *HE WASN'T HURT?*

28 no he wasn't hurt

29 so there you go

30 he's just mad <LAUGHS>

31 and it's just a miracle really

32 that he's still alive

33 but um he's always <LAUGHS> been mad like that

The second story, 'The Area Manager's Call', is a typical first-person narrative, where the narrator and the chief protagonist are one and the same person. This story comes from a conversation involving three young men in their twenties: a salesman, a computer engineer and a worker in a print shop. They are talking over a drink at the local pub. The narrator is Rob; Gary, whose comments are printed in italics, has previously worked for the same firm as Rob, so knows the people involved.

(2) The Area Manager's Call

1 did I tell you about that time when um . the area manager phoned
    me up?
2 *no* <ROB LAUGHS> *what, was it still JT?*
3 yeah,
4 just . we got this bloke at our place that's called John
5 and his days off on a Tuesday
6 and I answered the phone
7 it was the ex-D line
8 so it's li- like staff phoning in,
9 said 'hello it's John',
10 I said 'I tell you something mate,
11 it's fucking crap here today',
12 said, 'You're not missing anything',
13 said, 'The customers are ((stuffing xx)), it's dead,
14 bollocks,
15 I wish I wasn't here', <LAUGHTER>
16 and I wasn't getting a lot of feedback off him
17 so . 'I'm sorry,
18 what was it you wanted anyway?'.
19 He goes, 'I wanna speak to the manager,
20 it's John Taylor your area manager'.
21 'Oh right, OK' <SLOW AS IMPLICATIONS SINK IN>
22 Oh shit.
23 *<G LAUGHS> beaut*
24 I thought 'oh shit,
25 if there's a hole I'd be digging myself deeper.' <LAUGHS>
26 *yeah that's Rob Harrison* <PRETENDING TO BE ROB ON PHONE>
27 <LAUGHS> I mean what a twat.

What do these two examples show us about narrative structure? There have been many attempts to establish criteria which would define the well-formed story, in a wide range of disciplines, from literary criticism and folkloric studies to sociolinguistics. Aristotle's often quoted definition is deceptively simple: he states that a story is something that has a beginning, a middle and an end. Both the examples above seem to conform to this definition. When we read the transcripts, we understand them in terms of a beginning, a middle and an end, but are rather hazy about what we mean exactly by these terms.

Later commentators focus more on the internal structure of stories. Labov lists six potential components of narrative; Gergen and Gergen discuss five components; Bruner sketches out ten features of narrative.[2] What emerges from these discussions is consensus on two points. The first is that, to count as a narrative, there has to be a sequence of narrative clauses (clauses containing a verb in the simple past tense or, sometimes, the historic present tense) whose order matches the real-time order of the events described in those clauses. These clauses constitute the heart of the story, the 'narrative core' as I shall call it. The second is that, to count as a narrative, a story must have a point; it must have 'tellability'.[3] The worst thing that can happen to a narrator is that their story is seen as pointless; narrators need to avoid the 'So what?' challenge.[4] Let's examine the two stories in relation to these two key features.

'And He Went in to the Lion's Cage': The Narrative Core

'Jonesy and the Lion' has a narrative core of eight narrative clauses which are listed below (verbs are underlined):

(1a)
  8 and somebody <u>said</u> that they needed some electrical sockets in the lion's cage

  9 and they <u>said</u> that that would be his next task to put some electrical sockets in the- in the lion's cage

11 he just <u>went</u> and <u>picked up</u> the keys from the office one day

12 and he <u>went</u> IN to the lion's cage <LAUGHS>

14 and <u>started</u> drilling

17 and he <u>ended up</u> being chased around the cage by the- by the lion

22 so the um head or- the head keeper <u>discovered</u> what was going on

25 and eventually they <u>managed</u> to get him out of the cage

'The Area Manager's Call' also has a narrative core of eight narrative clauses:

(2a)
  6 and I <u>answered </u>the phone

  9 <u>said</u> 'hello it's John',

10 I <u>said</u> 'I tell you something mate, it's fucking crap here today',

12   said, 'You're not missing anything',
13   said, 'The customers are ((stuffing xx)), it's dead, bollocks, I wish
        I wasn't here',
17   so [*I said*] . 'I'm sorry, what was it you wanted anyway?'.
19   He goes, 'I wanna speak to the manager, it's John Taylor your
        area manager'.
24   I thought 'oh shit, if there's a hole I'd be digging myself deeper.'

Each narrative clause in these two stories has a simple past tense verb, apart from line 19 in the second, where the narrator switches to the historic present. The main difference between these two stories is in the stylistic choice of whether or not to use direct speech. The narrator of 'Jonesy and the Lion' chooses to tell his story without any direct speech to animate his characters; what people say is still foregrounded as significant (lines 8 and 9), but what is said is presented as indirect (reported) speech. For example, line 8 – *and somebody said that they needed some electrical sockets in the lion's cage* – could have been produced as *and somebody said 'We need some electrical sockets in the lion's cage'*. The narrator of 'The Area Manager's Call', by contrast, presents his story very dramatically, with seven of the eight narrative clauses involving direct speech (or the character's thoughts). This choice underlines the fact that this is a story involving the narrator himself; it is a significant episode in the continuing saga of Rob's life, and he demonstrates his first-hand knowledge of the event by reproducing the words of the main characters. (Of course, his audience is not expected to believe that these were the actual words spoken.[5]) Direct speech has a significant role to play in evaluation, that is, in getting the narrator's point across. So Rob's choice of words for himself and the Area Manager can be assumed to embody important messages to his audience about how to take the story.

Another interesting point about the second story is the narrator's use of the historic present tense in line 19 (*goes*). This marks the climax of the story, the moment at which the point of this story becomes clear. Recent analysis of the conversational historic present has claimed that it is the switch from past to present (or from present to past) which is significant, rather than anything intrinsic to the present tense itself.[6] So by making the switch at this dramatic moment, the narrator of this story signals to his audience that this is an important line. The final narrative clause reverts to the simple past tense.

'So He Was Outside the Cage': Narrative and Non-narrative Clauses

Another characteristic of narrative which is illustrated by these two stories is that they do not consist solely of narrative clauses with verbs in the simple past tense. They also contain non-narrative clauses which involve other kinds of verb phrase. Non-narrative clauses differ from narrative clauses in having either stative verbs such as *be* and *have*, or more complex verb phrases. William Labov calls these two types of clause 'narrative clauses' and 'free clauses';[7] he uses the term 'free' to capture the fact that, whereas narrative clauses have to occur in a specific order to match the order of events being described, non-narrative clauses are not so restricted in their placement. Background material about who, where and when ('orientation' in Labov's terms), for example, may be given at the beginning of a story, or may be added at some later point. Livia Polanyi opts for different terms: she refers to these two types of clause as 'event clauses' and 'state clauses'.[8] This terminology captures an important distinction between the two types of clause: while event clauses refer to one single moment in the past, state clauses 'encode states of affairs which persist over some interval of time in the discourse world rather than occurring at one unique discrete instant'.[9]

In each of the two stories, 'Jonesy and the Lion' and 'The Area Manager's Call', as we have seen, the core narrative consists of eight narrative clauses. The other clauses in these stories, the non-narrative free clauses, provide background information or evaluate the story. Line 20 in 'Jonesy and the Lion' is a good example of a non-narrative clause: *and well by this time there was quite a commotion in the zoo generally*. The verb *was* is a stative verb and describes 'a state of affairs which persists over some interval of time', unlike the verbs in the lines that precede and follow it (*ended up; discovered*). This line enables the narrator to give us a fuller picture of the situation developing at the zoo, and to make an important evaluative move: the word *commotion* signals that the narrator intends us to read the scenario he has described as chaotic rather than orderly. As the story reaches its climax, we get a series of non-narrative clauses: *so he was outside the cage you know, doing um whatever er lion um tamers do to keep the lion away from this guy*. Again we have a stative verb – *was* – in the main clause, followed by a non-finite clause introduced by *doing*, and this in turn has an embedded noun clause as object. The sequence is syntactically complex and contrasts markedly with the preceding simple narrative clauses. These two complex lines give us important background information about the head keeper but keep us in suspense about Jonesy's fate.

The opening of 'The Area Manager's Call' involves several non-narrative clauses which give important background information (lines 4–8 are given in (2b) below):

(2b)
4   just . we got this bloke at our place that's called John
5   and his days off on a Tuesday
6   <u>and I answered the phone</u>
7   it was the ex-D line
8   so it's li- like staff phoning in

Line 6 is the only narrative clause here, with the simple past tense verb *answered*. The verbs in the other clauses are *(have) got, is called, is, was, is, phoning*. None of them is a simple past tense verb: all these verbs refer to states rather than events, or to recurring events in the case of *phoning*. These lines are crucial in preparing the audience for the point of the story. It is vital if the story is to have its intended impact that story recipients understand that there is another John at Rob's workplace who was off work that day and who therefore might have phoned in on the ex-directory line. Other non-narrative clauses are line 22 *Oh shit* and line 27 *I mean what a twat*. Both are evaluative: they signal the narrator's attitude to the events in the story and orient the audience to the narrative point. Note that both these lines are verbless (apart from the discourse marker *I mean*), which again distinguishes them from the lines which constitute the narrative core.

'He's Just Mad': Breaching the Canonical Script

Besides having a narrative core, stories need to have tellability, that is, they need to have a point. What counts as 'having a point' will differ from culture to culture, but a fair generalization seems to be that stories involve 'deviations from expected norms'.[10] Jerome Bruner explains this in terms of the concept 'the canonical script'.[11] A canonical script is the unmarked script of everyday life, the way we expect things to be. For a story to be tellable, it must involve a breach of the canonical script.

The story 'Jonesy and the Lion' is a good example of breaching a canonical script. The story works – is tellable – because it is understood that in the canonical script you don't go into a lion's cage when the lion is there. The point of the story – *he's just mad* (line 30) – is irrefutable: anyone who breaches canonical scripts in this way can definitely be regarded as foolish, if not mad, and certainly Jonesy is lucky to be alive, as the narrator points out. The function of third-person stories like 'Jonesy and the Lion' is to confirm group values and attitudes, and in this case to affirm the three friends as an in-group with Jonesy positioned as the outsider. This construction of 'otherness' plays an important part in our maintenance of our sense of self. We assert who we are by establishing who we are not.

In the case of 'The Area Manager's Call', the canonical script would have Rob answering the phone and enquiring politely what the caller wants. However, for reasons Rob makes clear, he assumes he is speaking to another John, the John whose day off is on Tuesday, John who is an equal not a superior. He therefore lets off steam about work. To discover that you have told the Area Manager that *it's fucking crap here today* is a definite breach of the canonical script. The laughter and appreciative comments (e.g. *beaut*) that greet Rob's story demonstrate that his audience have no doubts about its tellability. Rob's own final comment *I mean what a twat* evaluates the story and makes the point that he, Rob, had put his foot in it in a big way. The function of this story is more subtle than that of 'Jonesy and the Lion'. At one level, the first-person narrator exposes his foolishness to his friends and declares himself to be *a twat*. At a more profound level, the story is a boast and fits a masculine tradition of stories involving achievement (even though the achievement here is 'laddish' rather than heroic).[12] This masculine tradition will be discussed further in the next chapter.

The stories in the conversations I've collected range from those which involve major breaches in the canonical script – cars breaking down, illness, fights – to those which deal more with the minutiae of life. But even when the events reported are less earth-shattering, even when the narrator is not saying 'this was terrifying, dangerous, weird, wild, crazy; or amusing, hilarious, wonderful',[13] it is still necessary to make clear that what happened was unusual. Otherwise the narrator runs the risk of having their narrative perceived as pointless, as not tellable.

The following is a nice example of a story about a relatively minor incident which makes extremely clear why it is tellable, by summarizing the point of the story forcibly in the last line. This story comes from a conversation involving three young men in their twenties. The narrator is Dan, and it is the second in a series of stories about false identity.

(3)   You Can't Not Know Your Name
1   Bad as my mate
2   [. . .]
3   So he went out last weekend right,
4   and he ended up going to Toff's.
5   Cos he's underage he borrowed his mate's licence yeah,
6   and they always ask you your post code,
7   so he had that memorized right.
8   So he got to the door and he goes 'Got any ID?'
9   Pulled up- pulled it out, give it to the doorman,
10   'What's your name?' <LAUGHTER>
11   And obviously like he'd been thinking about the post code over
       and over and over yeah
12   and he went 'oh shit' <LAUGHTER>
13   'TN5 7DR . that's a funny name.'
14   And he couldn't- he couldn't work it out right,
15   and he just stuttered after a while like that
16   going 'yeah'.
17   'What's your post code- post code?'
18   and he pulled that off perfectly
19   and he went 'Alright I'll let you in like'
20   Just one of those moments you know life's turned to shit like that.
21   It's like . you can't not know your name, all right
22   you might not know your post code right
23   but you can't not know your name.

In this story the narrator's friend has borrowed a friend's driving licence so that he can get into a club. (This false identity will 'prove' that he is old enough to be served alcohol.) In the expected script, the doorman asks what your post code is, so this friend has put a lot of effort into memorizing the post code on the driving licence. The climax of the story comes in line 10, when the doorman asks not for the post code but for the name (note how Dan's friends laugh at this point, demonstrating their understanding of the way the story is likely to go). The free clause in line 11, *And obviously like he'd been thinking about the post code over and over and over yeah*, is strongly evaluative: it stands out because of its syntactic complexity – adverbial plus complex verb phrase plus the repetition of *over*. It both keeps us in suspense and serves to explain why the protagonist becomes tongue-tied at this point. Finally, the story ends with the lines *It's like . you can't not know your name, alright, you might not know your post code right, but you can't not know your name.* The main point of the story is made twice here, and the canonical script is made explicit: it is acceptable to forget your post code but not acceptable to forget your own name.

Beginnings and Endings

The two components of narrative I have discussed – a core sequence of narrative clauses plus tellability – are indisputably key elements in our recognition of certain chunks of talk as 'stories'. Certainly they are key elements in the chunks of text I have identified as stories in the men's talk. However, there is still the problem of knowing where a story begins and ends. This is an issue not just for analysts but for all of us as speakers in the real world. In conversation we all tell stories, but that capability is a sophisticated part of our communicative competence. In order for the transition to be made from unmarked conversational interaction (or discussion) to story-telling, all participants at talk have to recognize the signals that announce that a story is about to be told. Similarly, for conversation to revert to discussion after narration is completed, all participants have to recognize the signals that mark the end of a story.[14]

Aristotle's definition of a story focuses on beginnings, middles and ends. In practical terms, what this means for speakers engaged in conversation is that as long as we can all recognize the beginnings and ends of stories, then the middles will take care of themselves. Of course, the middles of stories also have to be structured in particular ways to count as stories, as we have seen – but this is a problem solely for the narrator or for the narrator and co-narrators; it is not a problem of conversational organization.

'Did I Tell You About That Time When . . . ?': Questions as Narrative Beginnings

So how do we initiate stories? The two examples we have looked at both begin with a question. Example (1) arises from the narrator's question *d'you remember Jonesy?* In example (2), 'The Area Manager's Call', Rob's story can be said to begin with the question *Did I tell you about that time when the area manager phoned me up?* This question signals to Gary and Dan that Rob has a story to tell. Questions are frequently found as initiators of narrative, and, like this one, they can be used by speakers who have a story to tell as an initial move in taking the floor as a narrator. This initial move can be called a 'story preface': it announces the story to the story's potential recipients. Rob's question is followed by an answer from Gary which is itself a question: *no, what, was it still JT?* This question functions simultaneously to accept Rob's bid for the conversational floor (since this question effectively hands the floor back to him), and to claim solidarity in the storyworld being opened up, since Gary had previously worked for this firm and therefore knew the Area Manager in question. Rob responds to Gary's question with 'Yes', thus acknowledging Gary's shared knowledge and signalling acceptance of the floor.[15] He then proceeds to tell the story.

Gary's 'no' on its own would have been sufficient to grant Rob the conversational floor. In fact, no answer at all from fellow participants will not prevent a story being told, since by not taking a turn at talk fellow speakers signal that the floor is open to the narrator. (Paralinguistic signals such as nodding and looking at the speaker may also signal acquiescence.) The following extract from the opening of a story illustrates how a narrator's opening question may receive no verbal response. This example (example 4) comes from a conversation involving three men in their mid twenties, all involved in post-graduate study of one kind or another. They have been discussing drinking habits, and Tim starts talking about a difficult fellow art student called Robin.

(4) *Extract from* **The Paint Dispute**
 he just gets more- he just gets more Robinesque
 ((I mean)) he's quite happy- [*yeah*]
 he's quite difficult to handle [*mhm*]
→ did I tell you recently?
 he rea- he u- u- used up all- he used up a-
 like I had a palette with like loads of black paint on it
 and he used it all up
 and I said 'Get me some more paint'
 and he refused.

The question *did I tell you recently?* announces an upcoming story about the problematic Robin. Tim's friends orient to this narrative opening by *not* speaking, that is, by granting Tim the conversational floor. This contrasts with their behaviour in the chunk of talk leading up to the story, where two out of three statements made by Tim about Robin are met with minimal responses from his fellow conversationalists. So, as this example demonstrates, while a question signals that a narrative is on offer, such questions do not require a verbal response to function as narrative openings. (Notice, however, that in this particular example, gaining the floor with such ease seems to throw the narrator off his stride: he becomes noticeably disfluent at this point, making several false starts before getting into the swing of his story.)

Many stories in the conversations I've collected begin with a question. Other examples from the corpus are the following:

(5)   Do you remember that girl at Matt Hunter's party?
(6)   Did you see what I did this afternoon?
(7)   Do you remember Ivies [*a kind of shoe fashionable in the 1960s*] at all?
(8)   Shall I tell you a Nigerian anecdote?

In examples like these, where the question is uttered by the speaker who subsequently becomes narrator, the proposition contained in the question functions as an *abstract*[16] of the upcoming narrative. So in the story 'The Area Manager's Call', Rob's question tells his friends that he is offering to tell a story about *when the area manager phoned me up*. In the same way, the questions listed above announce that the person asking the question is offering a narrative about the girl at Matt Hunter's party, what I did this afternoon, and Ivy brogues, respectively. The last example – *shall I tell you a Nigerian anecdote?* – is less explicit in what it promises: while 'a Nigerian anecdote' is an abstract, it is an extremely general one, and it is incumbent on the narrator to provide further details without delay. This is what happens. The narrator goes on: *when we were in Cape Coast there was a guy there who was a German who had a Volkswagen*, and proceeds to tell a story about this German and his Volkswagen car.

Questions asked by a speaker other than the speaker-who-becomes-narrator can also initiate a story. In other words, some questions can function as invitations to *other* speakers to take the floor as narrator. The following are some examples from the corpus:

(9)   So what you done New Year's?
(10)   So how are your kids Steven?
(11)   You not been demolishing houses recently?

Many questions have the potential to be interpreted as invitations to tell a story, including routine greetings such as 'How are you?' and 'How's things?' But whether or not such a question initiates a narrative depends on the next speaker. The person to whom the question *So what you done New Year's?* was addressed could have answered 'Nothing', and the conversation would then have taken a different direction. Equally, Steven could have responded to his friend's question about his kids with a brief reply such as 'They're fine'. In these particular cases, analysis of the conversation shows that a specific question triggered a story, but it is important to note that this analysis is *post hoc*: while these stories are initiated by these questions, there was nothing in the question that meant a story *had to* follow.

Sometimes an invitation to tell a story will be rejected. In a conversation involving two friends, Geoff and Chris, Chris says to Geoff *I meant to ask you, I didn't know your Dad got remarried*. This roundabout way of asking *Did your Dad get remarried?* does not lead to Geoff telling a story, even though we get a few tantalizing details: *he asked me to sort of best man it which was a bit sort of hard*. Presumably because Geoff found his father's re-marriage 'hard', he chooses not to tell a story about it.

However, the evidence of the men's conversations is that speakers will normally work hard to produce a narrative when they are offered the floor. Example (12) gives the opening of the story initiated by the question *you not been demolishing houses recently?* This shows how the addressee struggles to orient himself to the question before coming up with an appropriate story. This extract comes from the same conversation as 'The Area Manager's Call'. Gary's question refers to an incident Rob has talked about, when he accidentally damaged a neighbour's wall. The question positions Rob as 'a person who gets into scrapes' (a role he plays up to in conversation with his friends, as the story 'The Area Manager's Call' demonstrates) and means that if he is to take up Gary's invitation to the conversational floor, he has to produce a story which matches the 'accidental demolishing of houses' scenario. (Gary's words are in italics.)

(12) *Extract from* **The Pornographic Video**
1   *you not been demolishing houses recently?* .
2   No, I've not done anything- ((I'm)) just trying to think what
      I've done lately (6.0)
3   Don't think I've done anything really that bad lately (2.0)
4   Oh yeah I have actually

    5 [*G laughs*]
→ 6 When we went out for this meal last week
    7 with Nick Staples
    8 um a customer . um . left a video . in a video recorder [*yeah*]
    9 and it broke in th- in there . . .

Rob's initial response to Gary's question (lines 2–4) shows him struggling to find something to say. Notice the long pause at the end of line 2: a 6-second pause constitutes a significant gap between turns and would normally suggest that a conversation was in trouble.[17] Here, it suggests that Rob's friends understand that Rob is searching for a relevant story to tell, and are prepared to give him time. Certainly, neither Gary nor Dan attempts to take the floor at this point. Line 3 shows us the work Rob is doing: when he says that he hasn't 'done anything bad' he reveals his understanding of Gary's question as being, pragmatically, an invitation to 'tell us another story about doing something bad'. Another, shorter pause follows, then in line 4 Rob announces that he does have a story to tell. This is met with laughter from Gary – laughter which signals acceptance of Rob's offer to tell a story. Rob then begins his story, which turns out to be an epic about a pornographic video which was Nick Staples' 'pride and joy', but which Rob inadvertently wipes out while trying to copy it. (This example will be discussed at greater length in chapter 3.)

This example demonstrates how all participants in conversation co-operate in constructing their conversation. Here, Gary asks the initial question and subsequently contributes supportive laughter and minimal responses; Dan says nothing (which in effect demonstrates acceptance of the course the conversation is taking); and Rob provides a relevant next story. In this way, all three share in constructing a narrative chunk at this point in their conversation.

'Can't Believe My Car': Other Forms of Beginning

Not all stories told in these conversations begin with a question. Stories often start with one or two clauses which summarize the whole story. Again, participants at talk need to orient themselves to the potential of such clauses: if these utterances are not recognized as a story abstract by others, then the narrator's bid for the floor will fail. Here are some successful examples from the corpus:

(13)   Oscar was very fucked off
       [This is the first line of a brief story about Oscar's anger and how the narrator defuses it]

(14)   I was about thirty when I first got pulled out of the Dartford Tunnel
       [This line begins a story about breaking down in the Dartford Tunnel]

(15)   never really had a run-in with a biker
       although one nearly killed me the other day
       [These are the first two lines of a story about nearly being run over by a motorbike while attempting to cross a busy road]

(16)   I heard a marvellous example today of er-
       of the you know sort of individual needs
       and the individual sort of concerns being just completely sort of
          destroyed you know
       just wiped away
       [These four lines begin a story to illustrate the way senior management don't respect staff at the narrator's place of work]

But opening lines are sometimes much less explicit than this:

(17)   A funny thing happened today
(18)   Can't believe my car

In these examples, the opening statement is evaluative: the evaluative clause announces a story and tells the audience how to orient to it (as funny in the first case, as incredible in the second). Other examples start with an orientation statement:

(19)   I know this girl called Debbie
(20)   I went to this customer's house the other day

These two examples give us details of characters and setting that will be important in the story that will follow, but they are abstracts only in a very basic sense: the first is to be a story about Debbie; the second a story about what happened to the narrator at a customer's house. They work as the first lines of stories because of our understanding of conversational norms: as a speaker you don't make an utterance like *I know this girl* unless you have something to say about the girl. In example (20) the phrase *the other day* functions like *once upon a time* as a conventionalized marker that a story is about to begin. Note that both these first lines use the deictic *this* to signal the significance of the characters mentioned (*this girl* and *this customer*). *This* in such contexts means topically salient rather than physically close to the speaker in a literal sense.

'And That Was the End of My Little Cortina': Endings

One of the tasks facing a narrator is to get back into real time, that is, into the now of the conversational present. 'Tellers must smooth the way as it were from the storyworld they have created back into the embedding conversation.'[18] This is done via 'exit talk'.[19]

Exit talk can take various forms: when the narrator comes to the last of the narrative clauses that form the core of the story, she or he can simply relinquish the floor to other speakers, and general talk will then re-establish itself. The following example is the last seven lines of the story 'The Paint Dispute' whose opening we looked at earlier (example (4)). Tim's story about the problematic Robin tells how Robin uses Tim's paint then refuses to replace it. The point of Tim's story seems initially to be about how angry he got with Robin, kicking a chair to pieces in his rage. But Tim's friends want to know whether Robin replaced the paint, and the story finally ends as follows:

(21)
19   *he still did- didn't get you more paint though?*
20   well in fact he did
21   I mean he took a while about it cos he kept saying 'I've got no money'
22   and I at one point lost my temper with him
23   I couldn't do it a second time
24   it was really pathetic
25   but in the end he gave- he gave me a tube of white.

Line 25 is the last narrative clause in the sequence of narrative clauses that tell us the story of Robin and the dispute over the paint, and it is also the last line of the story. It is not difficult to identify this as the final line of the story, given the story's opening abstract (*like I had a palette with like loads of black paint on it, and he used it all up*). Robin giving Tim a tube of white is clearly a relevant resolution of the conflict described in the story. Moreover, Luke's question in line 19 forces Tim to provide a resolution, which he does, at first briefly, in line 20, then more fully, in line 25. Between lines 20 and 25 we get some further action and the important evaluative line *it was really pathetic.* So by line 25 Tim's friends have been provided with an evaluation and a resolution.

What is interesting is to see how the three friends move from this point back into free-flowing conversation. The next chunk of their talk is given below in (22) (Luke's words are in italics, Jeremy's in italic capitals):

(22)

26 *but w- . do you share sort of- do you share ((palettes))?*

27 well no we don't [*L laughs*]

28 but I mean we just have palettes lying around and crap like that [*yeah*]

29 and usually- you know he's only seventeen and he- he's like a complete- he's like a disturbed child kind of thing [*oh right*]

30 and he's also very hyperactive

31 he just fucking uses whatever's around [*MHM*]

32 ((without)) any sense of the propriety ((xx)) [*MHM*]

33 but anyway that's- that's a really trivial-

34 *NO SENSE OF PROPRIETORIAL PROPRIETY*

35 yes <LAUGH> [*MHM*]

While Tim still holds the floor in this extract it is no longer the privileged narrative floor: Luke and Jeremy are very much involved and in line 34 Jeremy rounds off this exit talk with a clever play on words. The talk then moves on to another topic about photographs they need for a joint project.

This final section, the sequence of free clauses produced by Tim after the final narrative clause, could be described as a *coda*.[20] In this coda, Tim and his friends share in evaluating Robin and his behaviour. This talk also moves decisively from the past of the storyworld to the present of the ongoing conversation. Stories often end with a coda, that is, a non-narrative clause (or clauses) which bridges the gap between the storyworld and the now of the conversation that the narrative is embedded in.

The main function of a coda is to 'close off' the sequence of narrative clauses that form the core of the narrative: once we get to the coda there are no more clauses with verbs in the simple past. In 'The Area Manager's Call' (example (2)), the story ends as follows:

24 I thought 'oh shit,

25 if there's a hole I'd be digging myself deeper.' <LAUGHS>

27 <LAUGHS> I mean what a twat.

Line 24 contains the last of the narrative clauses which constitute the heart of the story. As well as giving us the last event in this particular storyworld, Rob's dramatization of his thought is used to evaluate what has happened. Rob expresses his horror at the position he had got himself into and portrays himself as someone who has made an appalling cock-up: he thus indicates that this is the appropriate evaluative stance for his listeners. Line 27, the coda, repeats this evaluation of what he has done, but from the standpoint of the conversational now rather than the past of the story. This one-line coda contrasts with the long coda in 'The Paint Dispute', but there is no ambiguity about this one line being the end of Rob's story, as his next words are *and the worst one was . . .* , words that announce a second story on the same theme.

Many stories end with a line like line 27 above, a line which is evaluative, and evaluative with such a note of finality that only a totally incompetent conversationalist would fail to realize that the story had come to an end. Here is an example from a story about a moment of genius on the sports field:

(23)   and it was just the most beautiful ball I've ever ever ever seen

The superlative adjective here is explicitly evaluative and the repetition of *ever* is highly emphatic. The next example comes at the end of a story about the narrator's car engine bursting into flames in the Dartford Tunnel:

(24)   and that was the end of my little Cortina

Both these examples of final clauses are in the past, but both use stative verbs and are clearly not narrative clauses. So although these two codas do not return us to the present, they signal unambiguously that the narrative past of the storyworld is at an end.

Example (25) gives the last four lines of a story about passing the driving test – after years of driving illegally without a licence ('he' in line 36 is the examiner):

(25)
36   he <u>said</u> to me 'I'm glad to tell you-' right,
37   I <u>thought</u> 'yeah you're glad to tell me that I've failed yeah' cos I'd been driving like a ((dangerous)) cunt,

38 but no, ((xx)) I <u>passed</u> man,
39 if he hadn't had that ring on him right I'd've kissed him
      <LAUGHTER>

Lines 36–8 are the last three narrative clauses, finishing the sequence of events which made up the narrator's experience of his driving test. The narrator skilfully breaks off in line 36 so we are left in suspense as to the outcome of the test. This is given in line 38, the resolution, and then line 39 provides the coda, a conditional sentence that very nicely evaluates the story and makes clear it is a story of triumph. It is highly taboo in mainstream British culture for a man to kiss another man: by claiming to have been tempted to infringe this taboo, the narrator makes clear to his audience that the story is to be evaluated as exceptional. The laughter that greets this final line demonstrates his audience's understanding that the narrative has ended.

Often, though, narrators provide codas that simultaneously close off the sequence of narrative clauses, evaluate the story and re-orient us in the conversational present. Here are three examples:

(26) it's the most disgusting thing I've ever seen
(27) it's flipping wonderful
(28) but that's the most exciting thing that's happened to me this week

All three examples use present-tense verbs that move us out of the storyworld into the now of ongoing conversation. All three are evaluative clauses which function as claims about tellability: to say that something is *disgusting* or *wonderful* or *exciting* is to mark it off from the unremarkable, the everyday. By finishing like this, narrators skilfully round off the narrative and assert the point of what has been told.

Codas can be more extensive, as we saw in example (21) 'The Paint Dispute', and as the ending of the story 'Jonesy and the Lion' shows:

(29)
29 so there you go
30 he's just mad <LAUGHS>
31 and it's just a miracle really
32 that he's still alive
33 but um he's always <LAUGHS> been mad like that.

The first line of this coda, *so there you go*, is a classic, like the one discussed by Labov, *and that was that*. It signals that the narrative is finished in a succinct and unambiguous way. The narrator then maintains his stance in the present (using present-tense verbs that bring us back from the storyworld past) and evaluates Jonesy's actions as 'mad', underlining how dangerous the situation was with the lines *and it's just a miracle really that he's still alive*. Finally the story ends with the line *but he's always been mad like that* which skilfully ties this particular episode of Jonesy's exciting life to earlier incidents, and so places the completed story firmly in the past while asserting its significance as a typical incident, not a one-off. In this sense, it fulfils the demands of a good coda, which 'leaves the listener with a feeling of satisfaction and completeness that matters have been rounded off and accounted for'.[21]

Sometimes this sense of satisfaction and completeness is achieved through speakers collaboratively ending a story. A good example is the following, from a story about a fellow worker at a large electronics retailers who took the insides out of a state-of-the-art electronic organizer and swapped them with the insides from his own, much older, organizer:

(30)
15 He was a dodgy bastard wasn't he?
16 he knew all the tricks though.
17 *Yeah but look what's happened to him now*
18 yeah now he's in prison.

Lines 15 and 16 evaluate the story of the man's doings and express an attitude of mixed disapproval and admiration. These could have functioned as the coda. But the narrator's co-participant at talk adds line 17, *Yeah but look what's happened to him now*, which enables the narrator to add *yeah now he's in prison*, making explicit their shared knowledge of 'what has happened to him'. These two lines give the story a much better point: this is now not just a story about a 'dodgy bastard' who was very clever with electronic gadgets, but a story that makes the point that people eventually get their just deserts. This much more universal point is achieved through the collaboration of two speakers.

'Only Twenty-five p': Gender and Story-telling

I do not think it is possible to read the stories discussed here without being aware of the gender of the narrators. They are men's stories, not stories in general. These narrators are doing many things simultaneously as they tell their stories. But one of the things they are doing is performing masculinity. Does this mean that their stories differ in structure from stories told by women?

The canonical story I have outlined in this chapter has been defined in relation to three criteria: first, it has a beginning, a middle and an end; secondly, it involves a narrative core consisting of a sequence of narrative clauses; and thirdly, it has a point (tellability). At first glance, analysis of a parallel corpus of all-female conversation suggests that all three criteria are met: stories told by women in conversation with other women have beginnings, middles and endings, contain a core series of narrative clauses, and make a point. Moreover, female narrators, like male narrators, bring their characters to life by using direct speech, position their characters in time and space, and communicate the tellability of their stories through evaluative devices of various kinds.

However, on closer inspection it seems that women's and men's notions of tellability might vary. Polanyi observes that 'what stories can be about is, to a very significant degree, culturally constrained: stories . . . can have as their *point* [sic] only culturally salient material generally agreed upon by members of the producer's culture to be self-evidently important and true'.[22] While both the men's and the women's narratives I've collected attest to membership of the culture which is Britain at the end of the twentieth century, some stories told by women suggest that women may have a different idea from men about what counts as culturally salient material.

Discussion of this aspect of story-telling has tended to be androcentric, with male norms interpreted as human norms. Labov, for example, talking about danger of death stories collected from Black male adolescents and pre-adolescents, asks why some stories are tellable and some are not. He argues that 'if the event [i.e. what the story is about] becomes common enough, it is no longer a violation of an expected rule of behaviour, and it is not reportable'.[23] He shows how narrators evaluate their narratives with adjectives such as 'terrifying, dangerous, weird' or 'funny' or 'unusual', not with adjectives like 'ordinary' or 'everyday'.

Yet women's stories are often precisely about the ordinary and the everyday. Women tell stories about seeing grain trains in the docks, about body hair, about forgetting to take a towel to school for PE, about buying a sundress, about comfortable shoes, about painting the ceiling. The following is a very short example, but one which makes

35

the point well. The narrator is Pat: she is telling her friend Karen about her shopping spree that morning (Karen's contributions are in italics).

(31) Ear-rings
→ 1 I went and bought some stupid things this morning in Boots,
   2 twenty-five p, <LAUGH>
   3 for twenty-five p you could be as silly as you want to couldn't you?
   4 silly aren't they?
   5 [...]
   6 oh what fun
   7 silly green nonsense
   8 children's bead ear-rings
   9 *you got green?*
  10 I've got a green jumper which I wear in the winter
  11 *yeah, that's fine*
  12 so I thought I would.
  13 I'm- am very fond of my green jumper,
  14 silly pair of green ear-rings to go with it.
  15 *why not?*
  16 it's a laugh
→ 17 there was another lady there looking through all the stuff when I was
  18 and she said to me, 'isn't it fun?', <LAUGH>
  19 and I said, 'Yes, only twenty-five p', <LAUGH>
  20 absurd.

The opening four lines operate as a kind of abstract, giving a summary of the story, which is that things were for sale at the ridiculous price of 25 pence. The middle section (lines 6–16) is more stream of consciousness than narrative: the narrator talks about the green ear-rings she has bought in the present tense. Only at line 17 does she revert to narrative proper, with an orientation clause introducing a new character (*another lady*), followed by two narrative clauses each introducing direct speech. The last line provides the evaluation: *absurd*. This evaluative adjective conforms to Labov's strictures on how a narrator presents their story as tellable – Pat's claim that her buying of a pair of ear-rings for 25p is 'absurd' demonstrates to her addressee that her story has a point. She implicitly appeals to a canonical script in which ear-rings cost more than 25p.

My interest in this story, and stories like it, lies in the fact that the subject matter differs so enormously from the kind of subject matter that is normally regarded as 'tellable' in men's stories. Even with its claim to absurdity, I suspect this example would fail as a story if told to a male audience. Or at the very least it might be met with puzzlement. Where is the heroism? What contest has the protagonist entered and won? What skill has been demonstrated? These questions can only be answered satisfactorily by adopting a gendered world-view, where a story about· buying something for very little can be regarded as tellable.

Narrative construction performs important gender work, and men and women are actively engaged in constructing and maintaining masculinity and femininity in their story-telling.[24] Given that masculinity and femininity are relational constructs (that is, they can only be defined in relation to each other), it is hardly surprising that the norms of men's and women's story-telling differ in some respects. After all, in telling a story, a male speaker is, among other things, performing *not* being a woman (just as a female speaker is performing *not* being a man).[25] Certain themes are typical of men's stories – heroism, conflict, achievement – but not of women's stories.[26]

It is important not to ignore these gender differences. Research into oral narrative has often relied on data collected from male speakers, and norms have been established which are assumed to account for the whole speech community. In the field of literary narrative, assumptions about what is 'normal' stretch back hundreds of years, and given the dominance of men in terms of access to literacy, it is not surprising that themes of heroism and achievement, of lone protagonists making epic journeys or struggling with a variety of foes, are the norm. Because of the prestige of the written in Western cultures, these literary norms inevitably have an impact on what we expect to find in oral narrative.[27] It seems that women's stories do not conform in every respect to these norms, but that does not mean they should be seen as deviant.[28]

Conclusions

This chapter has revealed the gendered nature of stories, but has also provided an introduction to narrative structure. I have discussed stories in terms of three features. The first is that there has to be a sequence of narrative clauses whose order matches the real-time

order of the events described in those clauses. These clauses constitute the heart of the story, the narrative core. The second is that a
story must have a point; it must have tellability. A third feature of
narrative which I have discussed at some length is that narrative can
be defined in terms of a beginning, a middle and an end (the Aristo-
telian definition).

While these features of conversational narrative are generalizable
across speakers, it emerges that tellability is variable in nature. In
other words, all speakers would agree that for a story to work as a
story, it must breach the canonical script, but what counts as canonical varies from sub-culture to sub-culture. In her paper on tellability,
Polanyi discusses differences between English-speaking and native
American narrative practices.[29] She argues that the differences in what
different groups can tell stories about reflect deep and vitally important differences in the way they view the world. It seems that such
differences are not confined to large, institutionally recognized speech
communities such as these, but may also be found within speech
communities at the sub-cultural level. Certainly it seems to be the
case that male and female speakers in Britain and in America differ in
their understanding of what is tellable.

Discussion of gender differences will be continued in chapter 5. In
the next chapter (chapter 3) I shall look more closely at the ways in
which masculinity is constructed in all-male talk. In particular I shall
look at the role played by narrative in men's performance of identity.

Notes

1 I shall follow the convention used by those who work on conversational
   narrative of presenting the story in numbered lines, each line correspond-
   ing to one of the narrator's breath-groups or intonation units, typically
   a grammatical phrase or clause (see Wallace Chafe, 'The deployment of
   consciousness in the production of narrative').
2 William Labov, *Language in the Inner City*, p. 363; Kenneth Gergen and
   Mary Gergen, 'Narrative and the self as relationship'; Jerome Bruner,
   'The narrative construction of reality'.
3 Bruner, 'The narrative construction of reality', p. 12.
4 Labov, *Language in the Inner City*, p. 362.
5 Deborah Tannen, *Talking Voices: Repetition, Dialogue and Imagery in Conversational Discourse*.
6 Nessa Wolfson, 'Tense-switching in narrative'; Joanna Thornborrow,
   'Principal, plausibility and the historic present'.

7   Labov, *Language in the Inner City*, p. 375.
8   Livia Polanyi, *Telling the American Story*, p. 17.
9   Ibid.
10 Ibid.
11 Bruner, 'The narrative construction of reality', p. 11.
12 See Jennifer Coates, *Women Talk*; Janet Holmes, 'Story-telling in New Zealand: women's and men's talk'; Barbara Johnstone, 'Community and contest: Midwestern men and women creating their worlds in conversational storytelling'.
13 Labov, *Language in the Inner City*, p. 371.
14 See Gail Jefferson, 'Sequential aspects of storytelling in conversation'.
15 As Harvey Sacks says: 'In storytelling you give them the floor to give it back to you' (*Lectures on Conversation*, p. 227).
16 Labov, *Language in the Inner City*, p. 363.
17 Harvey Sacks, Emanuel Schegloff and Gail Jefferson, 'A simplest systematics for the organisation of turn-taking in conversation'; Don Zimmerman and Candace West, 'Sex roles, interruptions and silences in conversation'.
18 Livia Polanyi, 'Literary complexity in everyday storytelling', p. 164.
19 Jefferson, 'Sequential aspects of storytelling in conversation'.
20 Labov, *Language in the Inner City*, p. 365.
21 Ibid., p. 366.
22 Livia Polanyi, 'So what's the point?', p. 207.
23 Labov, *Language in the Inner City*, pp. 370–1.
24 Coates, *Women Talk*; Jennifer Coates, 'Small talk and subversion'; Holmes, 'Story-telling in New Zealand'; Johnstone, 'Community and contest'.
25 R. W. Connell, *Masculinities*, p. 68; Michael Kimmel, 'Rethinking "masculinity"', p. 12; Michael Roper and John Tosh, 'Introduction' to *Manful Assertions*, p. 2.
26 See Coates *Women Talk*; Johnstone, 'Community and contest'; Kristin Langellier and Eric Peterson, 'Spinstorying: an analysis of women storytelling'.
27 After hearing a lecture on gender differences in narrative which included a great many examples from my data-base, a member of the audience commented that the men's stories seemed to him like 'real' stories, whereas the women's stories challenged his expectations.
28 Langellier and Peterson, 'Spinstorying: an analysis of women storytelling', p. 162.
29 Polanyi, 'So what's the point?', p. 227.

3

'So I Thought "Bollocks to It"': Men, Stories and Masculinities

When we talk with friends, one of the important things we accomplish is the maintenance of our sense of self. Talk with people we know well has the potential for 'the exchange of recognition',[1] as I've argued earlier. When we feel recognized, then our sense of who we are is affirmed. And since our sense of who we are is inextricably tied up with our sense of ourselves as male or female, then talk with friends also involves important gender work. Here are two male friends talking over lunch; the topic is mobile phones:

(1)

Chris:	Kate's just got a new one, got one of those tiny little Siemens ones with-
Geoff:	oh that are- that are about that big=
Chris:	=it's tiny . with WAP services
Geoff:	oh yeah
Chris:	it is pretty cool [. . .] and we've been having these endless discussions because she wants me to have the same phone as her
Geoff:	why?
Chris:	um on the basis that she won't read the manual and I will which means that-
→ Geoff:	you're a man you don't read manuals
Chris:	oh I do
Geoff:	<LAUGHS>
Chris:	only for the mobile phone I don't read it for anything else
Geoff:	ahhhh

Not only does this brief extract illustrate the way (young) men enjoy talking about modern technology, it also shows Geoff and Chris engaged in explicit gender work. Chris's remark that Kate wants him to get the same phone as her so that he can read the manual provokes Geoff to make an outright challenge: *you're a man you don't read manuals.* To begin with, Chris resists Geoff's challenge, countering with *oh I do.* But after a pause in which Geoff laughs, he backs down, amending his response to *only for the mobile phone I don't read it for anything else.* In other words, he aligns himself with Geoff's underlying proposition *men don't read manuals.*

The construction of identity and of masculinity is usually carried out less overtly than this. But even if most men do not spend time in conversation explicitly defining what men do and do not do, one of the functions of friendly talk is the re-assertion of the norms of masculine identity. In particular, in friendly talk men position themselves in relation to hegemonic masculinity. Story-telling plays a significant part in this. Telling stories not only allows us to give shape to our lives and to maintain our sense of self, it also allows us the possibility of exploring alternative selves. I intend in this chapter to analyse the stories the men tell each other in order to explore some of the tensions arising from competing versions of what it is to be a man today.

'And Now the Fucker Won't Start': Dominant Discourses of Masculinity

I want to begin by looking at four brief extracts from the men's stories, extracts which I have chosen because I think that, despite their differences, they all draw on dominant discourses of masculinity.

(2)   Car Wouldn't Start
[Four young men aged 18/19 in garden shed in Surrey: narrator = Sam; Jack's words in italics]

1   can't believe my car
2   it's ((2 sylls) [*really*]
3   mhm, speedo's fucked [*oh no*]
4   I was just about to-
5   wind[screen|wipers are fucked [*oh right*]
6   and now the fucker won't start [*oh no*]
7   [. . .]
8   I mean last time I just banged the bonnet [*yeah*]
9   and I mean it started up straight away [*yeah*]
10   and this time I was banging it and kicking it and shouting at it ((xxx)) [*oh my god*]

11 so then I- .hh I had a look at the fuses
12 and the fuses were all right
13 so I pulled the wires off
14 and cleaned them all up
15 and put them back again [*%fuck it%*]
16 did that three or four times
17 it still wouldn't start so-
18 *what a bastard*
19 ((xxx)) ((hope it)) starts first time tomorrow
20 [*Jack laughs quietly*]

(3) *Extract from* The Psion Swap*

[*Three men in their twenties talk in a pub in Somerset*]

1 yeah, like the most basic Psion he got was this one that he
   bought ages ago,
2 and he went and bought one from Argos
3 and totally swapped the cases over so he got like the new innards
   in his old case
4 and then took it back to Argos
5 and said he didn't want it any more <LAUGHTER>
6 and then later on he changed it for the upgraded version again at
   Curry's,
7 took all the serial numbers off,
8 switched them over and the badges,
9 and this customer brought this back,
10 and he said 'This is only a five twelve k'.
11 'Oh that's strange it's meant to be two megabytes'
12 cos he- it was a five twelve k
13 but he put the two megabyte stickers on there
14 and kept a five twelve k on his.
15 He was a dodgy bastard wasn't he?
16 he knew all the tricks though.
17 *Yeah but look what's happened to him now*
18 yeah now he's in prison.

[**A Psion is an electronic personal organizer*]

(4) *Extract from* Tablets and Drink

[*Two middle-aged men in a pub in Birmingham; narrator – Tom – is on tablets for a bad back*]

1 I'll tell you something
2 I had some of them fucking tablets

3 they're BASTARDS honest
4 and I went to the Eagle .
5 luckily it was only the Eagle
6 right?
7 and I got a little bit drowsy
8 [. . .]
9 and you know where Sandy road is. [B: *ahh*]
10 I was taking that fucking corner
11 and everything went . woozy
12 <u>you know what I mean</u> <FASTER>
13 so straight away ((then-)) pull into the fucking side eh?
14 started seeing double vision
15 so I pulls in to the side
16 and I thought well <u>I'll be all right in a couple of minutes</u> <FASTER>
17 I'd only had two pints
18 the next thing I knew were fucking four o'clock in the morning [*B laughs*].
19 and the fucking copper was knocking on the doo- . on the windscreen
20 [. . .]
   [*Tom is taken down to the police station and breathalysed. The police subsequently apologize and say he should have made it clear he was taking tablets for his back*]
21 and ever since then I've thought
22 well . if I can go without my fucking tablets
23 just taken the fucking three or four pints of beer
24 and they've picked me up
25 'I'm on the fucking <u>tablets</u>'
26 <u>and I can get a-fucking-way with it you know</u>. <LAUGHING>

(5) *Extract from* **The Good Samaritan**
[Two middle-aged men in a University office after work]
1 and I was doing in 1969 a dialect survey
2 of the languages round about a town called Yola
3 and . for our lunch with our interpreter one day we had sandwiches
4 and we decided after visiting this or that village in the area . to walk up to the top of one of these clusters of- of rocks and have our lunch,
5 this was about four hundred miles or so from Ibadan,
6 about a hundred and fifty miles from any sizeable town,

7   pretty remote one might think.
8   It took us about half an hour to wend our way up this jumble of
        very very large boulders,
9   and we got close to the very top,
10   and the top was obscured from us by a boulder,
11   we walked round this boulder
12   and there sitting on the top . was a European couple
13   with their backs to us,
14   as they heard us approach they turned round,
15   and lo it was my Vice-Chancellor and his wife.

These stories (or extracts from stories) obviously accomplish a lot
more than gender. Age is a significant factor in all of them: the first
two stories perform being young as well as being masculine, while
the last two perform being middle-aged. Class is also a significant
variable, with the differences between examples (4) and (5) being
very much to do with the social class of the two speakers. The narrator of 'Tablets and Drink' is a working-class Birmingham man for
whom the pub (the 'Eagle') is an extension of home; the narrator of
'The Good Samaritan' is a university academic who has got into the
habit of meeting his friend and colleague after work to chat – they
have agreed to tape these conversations because, like all linguists,
they can't resist collecting data.

But despite these disparities of age and class, there are some important commonalities. I shall discuss four of these: the topic of the stories,
the gender of characters in the stories, the attention to detail, and the
use of taboo language. These features of men's narratives all serve to
align men with hegemonic masculinity.

First, the topics of these extracts are stereotypically masculine:
they are about cars, about modern technology, about drinking, about
travel. Other stories from the conversations have topics such as
going out drinking, fighting, pornographic videos, sporting achievement. One of the functions of such topics is that they keep talk away
from the personal: very few stories in the conversations involve self-
disclosure of a kind parallel with that found in women's friendly
talk.[2]

Second, these extracts all portray a world peopled by male human
beings. The only woman mentioned in these four extracts is the Vice-
Chancellor's wife. If we look back at the examples in the last chapter,
the two stories that opened the chapter, 'Jonesy and the Lion' and
'The Area Manager's Call', both portray a world populated only by

men (and animals). Very few of the stories have female protagonists or even female characters. In the sub-corpus[3] of 68 stories that I have analysed, 94 per cent of the stories have male protagonists, and 72 per cent of stories depict an all-male world.[4] This corresponds to Barbara Johnstone's findings for men's narratives in Indiana, USA: 'when men are not the protagonists of their own stories, they tell stories about other men'.[5]

Third, these extracts display a great deal of attention to detail. For example, in (2), the narrator talks about his car in detail: he mentions the speedometer, the windscreen wipers, the bonnet, and the fuses, and tells us how many times he cleaned the wires. In example (3), the narrator talks about *two megabytes* and *five twelve k*, details which position him as technically competent. In (4), the narrator gives the name of the pub and of the road at the beginning of the extract, tells us he had *only had two pints*, and specifies the time the policeman knocked on his windscreen; in example (5), we again get lots of detail about place and time.[6] This attention to detail constitutes an important strategy in men's conversation: it enables men to avoid talk of a more personal nature. That this is often a deliberate strategy is revealed by the following observation from David Jackson's 'critical autobiography': 'I often turn to the sports page in the daily newspaper, concerning myself with the raw material for endless non-emotional non-conversations with other men . . .'.[7]

The detailed naming of objects, then, is one way the language of these stories accomplishes masculinity. The use of taboo words is another, one that is difficult to overlook, and which compares markedly with the language of the women's conversations and the language of the mixed conversations I have collected. To give an example, the word *fuck* and words deriving from it (*fucking*, *fucked*, *fucker*, etc.) appears 72 times in the stories in the all-male sub-corpus, 12 times in the mixed sub-corpus, and not at all in the all-female sub-corpus. Examples (6)–(12) give some more examples of taboo language from the men's stories:

(6)　we don't know what the fuck to do with the bastards ['Captain Cook']
(7)　they just fucked me about completely ['School Trip to France']
(8)　there was this fucking great vibrator ['The Vibrator']
(9)　like beating the shit out of me ['Big Brothers']
(10)　I was fairly pissed by the time we got to the fucking park if you remember ['Quadruple Jack Daniels']

(11)   cos I'd been driving like a dangerous cunt ['Lucky Thirteen']
(12)   he used to come out with so much bollocks like that ['Skin
          Disease and Stress']

Taboo language in these stories functions in many ways: it gives
verisimilitude to direct speech; it adds emphasis to points the narrator
wants to foreground; but most importantly it performs hegemonic
masculinity. Swearing and taboo language have historically been used
by men in the company of other men as a sign of their toughness and
of their manhood. Jock Phillips, in his classic account of early settlers
in New Zealand, writes that swearing 'signalled the colonial man's
readiness to live a hard and physical life and his unconcern for the
genteel formalities of civilised life. It also showed contempt for the
female world of manners.'[8] Swearing has played this role for men all
over the world, not just in the colonial setting. In the late twentieth
century there is ample evidence that taboo language is used in all-
male sub-cultures such as the army and in the rugby changing room
as well as in adolescent peer groups on the street as a way of constructing solidarity.[9] The extract from the talk of four male friends
under the influence of alcohol which this book began with ('We was
playing naked football the other night . . .') illustrates the ubiquity of
taboo language in informal all-male talk.[10]

Another highly significant function of the language in men's
narratives is its role in maintaining emotional restraint. Male inexpressivity is recognized as a major feature of contemporary masculinity, and is increasingly seen as problematic: 'we have learnt to use
our language to set a safe distance from our felt experience'.[11] David
Jackson claims that 'the non-adult public arena was dominated by
language routines that taught me to bury the language of personal
feeling'.[12] These language routines include swearing, boasting and
talking tough, and men's narratives often function as boasts and
construct a world peopled by swearing, tough-talking males. But
emotional restraint is also accomplished through the use of technical
vocabulary and formal syntax. 'The Psion Swap' (example (3) above)
is a good instance of a story that uses technical language: the technical vocabulary is skilfully used to make the story convincing, but
it also keeps the focus away from the personal and the emotional.
The use of more formal syntax as a way of accomplishing emotional restraint is more apparent in the narratives told by older well-
educated men, who swear a great deal less than their working-class
peers and also less than younger speakers of all classes. Example (5) is

a good representative of the narratives told by these older middle-class men.

What emerges from this analysis of a few examples is that a variety of resources are exploited to accomplish hegemonic masculinity: topic choice, the virtual exclusion of women from the storyworld, and linguistic patterns, both lexical and syntactic. All these features contribute to emotional restraint, one of the key values inherent in hegemonic masculinity.[13]

'I Did the Most Amazing Left': Stories of Achievement

Apart from emotional restraint, the other aspect of these stories which is most striking is their stress on achievement. Achievement is another key value of dominant masculinity. Story-telling has a major role to play in enabling male narrators to perform hegemonic masculinity through presenting themselves, or their male protagonists, as successful, as heroes.

Examples (13) and (14) are both tales of achievement and triumph:

(13) The Paint Dispute
[Three young men in their mid-twenties are talking at Tim's flat about a difficult art student. Narrator: Tim; Jeremy's words are in italics, Luke's in italic capitals]
1   did I tell you recently?
2   he rea- he u- u- used up all- he used up a-
3   like I had a palette with like loads of black paint on it
4   and he used it all up
5   and I said 'Get me some more paint'
6   and he refused [*what?*]
7   I- I told him to get me some more paint and he was going- he was going to refuse
8   and he could tell that I was getting more and more serious about it
9   cos he was getting more and more refuscy about it
10 *he y- y- YOUR paint?*
11 it was MY paint [*yeah*]
12 he was a complete cunt about using other people's paint
13 and in- in the end I had to- er in the end I got REALly annoyed with him
14 and I kicked a chair into bits
15 and then he r- he sort of . ran- ran out of the studio

16 and stayed away for <u>half an hour before coming back</u>
        <LAUGHING>
17 <u>back and sort of shaking</u> <u>my hand and being apologetic</u>
        <AMUSED>
18 and then-
19 [*HE STILL DID- DIDN'T GET YOU MORE PAINT THOUGH?*]
20 well in fact he did
21 I mean he took a while about it cos he kept saying 'I've got no
        money'
22 and I at one point lost my temper with him
23 I couldn't do it a second time
24 it was really pathetic
25 but in the end he gave- he gave me a tube of white.

(14) Amazing Left

[Three 16-year-olds are talking in Julian's room at boarding school]
 1 in the June in the- in the final of the Cup
 2 I did the most amazing left with this half-volley you will ever
        see.
 3 ((it)) came down
 4 it was like quite- it was quite like- quite a- quite high but quite
        hard
 5 it came down ((here))
 6 I had someone running up
 7 it was on my left so I didn't have time to ((1 word)) change
        ((feet))
 8 so I took it on the half-volley
 9 and it just went flying <EMPHATIC>
10 and Neil ran on from an on-side position
11 and he was away
12 and he ((was))-
13 and it was just the most beautiful ball <u>I've ever ever ever seen</u>.
        <EMPHATIC>

In both these examples, the narrator presents himself as the protagonist in a story where he performs heroically, whether in contest
with another person, or on the sports field. In 'The Paint Dispute', the
narrator is relatively modest about his achievement: the evaluative
clause *it was really pathetic* focuses on the inadequacy of Robin, the
other student, rather than on Tim's victory. However, we are left in
no doubt as to who came out on top in this dispute. Julian, in 'Amazing

Left', frames his story explicitly as a celebration of triumph with the phrase *the most amazing left* in line 2, and the final line *it was just the most beautiful ball I've ever ever ever seen.*

I also want to include an example from stories told by older speakers: a good example is a first-person narrative told by a middle-aged man about collapsing with acute appendicitis and having to survive with incredible stoicism a series of events which prevent him getting to hospital. The story is very long – 126 lines – so the following is only an extract from the epic tale:

(15) *Extract from* **Appendicitis**
[Three middle-aged men in a pub after work]
49   the next morning things were no better
50   so . I walked round the street a couple of hundred yards to the
        doctor's surgery
51   unfortunately . the doctor . lived out in Essex
52   and he'd been snowed in
53   so . I spent a couple of hours sitting around in his surgery
54   and then finally the receptionist says, 'Look you know,
55   the doctor isn't going to be able to make it till this evening,
56   he's stuck in the snow,
57   would you mind coming back'.
58   so I shuffled off around the street <LAUGHING>
59   and spent the day thinking . ((you know)) 'This is really getting bad',
60   because .hh oddly enough the sort of classic appendicitis pain
        didn't appear until very late
61   you know 'god only knows what is wrong with me,
62   but this is- this is definitely rough'.
63   So I spent the whole day um-
64   finally five or so . o'clock came round
65   and I staggered around the street again to the doctor's surgery
66   and this time I got to see him
67   and I was standing in front of him
68   and I was going like this
69   sort of swaying in the breeze
70   and he said 'I need to get you a bed,
71   suspected appendicitis' he said.

Tony is then whisked into hospital, where it becomes clear that he has a ruptured appendix and needs to be operated on immediately if he is not to die. Like examples (13) and (14), it is a tale of heroism, but heroism of a different kind. The protagonist has to endure a terrible ordeal; he becomes increasingly ill, and circumstances, such as bad weather, conspire against him. He comes through the ordeal with stoic fortitude. As we see from these examples, heroic behaviour can mean winning a dispute, or making a perfect move on the sports field, or bearing pain and coming through an ordeal.

There are other stories in the men's conversations which deal with pain or illness. Typically, the narrator will foreground the pain or the illness only if it serves to illustrate how brave the protagonist was, or how successful in outwitting a significant other. As example (4) illustrates, Tom's back pain provides the background to his story of getting the better of the police. His triumphant ending *and I can get a-fucking-way with it you know*, with its flamboyant use of *fucking* as an infix, makes explicit what his achievement is: the tablets he takes for his back mean that the police can't touch him for drinking and driving. Even though the background to Tom's story indicates that his back gives him a lot of pain (*I was in fucking agony with the back*), he chooses to frame it as an achievement story. In conversations involving women, stories of this kind, where the first-person narrator has a difficult time as a result of physical incapacity, are presented as disaster.[14] But male narrators, as we see here, shape their narratives into tales of triumph over adversity.

In her analysis of the stories told by male and female speakers in a town in Indiana, USA, Barbara Johnstone found that the men's stories emphasized *contest*.[15] Achievement in these stories, that is, the winning of the contest, was associated with the male protagonist acting alone. (By contrast, the women's stories emphasized *community* and the importance of acting in collaboration with others: women were portrayed as failing when they acted alone.) The stories in the conversations I've analysed seem to support her findings: in (13), Tim acts alone – and violently – to make Robin replace the paint he'd used; in (14), Julian is clearly part of a team, but the story celebrates his solo contribution; in the 'Appendicitis' story, the narrator portrays himself as battling alone against the odds.

The conversations also contain a subset of achievement stories which paradoxically tell of things going wrong, yet which function as boasts. The story 'The Area Manager's Call', which was discussed in chapter 2, is a good example of such a story. Like tales of heroism, these stories focus on the achievement of a lone protagonist in doing extraordinary deeds, but what is salient is how *bad* the protagonist has been, rather than how heroic. The following is another story in the same vein, again told by Rob to Gary and Dan in the pub. The beginning of this story has already been discussed in chapter 2.

(16)   The Pornographic Video
   1   *you not been demolishing houses recently? .*
   2   no, I've not done anything- ((I'm)) just trying to think what
          I've done lately (6.0)
   3   don't think I've done anything really that bad lately (2.0)
   4   oh yeah I have actually
   5   [*G laughs*]
→ 6   when we went out for this meal last week
   7   with Nick Staples
   8   um a customer . um . left a video . in a video recorder [*yeah*]
   9   and it broke in th- in there
  10 so Nick Staples got it out
  11 played it back and it's a porno film [*G laughs*]
  12 so he taped it [*G laughs*]
  13 and we were talking at this meal
  14 and he goes: 'oh I've got this porno film',
  15 I said, 'oh you'll have to let me borrow that film . Nick'
  16 and this is a bloke . that s- stays up . till . bloody twelve o'clock
          to watch the free ten minutes of soft porn on S-Sky [*G and
          D laugh*]
  17 so you can . imagine how sad this bloke is
  18 his pride and joy this tape
  19 he absolutely loves this tape to bits
  20 he's only just got it
  21 and he said 'Y- I'll let you borrow it
  22 but . just don't lend it out to anyone
  23 I want you to look after this tape
  24 I want it back in a couple of days'
  25 'Yeah, no problem,
  26 I'm- what d'you think I'm going to do to it
  27 I ain't gonna lend it out or nothing', no
  28 takes it home
  29 set the two video recorders up
  30 started taping it
  31 went back
  32 played it yeah
  33 brilliant
  34 thought 'I better get back to work'

35 press record
36 got back
37 and I thought 'oh I'll have a look,
38 see what it's like'
39 rewound it
40 pressed play
41 'this is MTV – strange'
42 got the other tape [*G laughs*]
43 'oh fuck, I've recorded MTV over it' <LAUGHS>
44 so I had to pluck up courage to tell him . that . I'd taped over
      his . bloody pride and joy video tape . with three hours <u>of</u>
      MTV <LAUGHING>
45 [*G and D laugh*]

Again this story tells of making a serious error: Rob presents himself as someone who gets into scrapes and who also manages to get out of them one way or another. In the case of this story, the scrape is explicitly framed as doing something 'bad' (line 3). His achievement here can be seen as a form of 'laddishness'. It seems that, in the modern world, 'behaving badly', that is, getting into minor scrapes, has positive connotations when associated with men.[16] Rob's story functions simultaneously to present him as someone who is an agent in his own life, but also as someone who makes mistakes, mistakes which he presents to his friends as something to laugh about, as proof of his laddishness. This mixture of openness and bravado can be found in many of the stories I've collected. They range from public school pranks told by schoolboys to each other, to potentially serious encounters such as being breathalysed by the police (see the extract 'Tablets and Drink', example (4)). In other words, these tales of bravado occur in conversations across the range I've collected and involve both younger and older men, and men from all social classes.

The story 'The Pornographic Video' is not just a laddish tale. It deals ambivalently with its subject, a pornographic video, depicting the video's owner as 'sad' for loving the tape, while telling a story about trying to copy the tape. In other words, the narrator positions himself (and his audience) as simultaneously interested in and not interested in pornographic videos. He portrays the video's owner as addicted to soft porn, while attempting to present his own attempt to copy the video as a laddish prank. This ambivalence reflects society's ambivalence: is watching pornography manly and therefore part of dominant masculinity? Or is it simply pathetic? While the story's main theme is a version of 'men behaving badly', like many of the stories it also deals with other, more complex, issues.

'More Leather Elbow Patches': Men Friends Having a Laugh

But there is more to men's talk than the construction and maintenance of hegemonic masculinity. One fact that all researchers agree on is that men have fun together. 'Having a laugh' is something which young males value very highly, to the extent that it is claimed that ' "having a laugh" is central to being acceptable as masculine'.[17] It goes on being an important theme of male friendship in adulthood, though it is more typical of younger men and of men employed in white- or blue-collar work than of older professional men. Male speakers use stories to narrate incidents when they 'had a laugh' as well as to entertain their friends. In other words, stories can be *about* having a laugh as well as being in themselves a way of having a laugh. Examples of the former are stories of laddish pranks such as 'The Area Manager's Call' (chapter 2) and 'The Pornographic Video' (example (16) above), while examples of the latter are humorous stories about crazy others such as 'Jonesy and the Lion' (chapter 2) or about unlikely incidents (a good example is 'A Double-Glazing Jehovah's Witness' which comes in chapter 4).

In the following brief example, two men friends play with the idea of a parallel world in which Chris had become an academic rather than a solicitor:

(17) If We'd Both Been Academics
Chris: I would've been going down the shops for more . leather elbow patches for my cardigan.
Geoff: <LAUGHS> yes and you would've been running a 386 machine and gasping at the graphics that that would produce.
Chris: a 386! I would've had a Style Writer or something.
Geoff: <LAUGHS> 'what's wrong with the old pen and paper?' <OLD MAN'S VOICE>

The two friends here collaborate in mocking the idea of the unworldly academic, rather in the style of the Monty Python 'sardine tin in the road' sketch ('. . . we used to live in a sardine tin in the road and were grateful . . .'). Each contribution takes a more extreme position and

Geoff's laughter demonstrates their amusement at this sustained bit of joking. (Of course, by mocking the technological naivety of academics, they simultaneously position themselves as technologically sophisticated.)

The next, longer, extract comes from a conversation in which three young men are discussing whether miracles are possible (all three are involved in their local church). In this example, Des reinterprets a Bible story with help from Jack and Hav (Jack and Hav's contributions are in italics):

(18) Miracles

1   But supposing that he raised someone from the dead?
2   [. . .]
3   It was a little girl [*yeah*]
4   and she was dead
5   he got to the house too late
6   when she was dead,
7   I can't remember all the . . .
8   And . he- he said- he said something ((to her))
9   *'Get up, ((xx)) stupid cow'*
10   and she got up,
11   she was alive.
12   But . when you think about how shit medicine was in those days [*mhm*]
13   I mean who says she was dead? [*yeah I know*]
14   she could have been in a coma [*yeah*]
15   and he could have like triggered something off
16   *she could have been lying*
17   she could have been lying
18   *she could have been really pretending*
19   **very very well**
20   **she could have been like-**
21   *'Right ((I'm gonna sort that out))'* <CLAPS HANDS> <LAUGHTER>
22   'I can't- I can't keep this up much longer, <SIMULATES GIRL'S HIGH VOICE> <LAUGHTER>
23   fucking stupid bearded cunt, <LOUD LAUGHTER>
24   go on, fuck off,' <LAUGHTER>
25   for fuck's sake, the bastard. <QUIETER>
26   'Get up' <SERIOUS VOICE> <LAUGHTER>
27   'Thank God for that, <REVERTS TO GIRL'S VOICE> <LAUGHTER>
28   oh, Jesus Christ <LAUGHTER> that was hard.' <LAUGHTER>

29 <u>Right, where's my fiver</u>. <NORMAL VOICE> <LAUGHTER>

30 But I mean let's face it,

31 medicine was crap. [*yeah*]

This story is typical of many in the conversations I've collected. Talk switches between serious and non-serious frames, and the men involved collaborate with each other to bring about the switches. This example is in two parts: the first (serious) part is a re-telling of a Bible story about a miracle; the second (non-serious) part involves a dramatized re-interpretation of the story. The link between the two parts (lines 12–20) is constructed by two speakers, Des and Jack. In the second part, Des's animation of the two main characters (the little girl and Jesus) through direct speech is greeted with almost constant laughter from the other two. Des's joking demand for payment (*right where's my fiver?*) recognizes that he has succeeded in amusing his friends. But his switch back to a serious frame in the next line *(But I mean let's face it, medicine was crap. . . .)* is achieved through the co-operation of Jack and Hav, who stop laughing.

Having a laugh, in conversations like this one, is something that is possible at any moment: any topic can be switched into a non-serious frame if all participants co-operate. This gives conversation a slightly manic feel, as more serious talk is always under threat. But note that switches sometimes don't come off. In line 9, Hav's intervention 'Get up, ((xx)) stupid cow' fails in its bid to shift to a non-serious frame. Des ignores Hav and completes his initial re-telling of the story. However, Hav's words provide the stimulus for Des to tell the story again entirely in dialogue, and allow Des the economy of simply saying 'Get up' in a more serious voice (line 26) to bring off the animation of Jesus in the story.

But these three friends are not just fooling about and having a laugh; they are also mulling things over. This brief extract shows them wrestling with the concept of 'miracle' and playing with alternative interpretations of this particular incident. Des's irreverent version of the story (lines 13–29) is framed by his proposition *medicine was crap* (introduced in line 12 as *when you think about how shit medicine was in those days*). This is a serious idea which allows them to 'explain' in rational terms the miracle of raising someone from the dead. Their fooling around allows them to explore alternative ways of understanding the Bible story.

I have noticed that in men's talk, 'having a laugh' often conceals other, more sensitive themes. For example, while men friends seem to enjoy sharing laddish stories of getting away with things, their tales of nearly getting into trouble allow them to be briefly in touch with the parallel world where things did *not* work out all right. For example, the story 'You Can't Not Know Your Name' (example (3), chapter 2), which deals with the narrator's friend nearly failing to get into a night-club because he couldn't produce the name on the driving licence, is at face value a funny story, as we see from the laughter of co-participants. But the story is funny precisely because of their aware-ness of how easily things could have turned out badly. Similarly, Tom's story of getting away with drinking and driving ('Tablets and Drink', example (4), this chapter) is superficially a story of bravado and of triumph over the police. Tom laughs at the climax of his story, but there is an important sub-text which deals with pain and suffer-ing: Tom has to take the tablets because his back gives him a lot of pain. In other words, men *do* deal with sensitive issues in their talk, but in a rather tangential way.

'I'll Beat All of That': Competition in Story-telling

Overtly, though, men's stories align them with hegemonic norms. The focus on achievement in men's stories means that narrative activity in all-male groups can be face-threatening in a way that it is not in all-female groups. Telling stories becomes in itself a competitive activ-ity, with speakers competing to boast about their triumphs or their cock-ups. For example, in the conversations, adolescent speakers compete to tell ever more extreme stories about getting drunk, young men (in their twenties) tell stories which exaggerate feats of aggression and getting the better of authority figures (e.g. by kicking down a door at work, about skiving off work, about a fight with a workmate), older men with a more working-class background tell stories about run-ins with the police, while older men with a more middle-class background vie with each other to appear widely read or well travelled or up-to-date in terms of technology and science – or even good wine. In one story sequence, the narrator of the second story begins his story with the words *tell you what, I'll beat all of that*, which explicitly labels his narrative as a competitive speech act.

In the case of younger speakers, this competitive element can be overt, with so-called friends ganging up on each other. The following extract comes from a series of boasting stories about drinking and getting drunk, told by three 16-year-old boys. It's the kind of narrative that Livia Polanyi calls a 'diffuse story' because the story isn't told as a neat chunk, but instead 'blocks of story materials [are] interleaved with blocks of conversation in which points of the story are discussed or amplified'.[18]

(19) *Extract from* Quadruple Jack Daniels
[Three 16-year-old boys at public school]
Henry: that evening you were in such a bad mood cos me and
    Robert were pissed and you weren't
Robert: I'm serious you know I've never seen you pissed
Julian: oh crap
Robert: I've never seen you pissed
Julian: how will that- hang on
Robert: how have you ever been pissed? <R AND H LAUGH>
Julian: oh fuck off
Robert: tell me now <MOCKING>
Julian: fuck you

This is a particularly vicious bit of competitive talk. Note how none of the speakers mitigates the force of their remarks with any face-saving devices. In particular, Robert's attack on Julian's drinking ability is a face-threatening act, pure and simple. Julian responds by swearing – *oh crap; fuck off; fuck you* – as a feeble attempt at counter-attack, but he can only lose face whatever he chooses to do. If he attempts to provide evidence that he has been drunk (which he does at another point), that still allows Robert the victory of having forced him onto the defensive.

A more subtle way of competing is to undermine another's story by adding a deflating comment at the end. In this way, the heroism of the current narrator-cum-protagonist can be punctured so that the next narrator is free to take the floor. The talk following the story 'Amazing Left' (example (14)) is a good example of this. After the narrator's triumphant *it was just the most beautiful ball I've ever ever ever seen*, one of his co-participants at talk asks, 'Who?'. The narrator answers, with considerable bathos, 'Me'. The question 'Who?' undermines the whole point of the story – if the addressees can claim not to know who the story is about, it fails as a piece of one-upmanship.

This strategy of deflation is also used by older speakers. For example, a middle-aged middle-class male tells a long story about a Volkswagen Beetle which was swept off a bridge into a river somewhere in Africa but which proves to be watertight and starts first time once it's back on dry land. The story is well constructed, but the narrator's friend adds comments both during and at the end of the story which undermine the narrator. The final section of the story is given in example (20).

(20) *Extract from* Watertight Volkswagen
84 The punchline of this tale was that he sent this reel of film which he'd taken back for developing in Germany
85 and had addressed it to his wife
86 and it arrived when his wife's-
87 it arrived at his home
88 and his wife saw the pictures before a letter from him arrived explaining what was ((up))
89 she was no end surprised to see her husband's Volkswagen in the middle of a river
90 *and no husband*
91 and no husband
92 all was well <IN HUSHED TONES>
93 *yes that seems to be the sort of thing one might attribute to the publicity department of Volkswagen*

The final comment here constitutes a highly unsupportive move; the narrator has invested time (this is one of the longer stories in the corpus) and creative energy in building a storyworld, in animating characters, in constructing a coherent plot. What the story-recipient is in effect saying is that he is not fool enough to think this is a genuine story, since in his view it is probably a fiction spread around by 'the publicity department of Volkswagen'. Although he is relatively indirect in making this accusation – he uses the hedges *seems, sort of thing*, and *might* and employs the impersonal pronoun *one* – this is still a 'So what?' move, and it therefore constitutes a serious challenge to the story's claims to tellability.

'Was He Beating You Up?': Collaborative Story-telling in Men's Talk

While competition is both a theme of men's stories and an aspect of male story-telling practice, men also choose sometimes to tell a story collaboratively. Collaborative narration involves skilful use of language because co-narrators need to anticipate each other's contributions accurately as well as to make contributions that are textually cohesive, that is, that fit the story so far. Collaborative narration can only occur where speakers know each other well, and have shared knowledge. It is much less common in all-male talk than in all-female talk, but can be a powerful means of expressing solidarity.

Let's look at two examples from the men's conversations. The first narrative to be discussed here is 'Carpet Tack Revenge', a story about a bully and how he was challenged and defeated. The story comes from a conversation involving five young men in their late teens who have met to smoke dope and chat in Jack's garden shed (something they do on a regular basis). The narrator, Jack, who is also the chief protagonist, initially seems reluctant to tell his story. The story emerges through the skilful use of questions which co-participants use to move the narrative along. It is given in (21) below (Jack's words are in normal typeface; other participants' contributions are in italics):

(21) Carpet Tack Revenge
1 *he used to beat you up? Mark?* [Hav]
2 yeah
3 *how comes?* [Hav]
4 cos he's- he- I dunno really
5 it was just-
6 ⌈I was just one of those . people-
7 ⌊*was he like- was he beating you up?* [Des]
8 yeah
9 I was one of those people
10 and he'd see me
11 and then he'd come over and beat me up [*Des laughs*]
12 *but he stopped after you stuck those nails in his back didn't he* [Will]
13 yeah that's right <LAUGHS>
14 *what happened- you stuck nails in his back?* [Mick]
15 yeah
16 *like what sort of nails?* [Mick]
17 er the ones you put in carpets
18 you know the sort of black ones
19 *tacks =* [Des]
20 *= tacks* [Mick]
21 yeah
22 *how did you tack a man in his back?* [Mick]
23 I just . got his shoulder
24 and got the nail there

25 and went like that into his shoulder blade
26 *what did he do?* [Mick]
27 he went 'aaaaghh'=
28 =*and hit you* [Mick]
29 =and ran off [*oh!*]
30 and then he didn't do it any more
31 *how big was he then?*
32 *how big was he?* [Des]
33 he was- he was well- not much-
34 well he was a year older than me
35 so
36 that's how much bigger he was

The construction of this chunk of talk is highly collaborative. The
background to the story emerges in general talk about a boy called
Mark who used to beat people up at school. Lines 1–11 provide
orientation, while it is Will's question *but he stopped after you stuck
those nails in his back* which signals the beginning of the story proper
and provides an abstract. This abstract is repeated in Mick's questions
What happened? you stuck nails in his back? and these questions are
designed to elicit the story. Jack's answer *yeah* confirms the abstract,
and is followed by a further question from Mick – *like what sort of
nails?* – which results in a vague answer from Jack (*you know the sort
of black ones*). Des collaborates here by providing a more precise term:
tacks. Mick repeats Des's term *tacks* and asks the key question *how did
you tack a man in his back?* It is only at this point (line 23) that Jack
starts to tell his story in recognizable short narrative clauses, each one
containing a simple past tense verb – this is the narrative core of the
story:

> I just . got his shoulder
> and got the nail there
> and went like that into his shoulder blade
> *what did he do?*
> he went 'aaaaghh'=
> =*and hit you* =
> =and ran off
> and then he didn't do it any more

Note that even this narrative core is told by two speakers, Jack and
Mick. Mick's contribution *and hit you* is a collaborative completion which

anticipates the resolution of the story. In fact, he anticipates wrongly, and Jack gives the actual resolution: *and ran off and then he didn't do it any more.* The story ends with the elicitation of further details about the bully which also function as an evaluation, since the bully being older and bigger casts Jack's action in an even more heroic light.

All five young men take part in the construction of this narrative, which makes it a remarkably collaborative endeavour. All participants seem fascinated by the story, and in particular, they are fascinated by the *details* of this violent episode in Jack's life. But they also seem aware that heroic action can make you vulnerable, an awareness which prompts Mick's faulty inference that the bully responded to Jack's attack with more violence.

Another collaboratively told story comes from a conversation involving seven young men in their twenties enjoying an evening in the pub. This third-person narrative describes a character who has been a workmate of most of the seven (several of them work for – or have worked for – a high street electrical goods chain). The young man at the centre of the story is clearly regarded as an oddity, and the story 'Strap 'Er On' tells of an episode when he delivers a television to a customer on the back of his motorbike. The collaborative telling of this story about him functions to build solidarity and a sense of shared norms. The chief narrator is Rob, but four other speakers contribute to the telling of the story (their contributions are in italics).

(22) 'Strap 'Er On'
[N.B. Underlined words are spoken with a broad Somerset accent]
1   this bloke called Phil at work
2   lives in <u>Taunton</u>
3   *<u>Taunton</u> yeah, Phil* [Craig]
4   and he calls his Mum
5   *'strap 'er on'* [Craig]
6   and he calls his Mum y- <u>our Gladys</u>
7   <u>our Gladys</u>
8   *Gladys* [Jeff]
9   and he s- he se- we went out for a drink
10 and he goes- yeah <LAUGHING>
11 he said- yeah 'that kid with the <u>gert big</u> <u>long arms</u>' <LAUGHS>
12 '<u>gert big thin arms</u>'
13 *yeah '<u>gert big thin arms</u>'* [Craig]
14 I said to him I said 'how can you have gert big thin arms?
15 they're either . big or they're thin

16   gert big thin it's not'
17   it doesn't-
18   *no, contradiction totally* [Johnny]
19   yeah
20   *ace* [Jeff]
21   and then he goes=
22   =*'gotta strap 'er on'* [Craig]
23   yeah, someone gets a um wide-screen tv,
24   nine hundred quid,
25   *that was hilarious that was, good story* [Gary]
26   I said 'yeah better put some bubble-wrap round hadn't we
27   might get damaged on the way'
28   'no don't worry
29   I'll just strap 'er on'
30   about half an hour later . 'bloody hell I've just had this tv
         delivered
31   and it looks like someone's kicked it to bits',
32   smashed all over <LAUGHING>
33   *it was in pieces literally it was*
34   *absolute bits.* [Craig]
35   I said 'so much for you just strapping 'er on'.
36   <LAUGHTER>
37   I always take the piss out of him
38   that was it what he said,
39   'don't worry, just strap 'er on'.

The collaborative feature of this story which stands out is repetition,
with significant words and phrases recurring throughout the story.
Craig repeats the names *Phil* and *Taunton* and Jeff repeats the name
Gladys. Craig also repeats the phrase *gert big thin arms*, while the other
key phrase *strap 'er on* occurs five times. Many of these words and
phrases are also repeated by the main narrator, Rob, so the overall
effect is one of very strong lexical cohesion. Co-participants also repeat
what Rob has said but in different words. Rob's words *and it looks
like someone's kicked it to bits, smashed all over* (lines 31–2) are echoed
by Craig in 33–4: *it was in pieces literally it was, absolute bits* (with
bits repeating Rob's *bits* from line 31). And Rob's representation of
himself as asserting that arms can't be both big and thin (14–16) is
supported by Johnny who says *no, contradiction totally*.

   Another feature of collaborative talk exhibited by this story is utterance completion, which can only be done when speakers know each

other well and which demonstrates shared knowledge and a shared world-view. Rob begins the utterance *and then he goes* (line 21) and Craig completes the clause with the words *'gotta strap 'er on'*. Gary greets this story abstract with the supportive comment *that was hilarious that was, good story*.

Rob, Craig, Jeff, Gary and Johnny all contribute to the telling of this story. What they achieve through this collaboration is a very strong sense of being an in-group. Many of the contributions demonstrate that several of those involved in telling the story were also witnesses to the events told in the story, or else have heard the story before and enjoy sharing in its re-telling. The talk that precedes the story makes very clear that the facts that constitute the eventual story are well known to several of the friends. This talk is reproduced in (23) below:

(23) *Talk preceding* 'Er On'

Craig:	<u>gert big arms</u> <LAUGHS>
<LAUGHTER>	
Johnny:	what's gert big arms
Jeff:	<LAUGHS>
Rob:	**there's this- there's this bloke, Johnny**
Craig:	**<u>'strap 'er on'</u> ((it makes you laugh))**
Rob:	I'm gonna take the emphasis off you
Jeff:	<LAUGHS>
Rob:	and we'll take the piss out of someone else
Craig:	<LAUGHS>
→ Rob:	this bloke called Phil at work
Jeff:	<LAUGHS>
Rob:	lives in Taunton

As this extract shows, it is Craig's quotation of the phrase *gert big arms* in a Somerset accent which triggers the telling of the story. Craig's utterances *gert big arms, strap 'er on*, and *it makes you laugh* all perform in-group work: they allude to a story that some of them know but others don't. Johnny, who is not a regular member of this group, asks *what's gert big arms?* Rob responds by announcing he will tell the relevant story (*there's this bloke, Johnny*) but positions Johnny as not one of the favoured few by going on *I'm gonna take the emphasis off you, and we'll take the piss out of someone else*. Rob's use of the pronoun *we* in *we'll take the piss out of someone else* also anticipates that the telling of the story will be shared by those in the know. In terms of lexical cohesion, note how Craig's quotation of the two key phrases from the story in this pre-story talk prepares his fellow speakers for their eventual use in the story itself. In fact, Craig is unable to restrain himself from quoting *strap 'er on* (line 5) at a moment which is not justified by the surrounding context.

The use by Rob and Craig of a Somerset accent in their representation of Phil's speech has an evaluative function: it distances them from him and makes him the butt of humour. West Country English accents stereotypically have the value of slow or stupid, and the co-narrators here take advantage of this possibility to characterize Phil as intrinsically different from them, as 'other'. The story (it is really two mini-stories on the same theme of Phil's stupidity) presents Phil as first making an illogical statement (*gert big thin arms*) and then making the decision to deliver a television to a customer by motorbike. Rob and his co-participants are able to present themselves, in contrast to Phil, as both logical (arms can't be both big and thin) and sensible (they anticipate the television getting damaged and suggest wrapping it in bubble-wrap). As Deborah Cameron has argued, the collaborative talk of young men functions to maintain or establish the in-group and to exclude others.[19] This story, with its focus on 'taking the piss' out of a particular other (Phil), allows co-participants to celebrate their in-group status and to enjoy the performance of their shared knowledge and shared values. Rob's words *I always take the piss out of him*, said in a coda to the story, position Phil as a permanent 'other', and show how important it is for in-group members to proclaim their difference from someone like Phil.

We can see that both these stories are constructed by more than one speaker and that collaboration is accomplished through a variety of means including repetition, collaborative completions and the use of questions. But these two stories, despite their collaborative structure, still embody many features that enable them to perform dominant masculinity. They deal with contest – physical contest in the case of 'Carpet Tack Revenge', verbal contest in the case of 'Strap 'Er On' (note Rob's coda: *I always take the piss out of him*). In 'Carpet Tack Revenge', the male protagonist comes out on top, while in 'Strap 'Er On', the narrator constructs the third-person protagonist as 'other'. The action takes place in the public arena in both stories, and the world they portray is inhabited exclusively by men (though Phil's mother is mentioned in passing). Both stories avoid emotion. Finally, there is attention to detail about inanimate objects: for example the co-narrators in 'Carpet Tack Revenge' work hard to name with precision the tacks used in the attack, while the television being delivered in 'Strap 'Er On' is described as *wide-screen* and worth £900.

It seems that collaborative story-telling enables men to jointly construct dominant masculinity, while simultaneously allowing them to express solidarity with each other. In 'Strap 'Er On', it is evident that the young men get a lot of pleasure out of their collaborative retelling of this story. 'Carpet Tack Revenge', by contrast, emerges as a collaborative narrative because Jack is initially so reluctant to tell the story. This seems to be because he is very aware of his non-heroic position at the beginning of the story. His statement *I was just one of those people* (line 6) declares rather fatalistically that some people are victims and some are bullies, and he was one of the former. Although his story eventually emerges as having a classic trajectory, with Jack getting his own back on the bully, throughout its shared telling there is an awareness of vulnerability that makes this an unusual story.

'He Was Quite Frightened': The Struggle to Express Vulnerability

Many of the stories we have looked at reproduce the dominant values of masculinity – emotional restraint, ambition, achievement, and competitiveness. But as we have seen in the story 'Carpet Tack Revenge', these values inevitably jostle for position with other, competing, values. We are all involved, whether we like it or not, in the ceaseless struggle to define gender,[20] and it is not the case that the men whose conversations I have listened to adopt the dominant discourses of masculinity at all times and without protest. Some of the stories reveal men struggling to reconcile competing discourses of masculinity.

The next story is a good example of this: in many respects this story performs conventional masculinity, but alternative discourses are voiced, and the discussion which follows the story shows the men struggling to reconcile these competing discourses. The story comes from a conversation involving four men, all carpenters, aged between 25 and 40, having a drink in a pub after work; the narrator is Alan.

(24) The Digger
1   should've seen Jason on that digger though
2   yeah he . he come down the ((park)) part
3   where it's- the slope

4   then he's knocking down the front wall
5   and there was this big rock
6   and he couldn't get it out
7   so he put a bit more . power on the thing
8   and . and the thing- the digger went <<SCOOPING NOISE>>
9   it nearly had him out <LAUGHS>
10 he come out all white.

This story constructs a dominant version of masculinity, where masculinity is bound up with physical strength. It tells of a man knocking down a wall, and using a huge and powerful machine to achieve this. The point of the story is that when Jason tries to employ more power to dig out the recalcitrant rock, he almost loses control of the machine.

The last line of the story, *he come out all white*, makes a subtle shift in perspective. 'To go white' is recognized as being a physical manifestation of fear, so in this line Alan portrays Jason not as a hero but as someone who nearly lost control of a powerful machine and who is frightened by the experience. Note that in lines 2–7 Jason is the subject of active verbs, but in lines 8 and 9, the climax of the story, the machine becomes the subject, with Jason becoming the object (*it nearly had him out*). This twist in the power relations between the man and the machine results in Jason *com[ing] out all white* in line 10.

As the following extract shows, two of Alan's co-participants orient to his evaluation of the story, but the third, Chris, resists. Example (25) presents the men's talk following Alan's story. Because this extract is not narrative, it needs to be presented in a different format: I have used stave format (as in a musical score) to allow the interplay of voices to be clearly seen. (Transcription conventions are given at the beginning of the book.)

(25) The Digger

```
 8   Alan:   it nearly had him out/ <LAUGHS> he come out all white/
     Chris:                     <LAUGHS>
     Kevin:                     <LAUGHS>
     John:
 9   Alan:
     Chris:  <LAUGHS>
     Kevin:           I bet that could be dangerous ⌈couldn't it/
     John:                                     ((⌊hurt himself/))
```

```
10  Alan:
    Chris:
    Kevin:   if it fell ⌈on your head))              it's quite-
    John:               ⌊he-            you know/ -
```
```
11  Alan:
    Chris:                          <LAUGHS> ⌈can I have some
    Kevin:   ⌈it's quite big/
    John:    ⌊he crapped himself/          he ⌊crapped himself/
```
```
12  Alan:
    Chris:   pot noodles please Kevin <SILLY VOICE>
    Kevin:                    <LAUGHS> ⌈no/
    John:                             ⌊did he have to sit down
```
```
13  Alan:           he- he- well . he was quite frightened ⌈actually/
    Chris:
    Kevin:
    John:   and stuff? .                                   ⌊I know/
```
```
14  Alan:           cos- cos-                        ⌈well yeah/
    Chris:                    was it for you as well ⌊mate?
    Kevin:
    John:   I must admit-
```
```
15  Alan:                                        ((well I still-))
    Chris:   did you go a bit white as well then did you?
    Kevin:
    John:                                                    god/
```
```
16  Alan:
    Chris:                                            don't get
    Kevin:
    John:   he was thinking 'god please don't wreck it'/
```
```
17  Alan:
    Chris:   any blood on it/ <SARCASTIC>
    Kevin:                          is that the one with all the loa-
    John:
```
```
18  Kevin:   lots of different things on it?
```

[Discussion continues about different types and sizes of diggers]

Kevin and John both orient to Alan's move to bring Jason's fear into focus: Kevin comments on the danger of such machines, while John surmises that Jason could have got hurt, and that he *crapped himself*, another physical manifestation of fear. Kevin's comments are met by taunting from Chris – at least, that is how I interpret Chris's remark *can I have some pot noodles please Kevin*. Chris uses a silly voice to say this and since at face value the remark is totally irrelevant, we have to use conversational inferencing to interpret it. Superficially this utterance is a polite request for food, the sort of thing you might expect somebody relatively powerless – a child, for example – to say to someone more powerful – a mother or a dinner lady. By saying this, is Chris implying that Kevin's utterances *I bet that could be dangerous couldn't it if it fell on your head, it's quite- it's quite big* would be more appropriate in the mouth of a caregiver or food-provider, i.e. in the mouth of a woman? Certainly, Chris seems to be trying to humiliate Kevin, to position him as being cowardly, a wimp, of being unmasculine. Perhaps by producing an utterance as irrelevant as this, he is implying that Kevin's utterances are equally out of place. Chris clearly finds Kevin's view of Jason's near-accident threatening. However, Kevin does not seem to be intimidated: he laughs and says *no* to Chris, meaning 'No you can't have any pot noodles', which defuses the challenge by treating it humorously.

John continues to explore the theme of Jason and fear with his question to Alan: *did he have to sit down and stuff?* This leads to Alan, who was an eye witness, admitting: *he- he- well . he was quite frightened actually*. Note the hesitations and false starts in this response, as well as the presence of several hedges: Alan is clearly uncomfortable with his answer. Predictably, given his taunting of Kevin, Chris now has a go at Alan with the direct challenge *was it for you as well mate?*, that is, 'was it frightening?' Alan replies, *well yeah*, with his *well* again signalling that this is a dispreferred response. Chris's subsequent question *did you go a bit white as well then did you?* ends with an aggressive tag. It is aggressive in that it demands an answer from Alan, and at the same time the repetition of *did you?* has overtones of motherese (*does he want his dindins, does he?*) which rudely suggests that Alan is behaving like a baby. Chris's question is highly face-threatening. His use of the phrase *go a bit white*, which picks up Alan's earlier utterance, mocks the euphemistic aspect of it and implies that to go white is un-manly. This question challenges Alan to align himself with Jason and, by extension, with un-manliness. Alan begins a reluctant response: *well I still-* before he is rescued by John's intervention: *god, he was thinking 'god please don't wreck it'*. John in effect answers for Alan with the claim that if Alan had gone white it was because he was worried about the machine. This utterance shifts the ground of the discussion by suggesting that the men's anxiety is to do with damaging the machine rather than with their own vulnerability. This interpretation of events is obviously more palatable to Chris, who here stands for hegemonic masculinity, but he still adds the sarcastic comment *don't get any blood on it* as if determined to wrong-foot Alan. But Kevin and John then steer the conversation into a discussion of exactly what kind of digger it was and how it compares to a fork-lift truck, an impersonal discussion involving lots of detail which re-establishes the solidarity of the group and their alignment with dominant norms of masculinity.

The tension and conflict in this short extract demonstrate how difficult it is for male speakers to discuss vulnerability, and how peer group pressure works to silence those who try to voice alternative masculinities.[21] Alan, Kevin and John attempt to explore their feelings, and thus to push at conventional gender boundaries, but violations of gender boundaries will always be resisted, and will be met with sanctions ranging from ridicule, as here, to violence.[22]

'Queerie': Masculinity and Homophobia

One significant way in which hegemonic masculinity is created and maintained is through the denial of femininity. The denial of the feminine is central to masculine gender identity.[23] As Adam Jukes puts it: 'the exorcism of all one's identifiable "feminine" or "mothering" qualities is essential to assuming masculinity'.[24] This means that men in conversation avoid ways of talking that might be associated with femininity and also actively construct women and gay men as the despised other. Hegemonic masculine discourses are both misogynistic and homophobic.

We all in part construct who we are through saying who we are not, but for men the denial of homosexuality is particularly salient; hegemonic masculinity is, in fact, heterosexual masculinity.[25] Deborah Cameron spells out the norm as follows: 'men in all-male groups must unambiguously display their heterosexual orientation'.[26] Younger males in my corpus are openly homophobic at times.[27] Example (26) is a story told by a male student to a friend about an evening out with his friend Bill:

(26) Queerie
[Two male friends, aged 19/20, narrator = Lee]
1   and er night before I left to come here right
2   I um ((xx)) Bill ((xx)),
3   I told you this.

4   I was driving down the road
5   and I've just seen this long hair little fucking mini-skirt.
6   I've beeped the horn,
7   this fucking bloke's turned round,
8   I've gone '<u>aaaggghhh!</u>' <SCREAMS>
9   <LAUGHTER>
10 Bill's gone 'what what what?',
11 'it was a bloke',
12 I've gone, 'turn round, turn round',
13 and he's turned round
14 and you could just see these shoes hiding under this car
15 and he must've thought we were just gonna literally beat the crap out of him.
16 [. . .]
17 I've driven past,
18 opened the window,
19 'come out, come out, wherever you are,
20 here queerie, queerie, queerie'.

This story operates on two levels: first, it tells of a series of events when the narrator and his friend pass someone who looks like a woman but who turns out on closer inspection to be a man dressed in a mini-skirt. More importantly, this story does important work in terms of establishing the narrator's identity: he positions himself as uncompromisingly heterosexual both through his initial interest in the person with long hair wearing a mini-skirt, and also through his horrified reaction when he realizes this person is actually a man. His fantasy that the cross-dresser feared they would 'beat the crap' out of him hints at the violent feelings unleashed by this encounter. The story ends with the narrator presenting himself as venting his fury at this subversion of conventional gender boundaries by shouting taunts and insults at the man (whether this actually happened or not is beside the point). This story demonstrates how powerful narrative can be as a tool of self-presentation and self-construction: the narrator is at an age when his sexual identity is still fragile and the function of this story is to establish his credentials as a 'normal' heterosexual man.

The next example, example (27), is an extract from a story in which two public schoolboys talk about a boy called Prendergast. Again, these 17-year-olds are still working to develop a more solid sense of their own masculinity, and this extract shows them struggling with what that means:

(27) *Extract from* **Throwing Stuff Out of Windows**
[Narrator = Henry; Julian's words are in italics]
1   he was talking about . being raped by Ralph, yeah? [*yeah*]
2   and he was going on about how he didn't see it- think it was
      actually that disgusting
3   *he is gay!* <INDIGNANT TONE>
4   and then- and then we said [. . .] 'didn't you think it was absolutely
      disgusting?'.
5   he was sit- he was just sitting there like not answering.

This discussion of an absent third person allows them to explore their attitude to homosexuality. Homosexuality is a live topic in British public
schools, as it is in all all-male institutions such as the army and men's
prisons. With no women in this social world, and with the dominant
discourses insisting that males are biologically programmed to 'need'
sexual gratification,[28] the taboos against homosexuality have to be very
strong, and in such institutions 'compulsory heterosexuality'[29] is rigidly
affirmed. The specialized language of such institutions is very revealing:
the slang of an in-group is a powerful bonding mechanism and areas of
'lexical density'[30] centre on women, sexual activity, homosexuality and
race. The misogyny and homophobia of such groups can literally be measured by the enormous numbers of pejorative words coined in these areas.[31]

In this extract, Henry seems prepared to explore what it means to
be 'raped'[32] and to mull over Prendergast's claim that this experience
was not necessarily disgusting. Julian, however, is quick to say *he is
gay*. What this statement asserts is that if someone describes a sexual
encounter with someone of the same sex as not 'disgusting', they must
be homosexual. This is a defensive move, and shows Julian's anxiety
to close down discussion. He wants to draw a clear line between people
who are gay and who consider same-sex activity to be not disgusting,
and 'normal' people who *do* consider same-sex activity to be disgusting.
Henry's story threatens to breach that neat dichotomy, since Prendergast appears to be a 'normal' boy like Julian and Henry and yet he
seems to be saying that his sexual encounter with Ralph was just 'an
experience'. Henry's response to Julian's outrage is noticeably disfluent:
he in turn feels threatened and he has to re-establish his credentials
as a member of the 'normal' camp. He does this by claiming that he
and his friends had asked *'didn't you think it was absolutely disgusting?'*,
a question that presupposes that it was 'absolutely disgusting'.

But despite Julian's strong reaction here, other parts of this conversation between these two friends, Julian and Henry, reveal a persistent homoerotic theme. For example, before Henry embarks on the story about Prendergast, a remark of Julian's casts light on the way the two boys are sitting in Henry's study-bedroom:

(28)   *Extract from* conversation preceding Closet Fags

Julian: ow ow like . OK the neck massage is great [*Henry laughs quietly*] but not when done by your feet [*Henry laughs*]
Julian: ⌈ng ng ng . . .)
Henry: ⌊ng ng ng . . .) [*both boys mimic the sound of an electric guitar*]

To judge from Julian's words, Henry has his feet on Julian's neck while they talk. The evidence that they are both relaxed about this physical contact is provided by their making those noises so typical of teenage boys, sounds imitating an electric guitar solo (made, presumably, while they pretend to play a guitar).

Later in the same conversation, Julian actually steers the talk round to a time in the past when they were suspected of being 'fags':

(29)   Closet Fags

Julian: I'd- I'd forgotten about that little . episode in M when everybody was convinced that we were closet fags
Henry: um that- but that- ((I mean)) that just- that ((was))- that's finished
Julian: that was just cos every second minute I was . popping along to your room [. . .]
           yeah it's also like the way- you know it's what Robert dines off is the fact that .hh Lynch climbing into your bed and like no insult but I really couldn't **climb into your bed in the morning**
Henry: **yeah that- that was fairly** that was unfortunate I agree
Julian: I really couldn't climb into your bed in the morning
Henry: <LAUGHS>
Julian: I'm sorry, it would have to be very cold
Henry: <LAUGHS> yeah that was unfortunate, does he still go on about that?
Julian: yes <BORED DRAWL>
Henry: really?
Julian: yes <BORED DRAWL>
Henry: %god%

[Note: utterances appearing between asterisks ** were spoken at the same time]

This chunk of talk does very important work in negotiating their relationship. They establish that they are not 'closet fags', even though people thought they were. They look at why people made this assumption, and also consider the problems caused for Henry by Lynch's escapade, which according to Julian is still a topic of conversation. Julian's light-hearted banter about why he chooses not to get into bed with Henry in the morning suggests that while it is important for him to state that this is *not* what he wants to do, he still chooses to talk about what he would not do, and to say it twice. He even jokes *I'm sorry, it would have to be very cold,* implying that in certain circumstances he *would* get into bed with Henry.

For younger speakers, the work of asserting their heterosexuality, that is, of asserting not-homosexuality, is an important part of their everyday construction of themselves as men. These few examples show that this can vary from virulent homophobia (as in example (26)) to more relaxed discussion and negotiation of sexual identity (as in the last example). In all these examples the dominance of heterosexual masculinity is apparent, as is the tension between heterosocial and homosocial norms.

'Makes You Vulnerable Though': Self-disclosure

Finally, I want to look at self-disclosure in all-male talk. As I've said, the majority of the stories in the conversations are first-person narratives, that is, the narrator and the chief protagonist are one and the same person. First-person narratives in all-female talk very often involve self-disclosure, because the narrative will tell of an event that occurred in the speaker's life, usually very recently, which had some kind of emotional impact. Men's first-person narratives, by contrast, focus more on achievement and triumph, or on the more banal happenings of everyday life, and are not designed to reveal feelings or to lead into talk where feelings can be compared and discussed. The only stories I could really label as self-disclosing came in conversations involving older rather than younger men, middle-aged men who seem more solid in their masculine identity.

Example (31) is an example of a story involving self-disclosure. The participants in the conversation that this story comes from are four middle-aged middle-class men in the pub after work. They are having a general discussion about peaks and troughs in social history.

Example (30) gives a brief chunk of the preceding conversation to contextualize the story:

(30)

Brian: we keep having this idea that things are going to get better, which was an earlier part of the conversation

Tony: yes

Brian: it's paralleled by this- I think what tends to happen, you-you ((just)) have peaks and troughs, you know the thing goes- there's a wave, it does- it doesn't suddenly turn into an exponential growth pattern

Pete: right

Brian: you know it goes up and it comes down again ** you know and I think-**

Pete: but **do you think- do you** think- but do you think that there's a- within the p- peaks and troughs, do you think there's a- there's a upward or a downward trend?

Brian: well at the moment . . .

At this point Brian gives an example from his own life (note how it is Pete's question that allows Brian this opportunity):

(31) Suicidal

→ 1   well at the moment ((I mean)) this is partly personal

2   cos I mean I- my own life sort of has been [*ah*] up and down

3   and I've . you know sort of- . if you'd t- if you'd had this conversation with me about a term ago

4   I mean I was just about as down as you could get

5   because I'm er- really was quite seriously suicidal

6   and . it HAS come up again

7   you know my life HAS improved/ [*mhm/ mhm/*]

8   ((xx)) it hasn't actually got any better

9   but my attitude to it and psychologically I'm a lot straighter and clearer about what's going on

10   so it has picked up

11   and it was just literally a case of hanging on in there

12   I mean about . towards . about the middle of last term

13   I quite seriously- . I went out and I bought a big bottle of pills

14   they were codeine and aspirin mix

15   and a bottle of whisky
16   and I went and sat on Twickenham Green
17   and I was going to kill myself [*mhm*]
18   I was going to eat the pills and drink the whisky
19   well it was only a little bottle of whisky <GREATER SPEED>
20   sitting there y'know TOTALLY just about as depressed as you
         could possibly get
21   and then I just thought 'you stupid sod'
22   so I threw away the pills
23   drank the whisky
24   and went home
25   [*everyone laughs*]
26   but y'know that was the turning point
27   I started coming up again <LAUGHING QUALITY TO VOICE>
28   [Pete: *good*; Tony: *good*]

This rare example of a man talking about a difficult moment in his life is introduced with some tentativeness. First, he warns his fellow conversationalists that he is about to talk about something *partly personal* (the hedge *partly* here is semantically nonsense, but functions to soften the force of his utterance and protect his addressees' face). Second, he ties his story in very carefully to the theme of *peaks and troughs* which has been established in the preceding conversation. This careful tying-in of his story to the more general conversational theme reveals his anxiety about telling the story, anxiety which is expressed in the many hedges which appear in lines 1–5 (three tokens of *I mean*, two tokens of *sort of*, and one each of *you know* and *really*). This density of hedging is unusual in men's talk (but is typical of all-female conversation where sensitive topics are under discussion). After this he seems to settle down to tell his story, perhaps reassured that his fellow conversationalists have not raised any objections.

However, the reactions of the other men – laughing with Brian at line 25, then saying 'Good' after Brian's coda – express both relief and embarrassment. They do not seem very comfortable with Brian's self-disclosure, and this interpretation is borne out by a conversation which takes place the following week involving just Pete and Tony. Pete and Tony arrive at the pub ahead of their friends, and mull over Brian's self-disclosing behaviour the previous week. Example (32) gives an extract from this conversation:

(32) Englishness

Tony: I don't know Brian THAT well, but every time I've met him, he's been pretty . free with whatever happened to be on his mind at the time

Pete: I don't know many people like that . you know who are able to sort of [*no*] just tap into . their- I don't know their situations their problems, I know I take a long time to sort of er . warm to people I think=

Tony: =you . might wonder really how he . overcame the- the education that the rest of us obviously ⌈succumbed to <LAUGHS>

Pete: ⌊<LAUGHS> yeah %yeah%/
(1.0) I think I must be quite a typical Englishman in that sense/ being quite sort of er-

Tony: I k- I'm less English than I was <LAUGHS>

Pete: is that because you've been ab- abroad?

Tony: no ⌈((xx))

Pete: er ⌊how did you- how did you manage to- to become less English?

Tony: I think it's because I decided that- . that (1.0) I ((really)) didn't like this way of relating to people very much and that . life actually would be . improved by . people being more open with each other . not that I'm . brilliant at it <QUIET LAUGH>

Pete: makes you vulnerable though don't you think? . um don't-don't you feel vulnerable? . sometimes?

Tony: yeah but . I suppose that . that's a useful reminder really isn't it ((I mean)) vulnerability is er- (1.0) all the- all the- the- the masks and so on are supposed to keep vulnerability at bay but . .hh they only do this at a very high cost

Pete: yeah I suppose that's another kind of pain isn't it

Tony: yeah

Pete: you know putting up barriers, distancing yourself, and maybe- . maybe more damage is done that way than actually=

Tony: =it's not impossible

This is an extraordinary stretch of talk. I have found nothing comparable anywhere else in the conversations in the corpus. Pete and Tony not only address a topic that demands reflexivity, something men normally avoid; they stick to the topic and explore the issues that arise from it in a way that is relatively common in women friends' talk but is extremely rare in all-male talk. It is probably significant that there are only two speakers present: this conversation arises when two friends meet in the expectation that other friends will join them. When three or more males meet, it seems that peer group pressures make talk of this kind difficult, but where there are just two males, then a kind of intimacy is possible that is precluded otherwise.[33]

Pete and Tony make some fascinating observations on men's talk (though note that they gloss male inexpressivity as 'Englishness' and seem to overlook the gendered nature of the masks they are forced to wear). Tony argues for greater openness, which Pete responds to with a series of three questions: *makes you vulnerable though don't you think? . um don't- don't you feel vulnerable? . sometimes?* Pete obviously feels vulnerable just talking like this, but wants to question Tony's assertion that it is better to be more open. Tony accepts that being open can make you vulnerable, but pursues his line of thinking by asserting that vulnerability is not necessarily bad but may be a useful reminder of our humanity. While feeling vulnerable can be uncomfortable, wearing masks all the time is a much worse option. Tony here voices an alternative discourse which challenges hegemonic masculinity and asserts the value of emotional honesty and openness.

The Masculine 'Mask of Silence'

The metaphor of the mask which Tony voices is a powerful one, and seems to express the experience of many men. Andrew Tolson, for example, describes conventional male interaction as follows: 'we would fall into the conventional "matiness" of the pub, a mutual back-slapping, designed to repress as much as it expresses. It was impossible to talk to other men about personal feelings of weakness or jealousy. A masculine "mask of silence" concealed the emptiness of our emotional lives.'[34]

The phrase 'to mask up' is an expression coined by male prisoners to describe 'the conscious adoption each day of a defensive emotional wall that provides a barrier between the man's real feelings and the outward facade he presents to the inmate group'.[35] This 'mask' takes the form of an extreme kind of tough masculinity where the concealment of all traces of vulnerability is viewed as an essential part of men's self-presentation. Much earlier in the twentieth century, a very different kind of male, a member of the privileged Bloomsbury group in England, Leonard Woolf, wrote about the mask he felt forced to adopt: 'I suspect that the male carapace is usually grown to conceal cowardice. . . . It was the fear of ridicule or disapproval that prompted one to invent that kind of second-hand version of oneself which might provide for one's original self the safety of a permanent alibi.'[36] It is this 'kind of second-hand version' of self which Tony challenges in his bid for fuller, more honest interpersonal interaction.

Conclusions

In this chapter I've looked at only a fraction of the stories told in the men's conversations, but I have tried to show how narrative is used in all-male talk to construct and maintain masculine identity. Conversational narrative is our chief means of constructing the fictions that are our lives and of getting others to collude in them. Story-telling also allows us to order or to re-order our everyday, normally taken-for-granted experiences. So while story-telling reinforces hegemonic masculinity, it can also provide a space where what is normally taken for granted can be questioned or challenged.

The examples I have looked at show men constructing themselves as achievement-oriented, competitive and unemotional; but also exploring more feminine sides of themselves. The opening sections of the chapter looked at canonical narratives, where men triumphed over adversity as lone heroes or 'got away with' laddish pranks. I contrasted competitive aspects of male story-telling with the collaborative construction of narrative found in some all-male groups. Story-telling can also be the locus of men's struggle to express vulnerability, but in all-male contexts, most men want to avoid appearing weak, and collude in the denial of the feminine. Most men in most conversations avoided self-disclosure, but a few men took the risk of engaging in a more self-reflexive discourse, in place of the back-slapping camaraderie more typical of male friendship.

As Michael Roper and John Tosh put it: 'Despite the myths of omnipotent manhood which surround us, masculinity is never fully possessed, but must perpetually be achieved, asserted and renegotiated.'[37] What I have tried to do in this chapter is to show some of the ways that conversational narrative is used by male speakers as a way of achieving, asserting and renegotiating the conflicting masculinities available to them at the turn of the century.

Notes

1 Jessica Benjamin, *The Bonds of Love*, p. 12.
2 See Jennifer Coates, *Women Talk*.
3 In order to give some statistical backing to my observations, I've done a detailed analysis of a subset of the narratives in my conversational data: this subset consists of 68 stories selected so as to give full coverage of all 32 conversations, with more or fewer stories being selected depending on the total number in that conversation, so, for example, a conversation containing only one or two stories will have just one in the subset, while a conversation containing eleven or twelve stories will have three or four in the subset. Stories chosen cover the whole range from minimal narratives of two lines to very long stories of 165 lines.
4 Table 3.1 summarizes the gender of characters in the all-male sub-corpus of 68 stories (only 67 appear in the total here because in one story – 'Overheard between Two Cleaners' – the gender of the two cleaners is not clarified). (Percentages have been rounded up to the nearest whole number, which means that totals are sometimes more than 100.)

Table 3.1 Distribution of characters by gender in the sub-corpus

	Male	Female	Both	Total
Gender of protagonist	64 (96%)	3 (5%)	0 (0%)	67
Gender of other characters	48 (72%)	1 (2%)	18 (27%)	67

5 Barbara Johnstone *Stories, Community, and Place*, p. 67.
6 This is precisely what Barbara Johnstone found in her analysis of stories told by white middle-class males in Indiana, USA (see Johnstone, *Stories, Community, and Place*; Barbara Johnstone, 'Community and contest: Midwestern men and women creating their worlds in conversational storytelling').
7 David Jackson, *Unmasking Masculinity*, p. 221.
8 Jock Phillips, *A Man's Country? The Image of the Pakeha Male – a History*, p. 32.
9 Jackson, *Unmasking Masculinity*, p. 156; Koenraad Kuiper, 'Sporting formulae in New Zealand English: two models of male solidarity'; William Labov, *Language in the Inner City*; Bruce Moore, *A Lexicon of Cadet Language*.
10 All the extracts quoted in Gough and Edwards' analysis of men's talk contain taboo language (see Brendan Gough and Gareth Edwards, 'The beer talking: four lads, a carry out and the reproduction of masculinities').
11 Victor Seidler, *Rediscovering Masculinity*, p. 63 (see also Joseph Pleck, 'Men's power with women, other men, and society').

12   Jackson, *Unmasking Masculinity*, p. 156.
13   See R. W. Connell, *Masculinities*; Adam Jukes, *Why Men Hate Women*; Seidler, *Rediscovering Masculinity*; Andrew Tolson, *The Limits of Masculinity*.
14   For an example, see the story 'Cystitis' in Coates, *Women Talk*, pp. 104–5.
15   Johnstone, *Stories, Community, and Place*; 'Community and contest'.
16   'Behaving badly' is problematic for women, who are constrained by social pressure to be 'nice'. But talking about 'behaving badly' does happen in all-female conversation. See Jennifer Coates, 'Women behaving badly'.
17   Stephen Frosh, Ann Phoenix and Rob Pattman, *Young Masculinities*, p. 205 (see also discussion on p. 104).
18   Livia Polanyi, *Telling the American Story*, p. 66.
19   Deborah Cameron, 'Performing gender identity: young men's talk and the construction of heterosexual masculinity'.
20   Chris Weedon, *Feminist Practice and Poststructuralist Theory*, p. 98.
21   See Seidler, *Rediscovering Masculinity*.
22   Leonora Davidoff and Catherine Hall, *Family Fortunes: Men and Women of the English Middle Classes 1780–1850*, p. 29.
23   Connell, *Masculinities*, p. 78; Frosh, Phoenix and Pattman, *Young Masculinities*, p. 77; Michael Roper and John Tosh, 'Introduction' to *Manful Assertions: Masculinities in Britain since 1800*, p. 13; Lynne Segal, *Slow Motion: Changing Masculinities, Changing Men*, p. 15; Tolson, *The Limits of Masculinity*, p. 19.
24   Jukes, *Why Men Hate Women*, p. 43.
25   Cameron, 'Performing gender identity'; Timothy Curry, 'Fraternal bonding in the locker room: a pro-feminist analysis of talk about competition and women'; Gough and Edwards, 'The beer talking'; G. M. Herek, 'On heterosexual masculinity: some psychical consequences of the social construction of gender and sexuality'.
26   Cameron, 'Performing gender identity', p. 61.
27   Stephen Frosh, Ann Phoenix and Rob Pattman found this in relation to the London schoolboys they interviewed: 'Homophobia is one clear marker of much emergent masculinity in this age group, suggesting that the struggle to establish oneself as "normatively heterosexual" is a very significant feature of identity formation for these boys' (*Young Masculinities*, p. 258).
28   Wendy Hollway, 'Heterosexual sex: power and desire for the other'.
29   Adrienne Rich, 'Compulsory heterosexuality and lesbian existence'.
30   'Lexical density' is a term used to refer to a significant clustering of words (see Moore, *A Lexicon of Cadet Language*, pp. xvii–xviii).
31   See Moore, *A Lexicon of Cadet Language*; Diana Looser, 'Bonds and barriers: language in a New Zealand prison'.
32   The boys' use of the word 'rape' is problematic: there is no way of knowing exactly what had taken place between 'Ralph' and 'Prendergast',

but frequent listening to this passage on the tape suggests to me that the word does not have the same (extremely negative) meaning as it would have in, for example, a feminist context. Henry's choice of this word may be influenced simply by his wish to imply that Prendergast had not *chosen* to take part in this sexual encounter.

33 The difference between two and three participants in friendly conversation seems to be highly salient for male speakers. A male friend of mine told me that he has two good friends who he goes running with, and that when he runs with either of them on their own, conversation is personal and engaging, but when all three of them run together, conversation is impersonal and stilted.

34 Tolson, *The Limits of Masculinity*, p. 10.

35 Diana Looser, personal communication, October 1999.

36 Leonard Woolf quoted in Segal, *Slow Motion: Changing Masculinities, Changing Men*, p. 108.

37 Roper and Tosh, 'Introduction' to *Manful Assertions: Masculinities in Britain since 1800*, p. 18.

4

'Bad as My Mate': Stories in Sequence

Narrative, as the last chapter demonstrated, plays a key role in the construction of masculinity. It can also play a key role in the construction and maintenance of friendship. Stories don't necessarily occur as isolated chunks in the middle of conversation. Often a story will be followed by another story on the same theme. In this chapter I want to focus on the role of story sequences in talk among male friends. Telling a second story involves co-participants in paying careful attention to what each other is saying. As Harvey Sacks puts it, telling a relevant second story says 'My mind is with you'.[1] This capacity of sequential story-telling to testify to the closeness of participants means that it can be a powerful way of 'doing' friendship.

The following brief extract comes from the beginning of a story told by Dan to his friends, Gary and Rob:

(1) *Extract from* **You Can't Not Know Your Name**
1   Bad as my mate,
2   he went out-
3   so he went out last weekend right,
4   and he ended up going to Toff's [*a club*] . . .

Unlike stories we have looked at in previous chapters, this story is not initiated by a question such as 'Did I tell you what happened to my mate last weekend?', but by the utterance 'Bad as my mate'. This utterance aligns Dan's story carefully with the story that has just finished, Rob's story about something 'bad' that he had done at work. By using the word 'bad' Dan signals the theme in Rob's story which he is orienting to, and by linking a new character, 'my mate', to the notion of 'badness', he announces the protagonist of his upcoming story. In other words, unlike most of the stories we have looked at, this is a *second story*, a story which is carefully designed to follow a previous story. As long as it has a topical link with the first story and is contiguous (occurs close to the first story), a second story will be perceived as being in sequence.

The tendency for stories to occur in clusters has been commented on by a wide range of researchers:[2] 'stories come in clumps' and 'clumped stories have an apparent similarity between them'.[3] In the conversations I've collected, over a third (35 per cent) of the stories occur as part of a sequence of stories.

This of course begs the question: what counts as a second story? For stories to count as being in sequence, I have applied the two defining criteria mentioned above: first, there must be a topical link between the stories, and second, the stories must be contiguous. There are several examples in the data-base of stories which are on the same general topic but which are separated from each other by multi-party discussion among the participants, and I have not counted these as a sequence of stories. An example is a conversation involving three college lecturers who are discussing men and clothes. This topic is sustained for nearly half an hour and in the course of discussion five narratives are told. These range from personal stories about wearing a dinner jacket sprayed with glitter to a story about female students who couldn't afford dresses making their own ballgowns. In no case are two stories told one after the other; that is, they are not contiguous. This is the main reason I have not counted them as constituting a sequence. But the other main reason is that these stories lack the quality displayed by a 'true' sequence of stories where the second narrator orients very carefully to the story told by the first narrator. In other words, these stories do not function as a display of closeness.

'He Looked Like a Completely Different Person': Story Sequences in the Men's Conversations

Story sequences can in theory go on as long as participants can produce relevant next stories. In my data-base the longest sequence is of seven stories and there are two sequences of five stories.[4] Let's look at brief outlines of a few of these sequences.

Story sequence A: False identity

Participants: three men in their twenties (Rob, Gary and Dan)
Context: pub in Somerset

'Bad as My Mate'

Rob tells a story about pretending to be somebody else when talking to a customer on the phone at work, and then Dan and Gary tell stories on the theme of false identity.

STORY 1:   Avoiding sales (Rob)
STORY 2:   You can't not know your name (Dan)
STORY 3A: Mike's middle names (Gary)
STORY 3B: Mike's parents fucked him about (Dan)

Story sequence B: Car breakdown

Participants: three men in their thirties/forties (Len, Joe, Steve)
Context: tea break at a car repair workshop in the home counties
After some general discussion about the RAC and car breakdown, Len tells a story about seeing an Asian family pushing their broken-down car along the motorway. This is followed by another story about a breakdown involving an Asian family (both these stories have racist overtones). The final story is a first-person narrative told by Len about breaking down in the Dartford Tunnel.

STORY 1: Asian family pushing car (Len)
STORY 2: Overcrowded minibus (Joe)
STORY 3: My little Cortina (Len)

Story sequence C: Peter at church

Participants: three males aged 18/19 (Des, Hav, Jack)
Context: shed in the garden of Jack's house, Surrey
This group of teenage boys are all involved in the local evangelical church and they have been discussing Peter, a key adult figure in the church. The first story is a minimal narrative about Peter, and this leads into Hav's story about meeting Peter and hardly recognizing him because he looked so different. This is followed by two more stories about Peter, both about his skin problems.

STORY 1: He used to treat you like a little kid (Des)
STORY 2: He looked like a completely different person (Hav)
STORY 3: Skin disease and stress (Jack)
STORY 4: Christian camping trip (Des)

Story sequence D: Coincidence and probability theory

Participants: three men in their forties (Tony, Brian, Pete)
Context: pub in Richmond
  Brian tells a story about helping out a friend who had broken his foot and needed information on probability theory. He follows this with two more stories which involve coincidence, and Tony then adds a fourth story on this theme from his own recent experience.

STORY 1:   Keith's foot and probability theory (Brian)
STORY 2:   Double-glazing Jehovah's Witness (Brian)
STORY 3:   Loons and shopping trolleys (Brian)
STORY 4:   Jazz workshop (Tony)

Story sequence E: African stories

Participants: two male lecturers in their thirties (Andrew, Paul)
Context: university office after hours
  Andrew tells a story about an event which occurred when he was working in Nigeria, and he follows this with another story about his time there. Paul then tells a general story about the television series 'Roots' and follows it with what he calls a 'Nigerian anecdote'.

STORY 1:   German visiting lecturer (Andrew)
STORY 2:   The good Samaritan (Andrew)
STORY 3:   TV drama 'Roots' (Paul)
STORY 4:   Watertight Volkswagen (Paul)

  These examples of story sequences demonstrate a wide range of variation. Sometimes, all participants are involved in the story sequence; sometimes they are not. In all the sequences discussed here, one speaker tells more than one of the stories in the sequence, but this speaker is not necessarily the one who initiated the sequence. Table 4.1 sets out the patterns (where 'speaker A' is used to refer to the participant who told the first story in the sequence, 'speaker B' for the second narrator, and so on).
  As table 4.1 shows, second stories are sometimes told by the same narrator rather than by a different narrator (sequences D and E illustrate this pattern). In my corpus thirty-three of the seventy-one story sequences involve the same narrator telling two or more stories in sequence, that is, nearly half of the sequences exhibit this pattern.

Table 4.1 Patterns of sequencing

	Story 1	Story 2	Story 3	Story 4
Sequence A	speaker A	speaker B	speaker C	speaker B
Sequence B	speaker A	speaker B	speaker A	N/A
Sequence C	speaker A	speaker B	speaker C	speaker A
Sequence D	speaker A	speaker A	speaker A	speaker B
Sequence E	speaker A	speaker A	speaker B	speaker B

There are even sequences which involve only one narrator, and these range from sequences of just two stories to as many as five stories. This phenomenon – of a speaker telling five stories in sequence – occurs twice in the corpus in two very different conversations (one involving young working men, the other middle-aged middle-class men). In one case the sequence consists entirely of these five stories; in the other case the five stories from one speaker are followed by two from another speaker. This finding suggests that in the talk of all-male friends, one speaker dominating talk by telling a sequence of stories is acceptable in a way it would not normally be in all-female talk (I shall take up this point in chapter 5).

I want now to look in more detail at two of these story sequences, first, to see how they are co-constructed by speakers; second, to answer the question, do second stories differ in structure from first stories?; and third, to examine the ways in which men friends construct solidarity through telling second stories.

'I Did That Loads of Times': An Example in Detail

I shall look now in detail at Story Sequence A, the 'False Identity' sequence. Example (2) below presents the first of the four stories which constitute this sequence. Rob, Gary and Dan have been talking about their experiences in an electronics store where they have all worked at different times. An indirect reference to the practice of giving a false name when pressed by a customer triggers the following story from Rob. (The three friends are having a drink in the pub after work.)

(2) Avoiding Sales
1   There was one that I did,
2   was this customer,

3   was on the phone,
4   and I was setting up a satellite system that they wanted to buy,
5   not doing these satellites
6   because it's a hell of a lot of discount on your number,
7   plus . a lot-
8   it's very time-consuming.
9   'Who shall I ask for when I come in?'
10 and I er- nearly said my name
11 'Joh-n, Joh-n', <LAUGHS>
12 just came out,
13 'John' <R AND G LAUGH>
14 And then afterwards 'I bet he'll have a go',
15 thought, 'Oh fuck it' <G LAUGHS>
16 I've done it a couple of times.
17 [G: *it's all right, I did that loads of times*]
18 'Who shall I ask for when I come in?'
19 'Jo- John'. <G LAUGHS>
20 I thought 'look around and hope no-one can see you'.
21 John.

We can see how Gary aligns to this story, laughing at the climax of the story (lines 13 and 15) and again when Rob recycles the climax (line 19). His comment *it's all right, I did that loads of times* (line 17) is supportive in that it reassures Rob that what he has done is not abnormal (since Gary has done it *loads of times*). But perhaps Rob feels that this response focuses too much on Rob's mock anxiety about his action rather than on his self-presentation as 'a bit of a lad' (see the story 'The Pornographic Video', example 16 in chapter 3). This could explain Rob's repetition of the last bit of his story in lines 18–21, which omits him worrying about the customer coming in (lines 14–15) and instead presents him as thinking *'look around and no-one can see you'*, which has more bravado than the first version.

Dan, who produces a second story to follow this first story, mistimes the beginning of his story, because he assumes that line 16 *I've done it a couple of times* is the last line of Rob's story. Example (3) shows how this transition takes place.

(3)

1	Rob:	I've done it a couple of times/	
	Gary:		it's all right/

```
2  Rob:                                              ⌈'who
   Gary:   I did that loads of times/               |
→  Dan:                        bad as my mate ⌊((xxxx
3  Rob:   shall I ask for when I come in?'/ Jo- John/
   Gary:                               <LAUGHS>
   Dan:    xxxxxxxxxxxxxxxxxxxxxxxxxx))
4  Rob:                 I thought 'look around and hope no-one
   Gary:
→  Dan:    he went out/
5  Rob:   can see you'/ John/
   Gary:
→  Dan:                    so he went out last weekend right/
```

The opening line of the second story *bad as my mate* orients it carefully to the first, and announces that what Dan is taking as salient from the first story is that Rob did something 'bad'. 'Behaving badly' is a strong theme in the narratives of younger men in the corpus, and is viewed as a positive way of 'doing' masculinity (as we saw in the last chapter). He also announces that the chief protagonist in the story – who will play a parallel role to Rob in the first story – will be his mate. His next words are inaudible (because Rob is talking simultaneously) and his utterance *he went out* is ignored by Rob who continues with the end of his story.

Dan finally establishes a narrative floor with the line *so he went out last weekend right* and proceeds to tell the story 'You Can't Not Know Your Name' (first discussed in chapter 2, p. 23); the story is given again in (4) below.

(4)   You Can't Not Know Your Name

1   Bad as my mate
2   [. . .]
3   So he went out last weekend right,
4   and he ended up going to Toff's.
5   Cos he's underage he borrowed his mate's licence yeah,
6   and they always ask you your post code,
7   so he had that memorized right.
8   So he got to the door and he goes 'Got any ID?'
9   Pulled up- pulled it out, give it to the doorman,
10 'What's your name?' <LAUGHTER>
11 And obviously like he'd been thinking about the post code over
        and over and over yeah

12 and he went 'oh shit' <LAUGHTER>
13 'TN5 7DR . that's a funny name.'
14 And he couldn't- he couldn't work it out right,
15 and he just stuttered after a while like that
16 going 'yeah'.
17 'What's your post code- post code?'
18 and he pulled that off perfectly
19 and he went 'All right I'll let you in like'.
20 Just one of those moments you know life's turned to shit like that.
21 It's like . you can't not know your name, all right
22 you might not know your post code right
23 but you can't not know your name.

At this point Gary starts a third story on the same theme (of pretending to be someone you are not). The transition from Dan's to Gary's story is given in (5) below.

(5)
_ _
1   Dan: you might not know your post code right/
    Gary:
    Rob:
_ _
2   Dan: but you can't not know ⌈your name/
→   Gary: ⌊outside   ⌈of Beadle's/
    Rob: ⌊fucking hell/
_ _
3   Dan:
    Gary: outside of Beadle's/ Mike's driving licence/ 'What's your
    Rob:
_ _
4   Dan: <LAUGHS> you can't think about it/
    Gary: middle name?'/ shit/ um-
    Rob: <LAUGHS>
_ _
5   Dan: ⌈it's too obvious isn't it?
    Gary: ⌊yeah but the thing is/   the worst thing was that
    Rob:
_ _
6   Dan: yeah/
    Gary: Mike's parents fucked him about/   ((xx)) name/
    Rob:
_ _

Gary's utterances: *outside of Beadle's/ Mike's driving licence/ 'What's your middle name?'/ shit/* could be seen as an abstract for an upcoming story, or, more radically, it could be argued that they *are* the story. After all, given that we have had Dan's story, it is easy to make sense of Gary's telegraphic utterances: we assume that Beadle's, like Toff's, is a club; that Gary, like Dan's mate, has borrowed a friend's driving licence as ID; that the doorman asks *What's your middle name?* (just as the Toff's doorman asked *What's your name?*), and that this question is problematic in some way since Gary's response (like that of Dan's mate) is *shit.* Dan's and Rob's laughter (stave 4) shows that they have understood Gary's elliptical story. Dan adds the supportive comment *you can't think about it, it's too obvious isn't it?* to show his alignment with the point of Gary's story (which matches the point of his own story perfectly), the point being that you can't hesitate when asked your name because you can't not know your name.

At this point Gary adds: *yeah but the thing is, the worst thing was that Mike's parents fucked him about.* This proposition – that Mike's parents fucked him about – provides the abstract for another story, one that Dan, rather than Gary, proceeds to tell. Perhaps Dan feels that Gary's statement on its own is insufficient for Rob, who does not know Mike as well as the other two, and who therefore may not be familiar with the story behind Mike's name and how his parents 'fucked him about'. Dan's story is given in (6) below.

(6) Mike's Parents Fucked Him About
1 For fucking sixteen or seventeen years of his life right
2 Mike's parents told him he had John Luke as his middle names
3 they said his middle names were John Luke right,
4 and when he turned seventeen or eighteen
5 they said it's Michael John Luke Honeyman
6 and they- and his Mum goes, 'You haven't got any middle names by the way'
7 So all the things he'd applied for, right,
8 all his driving licence
9 everything had it on there, right,
10 and it was bullshit. <LAUGHS>

This story makes clear why Mike's name is an issue and why there could be doubt about what name might be on any given document. At the conclusion of Dan's clarificatory tale, Gary resumes his story, that is, he fleshes out what he had said before:

(7)
1 cos I was- I was stood there
2 and he was like 'What's your middle name?',

3   alright, well fuck,
4   has it got his middle name on there or hasn't it?
5   I said 'Well I don't know,
6   if there's a middle name on there it'll be this,
7   if there isn't it's that'. <LAUGHTER>

Although I have talked so far of a series of four stories, it would be more accurate to say that this is a series of three stories with a fourth story embedded in the third. In other words, while the second and third stories ('You Can't Not Know Your Name' and 'Mike's Middle Names') are both second stories in the sense I defined earlier, the fourth story ('Mike's Parents Fucked Him About') is not: it does not 'follow on' from any other story but rather expands on a key point in the story 'Mike's Middle Names'. So this fourth story functions as part of the orientation in story 3. Story 3 could in fact be presented as follows (with Gary as the narrator and Dan's contributions given in italics):

(8)   Mike's Middle Names
1   outside of Beadle's,
2   outside of Beadle's,
3   Mike's driving licence,
4   'What's your middle name?',
5   Shit.
6   *<LAUGHS> you can't think about it,*
7   *it's too obvious isn't it?*
8   yeah but the thing is,
9   the worst thing was that Mike's parents fucked him about [*yeah*]
10 ((xx)) name.
11 *For fucking sixteen or seventeen years of his life right*
12 *Mike's parents told him he had John Luke as his middle names*
13 *they said his middle names were John Luke right,*
14 *and when he turned seventeen or eighteen*
15 *they said it's Michael John Luke Honeyman*
16 *and they- and his Mum goes, 'You haven't got any middle names by the way'*
17 *So all the things he'd applied for, right,*
18 *all his driving licence*
19 *everything had it on there, right,*
20 *and it was bullshit. <LAUGHS>*
21 cos I was- I was stood there

22 and he was like 'What's your middle name?',
23 alright, well fuck,
24 has it got his middle name on there or hasn't it?
25 I said 'Well I don't know,
26 if there's a middle name on there it'll be this,
27 if there isn't it's that'. <LAUGHTER>

This story both exemplifies the careful work done to create following-on stories and the way speakers co-operate in talk. While Dan's embedded story is not part of the series of stories on false identity, it provides crucial background information for Gary's story and thus helps Gary's story to be a successful second story, successful in the sense both that it works as a story (has a point) and that it works as a second story to the preceding story.

'Mike's Middle Names': Second Stories

Gary's story 'Mike's Middle Names' is a good example of the economy that can be found in second stories. Harvey Sacks argues that while one criterion of what it is to be a 'story' is that it takes more than an utterance to produce, second stories are the exception to that rule.[5] Gary's second story here takes more than an utterance to produce, but it is structurally quite different from the stories that precede it. Rob's first story, 'Avoiding Sales', like the stories 'Jonesy and the Lion' and 'The Area Manager's Call' discussed in chapter 2, has all the elements expected of a fully fledged narrative: it starts with an abstract (line 1), then provides orientation (who, where, when and other background information) in lines 2–8. The narrative core is told mostly through dialogue in lines 9–15, and is then repeated in lines 18–21. The story has a clear point: the canonical script would have Rob giving his real name to the customer (and Rob alludes to this possibility in his story – *I nearly said my name* (line 10)) but he breaches the script by giving a false name. The story is evaluated through his representation of his thoughts at the time: line 15 *thought 'Oh fuck it'* frames the protagonist as someone who is prepared to risk the consequences of his deception; line 20 *I thought 'Look around and hope no-one can see you'* presents him as well aware that what he has done is a breach of the canonical script but hoping to get away with it. This sense of 'getting away with it' is a significant theme in men's stories, as we have seen.

The second story in this sequence, 'You Can't Not Know Your Name', is also a fully fledged story, with a narrative core and an explicitly made point. This means that this sequence of three stories consists of a first story, a second story that is structurally very like a first story, and a third story which is structurally different from a first story. Why should these two 'second stories' (stories 2 and 3) differ like this? It seems to me that this variation in fullness between the two stories relates to how thematically coherent they are with the preceding story.

Let's look now in detail at the way these two stories achieve 'second storyhood' and also at the ways they differ. The first of them – 'You Can't Not Know Your Name' – opens with the line *Bad as my mate*. This is a good example of the work required of second story-tellers if a story is to be perceived *as* a second story. It has been an important insight into stories in sequence in conversation that it is the work done by the second storyteller which creates the sense that the stories are in sequence.[6] In other words, the teller of the first story cannot pre-ordain in any way that someone will tell a second story, or what angle that second story will take. This may seem like stating the obvious, but given that analysts come at any given series of stories after the event – as part of a conversation on audio-tape or as a transcript on the page – it is easy to see them as structures involving two or more parts (stories), and to ignore the fact that the first story could have stood alone. As Galloway-Young puts it: 'The appearance of thematic continuity is reconstituted backwards, the constitution of the pair of stories not being what is intended by the first but what is foregrounded by the second.'[7]

Dan's words *bad as my mate* foregrounds 'badness' as the theme to be oriented to in Rob's story and so prepares his co-participants for a story which will parallel Rob's in telling about someone who be-haved 'badly' in some way. The word *bad* not only orients to Rob's behaviour where he does not perform as the 'good' salesman, but also picks up the tone of *fuck it* that characterizes stories of this kind which revolve around laddish pranks which have the potential for landing the protagonist in trouble. The syntactic structure *as . . . as* (in the line *[as] bad as my mate*) explicitly sets up a comparison between the protagonist of this second story and the protagonist of the first, and foregrounds the parallelism between them in that both take on an assumed identity. But in other ways the stories are not very parallel. They have very different settings – the first is set in the workplace during working hours, the second is set outside a club outside working hours – and the protagonists have very different motives for assuming a false identity. Moreover, Rob chooses a name, John, that belongs to no-one in particular but which has the virtue of being a common name: his main aim is to avoid having to deal with a particular customer if he comes to the shop in person. By contrast, Dan's mate pretends to be a specific person, a friend who has a valid driving licence, and thus has no choice about what name he has to assume. All these differences mean that Dan has to work hard to give his audience enough information to follow his story, since they can't infer this information from the previous story.

A more topically coherent second story to Rob's would be one on the theme of laddish pranks where a narrator told a second story about some minor episode of malpractice he had been involved in. This is precisely what we find in another series involving Rob ('The Pornographic Video 1' and 'The Pornographic Video 2'), though in this case both stories are told by Rob.

If we compare the second and third stories in the sequence ('You Can't Not Know Your Name' and 'Mike's Middle Names'), we can see that they are topically very coherent. Both stories take place outside a nightclub, in both stories the narrative core involves the interaction between the protagonist and the doorman, and in both the point of the story is that 'you can't not know your name'. This very close parallelism means that the narrator of 'Mike's Middle Names' doesn't feel obliged to provide any linking utterance (to show the audience how he is orienting to the previous story). Instead he launches straight into his story, keeping rigorously to the structure set up by Dan in the previous story. He does not even use the pronoun 'I', so superficially this is a story without a named protagonist, but speakers will assume that where a storyteller ellipts or omits the subject of narrative clauses, then the subject is likely to be 'I'.

The five lines that open Gary's story involve a great deal of ellipsis: not only is there no subject in these clauses, there are no verbs either. We hear lines 1–3 as orientation and lines 4 and 5 as narrative clauses because we supply past tense verbs as follows:

1   *I was* outside of Beadle's,
2   *I was* outside of Beadle's,
3   *I had* Mike's driving licence,
4   *The doorman asked* 'What's your middle name?',
5   *I thought* Shit.

We are able to do this because we have just heard the previous story. We can fill in the gaps from details that were given in full in 'You Can't Not Know Your Name'.

You Can't Not Know Your Name	*Mike's Middle Names*
1 So he went out last weekend right, and he ended up going to Toff's.	outside of Beadle's
2 Cos he's underage he borrowed his mate's licence	Mike's driving licence
3 So he got to the door and he goes 'Got any ID?' Pulled up- pulled it out, give it to the doorman, 'What's your name?'	'What's your middle name?'
4 and he went 'oh shit'	Shit.

The only changes that the second story introduces are: (1) the setting is a nightclub called Beadle's not Toff's; (2) the protagonist is the narrator, Gary, not Dan's mate; (3) the driving licence belongs to Gary's friend Mike; (4) the doorman asks him what his middle name is. The first three of these changes are trivial: the story hinges on the fourth change, the fact that it is Mike's *middle* name that needs to be known. The audience to the story 'You Can't Not Know Your Name' can work out from their own cultural knowledge why it is that the protagonist is expected to know his name and why, in the circumstances, such a question might throw someone who was prepared for a harder question. However, in the following story, the reason that Mike's middle names are problematic is in-group knowledge, knowledge available to Gary and Dan but not necessarily to Rob. It is presumably for this reason that the embedded story 'Mike's Parents Fucked Him About' is told.

What this discussion of a particular story sequence demonstrates is that it is not possible to make sweeping generalizations about the shape of second stories. They can only count as second stories if they are thematically coherent with the preceding story, but thematic coherence is an elastic concept. The second narrator may have to work quite hard to establish his story as a second story; or, as in the case of 'Mike's Middle Names', the second narrator may feel able to tell his story in an abbreviated form because it follows the pattern of the preceding story so closely.

'These Peculiar Coincidences': Second Stories Told by the Same Narrator

In this section, I want to look at second stories where the narrator remains the same: does this have any effect on the structure of the stories? I shall look at stories 1, 2 and 3 in the sequence 'Coincidence and Probability Theory'. The sequence begins with Brian telling the story 'Keith's Foot and Probability Theory', which is about helping out a friend who had broken his foot and needed information on probability theory. The story is given in (9) below.

(9) Keith's Foot and Probability Theory
1   In the last couple of days I've had so many odd things happen
2   I mean I got a phone call from-
3   you know- do you know Keith who works round in Business Studies? [*Tony: no*]
4   no, he's ever such a nice bloke
5   and he's um- he's been very helpful, very friendly
6   and er he's on partial secondment to do an MA- um MBA
7   and er got a <u>phone call about half-past seven</u> <CHUCKLING> . couple of days ago
8   and he said er 'Brian' you know 'can you come and- come and help me'
9   I said- I said, '((well)) I'm going to work'
10 he said er- he said 'well all right, can you- can you come round tonight?'
11 so I said 'well I suppose so,
12 what do you want me to do?'
13 He said 'Well I dropped . a carving board on my foot'
14 and I- I- I said 'Look . I can't quite see what you know-'
15 said you know 'I haven't got a car
16 cos my wife's nicked it,
17 you know that . um <LAUGHS>
18 what can I do about your foot?'
19 and he said, 'I want to know some stuff about probability theory'
20 <LAUGHTER>
21 so I said 'Keith you are not talking straight,
22 please explain'
23 and <LAUGHING> he said what'd happened is that
24 he had to produce this um assignment for the next day

25 and because he had to go to the hospital because of his . broken toe
26 he wouldn't have time to read up the book on probability theory
27 and he knew that I knew the probability theory
28 and would I come round and explain it to him,
29 and it's the only time in my life I've cured somebody's toe by probability theory
30 <LAUGHTER>
31 ((was)) absolutely dotty <LAUGHING>

This story is preceded by a few lines from Brian which frame the story as being about coincidence:

> I started thinking a lot about these peculiar coincidences
> and um (1.5) some very strange things happen
> ((I mean)) apart from that thing with the- the Dutch form earlier
> → in the last couple of days I've had so many odd things happen.

These four lines include a repeated theme: the phrase *peculiar coincidences* is picked up by the clause *some very strange things happen* and this general claim is then pinned down in the first line of the story, *in the last couple of days I've had so many odd things happen*. This line can be described as a story proposition[8] and requires a story to substantiate the claim made in the proposition. This line also places the story in time (*in the last couple of days*) and moves us away from the conversational present into the past of the storyworld.

The narrator now has to tell a story about something strange or odd happening which involves coincidence. Line 29 – *and it's the only time in my life I've cured somebody's toe by probability theory* – functions to frame the story and to spell out exactly what the coincidence is. The final evaluative line *was absolutely dotty* both rounds off the story and, through its semantic cohesiveness with the opening adjectives *strange* and *odd*, asserts that the story has delivered what was promised at the beginning.

Brian then continues to talk about Keith and launches into another coincidence story where Keith is the protagonist. This is the story 'A Double-Glazing Jehovah's Witness', given in (10). (Pete's comments are in italics; Tony's in italic capitals.)

(10)   A Double-Glazing Jehovah's Witness
1 actually he- he came down and that's- he-
2 something happened to him.

3   I mean I- I been collecting these sort of silly coincidences

4   we- we started talking about them

→ 5   and lovely thing that er he came up with

6   was about three weeks ago

7   he had somebody come to the door

8   and um . and this is justified

9   Gwen his wife is er you know- she- she confirms that it's absolutely true

10   er <u>he- he'd gone down</u> <LAUGHING>

11   and this bloke was sort of doing this . whole business about you know sort of

12   'oh I'm doing this survey, this questionnaire you know, we um-'

13   and after a little while he said 'Look come on I'm not daft.

14   Why don't you just tell me what you're trying to sell me,

15   cos you're trying to sell me something,

16   and I'll tell you whether I want to know about it or not'.

17   He said, 'OK, I'm trying to sell you . double glazing'.

18   <LAUGHTER>

19   ((anyway)) and he- and he said <LAUGHING> so Keith then said,

20   'Well as it happens I- I'm . quite interested in double glazing <LAUGHTER>

21   Now, that's fine', you know,

22   and he'd been quite rude to him,

23   he said 'you can come in and sit down',

24   and then he felt a little bit guilty

25   after a little while

26   cos he's a nice guy

27   and he said- he said, 'I didn't mean to be rude to you',

28   he said, 'but I rather feared that you might be a Jehovah's Witness',

29   and he said, 'I am'.

30   <LAUGHTER>

31   and Gwen told me that ((she xx)) hearing this <LAUGHTER CONTINUES>

32   and thinking 'Aaahhh!!!'.<LAUGHS>

33   *brilliant*

34   **double- a double-glazing ⌈Jehovah's Witness

                                   ⌊*Jehovah's Witness*

35   oh [*GOD*]

36 I mean short of having a living Mormon trying to extend your
      loft
37 you can't do much else can you.
38 ((it's- it's-)) flipping wonderful.
39 *brilliant*
40 <LAUGHTER>**

[The final section between ** and ** is accompanied by continual laughter from all participants]

The story 'A Double-Glazing Jehovah's Witness' counts as a second story since it is contiguous with the first story ('Keith's Foot and Probability Theory') and is thematically coherent with it. Tony and Pete contribute to its success as a second story by demonstrating their alignment with its theme: they add supportive comments ('brilliant', lines 33 and 39; 'god', line 35), they laugh at key moments, and Pete even co-constructs the climactic line ('a double-glazing Jehovah's Witness', line 34). But as the lines preceding the story show, Brian feels the need to introduce the theme of 'silly coincidences' again before telling this second story, even though this theme has been well established by the first story.

Some analysts have argued that where a second story is told by the same narrator as the first story, the 'point' need not be repeated,[9] whereas others claim that the possibility of not repeating the point holds true for *all* second stories.[10] But the evidence of my data is that these claims are incorrect. Story (8), 'Mike's Middle Names', relies on co-participants knowing that the point of the story can be carried over from the previous story, that is, *you can't not know your name*. This second story is told by a different speaker from the preceding story. By contrast, the story 'A Double-Glazing Jehovah's Witness' is told by the same narrator who told the preceding story, yet here the narrator repeats the key phrase *silly coincidences* (worded as *peculiar coincidences* in the first story) to frame the story, as if he cannot rely on his audience assuming that the point made at the beginning of the first story – *some very strange things happen* – is still in place. (It may be that the narrator feels he needs to underline the link between the two narratives to justify his holding on to the floor to tell a second story.)

Certainly Brian and his friends collaborate to maintain the salience of the coincidence theme. After Brian's evaluative closing line *it's flipping wonderful* and Pete's comment *brilliant*, there is general laughter before the following brief discussion involving all three friends:

(11) *Extract from 'Coincidence' Sequence*

Brian: I- you- you know ((xx)) I like to store these little things up,
        you know when I'm- when I'm doing probability theory

Pete: yeah

Brian: with different people, say- say to them 'just because some-
        thing is unlikely, doesn't mean to say that it won't happen'

Tony: in fact you might almost say that the more unlikely a thing is,
        in a paradoxical sort of way, the more likely it is to happen

Here we see the work co-participants do to co-operate in story-telling. They reflect on the general theme of coincidence, while Brian again makes the link with his professional interest in probability theory. Tony's bold statement *in fact you might almost say that the more unlikely a thing is, in a paradoxical sort of way, the more likely it is to happen* could have led on to further discussion, but in fact it triggers Brian's third story. Tony's statement moves the focus on from the more general 'some very strange things happen' (which was said before the first story, 'Keith's Foot and Probability Theory') to the idea that extraordinarily 'unlikely' things may in fact be expected to happen. Brian responds by telling the story 'Loons and Shopping Trolleys' which is a (very funny) story about an extremely unlikely juxtaposition of people and events, so showing great sensitivity to the nuances of Tony's comment. The story tells of a woman in a super-market who gets herself caught up in the wheels of her shopping trolley because her trousers ('loons') have such wide hems, and who asks for help from a woman on the other side of the frozen food counter who turns out to be in the same position. The story is given in (12) below.

(12) Loons and Shopping Trolleys

1   ((there was)) another nice one
2   cos it sprang to mind
3   the other- the other one that er-
4   once I started thinking about it
5   cos I started trying to . go through this
6   ((you know)) it's- it's on the back of my mind at the moment
7   I remembered a story . way back er . when I was living in
      Brighton
8   and somebody told me
9   woman called Catherine
10 not Catherine that we know but another one

11 do you remember the days of tight-fitting . trousers with flappy
       bottoms? [*mhm*]
12 you know, loons [*mhm*]
13 anyway . she had been going to shop to buy frozen food in
       Sainsburys
14 and she's pushing . the trolley along
15 I think it's delightful
16 pushing the trolley along
17 anyway her loons . had got hooked into the wheels of the trolley
18 <LAUGHTER>
19 so that she couldn't push any further <LAUGHTER>
20 but the trouble is
21 because they were so tight
22 she couldn't therefore bend down . to get them out <T AND P
       LAUGH THROUGHOUT>
23 so she was totally stuck <LAUGHTER>
24 she couldn't act- she couldn't go forward, she was stuck
       <LAUGHTER – T HELPLESS>
25 so no no this- <IMPLYING HE HASN'T REACHED PUNCH LINE YET>
26 the- the bit that really got me . is that-
27 you know with er . frozen food counters
28 you know you can usually see through
29 and she could see that there was somebody on the other side
30 so she said- did the 'Pssst! Pssst' <LAUGHTER>
31 somebody on the other- moved a few ((xx)) or heard a ((xx)) <P
       GUFFAWS>
32 and er . so she- she ((said)) through to this other woman on the
       other side <LAUGHING>
33 she said, 'This sounds very silly
34 but um . I'm in an embarrassing situation
35 um . I've managed to get myself completely locked into my
       trolley by my trousers <MIMICS WOMAN'S VOICE> <T AND
       P LAUGH>
36 and the woman on the other side said
37 'So have I'
38 <ALL LAUGH>
39 ((I say you see)) I think it's a absolutely stunning idea
40 [*P: beautiful/ T: wonderful*]

Lines 24–6 are interesting: line 24 *she couldn't act- she couldn't go
forward, she was stuck* is greeted with laughter by both Tony and Pete,

with Tony being helpless with laughter. Brian then says *so no no this-
the- the bit that really got me . is that-* and then proceeds with the story.
It is as if he interprets Tony and Pete's laughter as marking what they
take to be the climax of his story, whereas he as narrator is strongly
aware that he not only has to produce a story about something 'strange'
or 'unlikely' (which he has done) but he also has to keep to the
theme of coincidence (which he has not yet done). This hiccup in the
middle of his story displays the sensitivity of narrators to maintaining
thematic coherence.

Although all three stories tell of strange coincidences, they are very
different in other ways. They have different, non-parallel protagonists
(the narrator in the first, the narrator's colleague in the second, and
two unknown women in the third). The first story is a first-person
narrative, while the other two are third-person narratives. The first
is also a participant narrative,[11] that is, the narrator was a participant
in the events narrated. Participant narratives are not restricted to
first-person narratives, that is, third-person narratives can be participant narratives. But stories 2 and 3 in the sequence here are non-
participant narratives: the narrator was not a participant in or a witness
to the events described (though he works hard to show his closeness
to those involved in the second story, particularly in his comments
about what Keith's wife said). Non-participant narratives are said to
be rare in spontaneous conversation among friends,[12] and this is
supported by my data, with these two coincidence stories being two
of only fourteen non-participant stories in my corpus. In spontaneous
talk among friends, eye-witness knowledge of events is valued and
the first-person narrative of personal experience is the most common
form of narrative found. But occasionally a speaker will tell a story
where s/he was not a participant, and such stories can play an important role in establishing group values (see, for example 'Jonesy and
the Lion', chapter 2, example (1)) or in entertaining co-participants
(the two stories under discussion here can be seen to be highly successful in this sense from the evidence of co-participants' appreciative
comments and their laughter).

But the order in which Brian tells this series of stories is not
random: he begins with a personal story, a first-person narrative;
he then tells a second story on the same theme where the protagonist, Keith, was one of the two main characters in the first story.
Only after the success of this second story is he emboldened to
embark on a third story where he has no first-hand knowledge of
the events recounted, but where he is at pains to name his source

(Catherine) and to specify where he was living when he heard the story (*I was living in Brighton*). The majority (66 per cent) of non-participant stories in the conversations I've collected occur as second stories, which suggests that in friendly conversation the norm is for first stories (by which I mean stories which stand alone as well as stories which subsequently become first in a series) to be participant narratives.

This analysis of second stories told by the same narrator shows that the work needed to establish a second story varies depending on how closely the second story follows the pattern of the first. This is true regardless of whether a second story involves the same narrator or a different one. While all second stories must be thematically coherent with a first story, this allows narrators of second stories a great deal of scope. Second stories may match the first story in terms of general theme (coincidence in the case of 'The Double-Glazing Jehovah's Witness' and 'Loons and Shopping Trolleys') or just in terms of the oddity of a particular (non-present) individual (Peter in the case of the 'Peter at Church' sequence). At the other end of the scale, a second story may orient so closely to a first story that the parallelisms between the stories hold at every level: theme, setting, characters, events. The story 'Mike's Middle Names' is a good example of such a second story. What is striking about second stories of this latter kind is that narrators can exploit the sequential positioning of their story by leaving out much that would be necessary in a first story since they can rely on listeners to infer what is needed from the preceding story.

'Second story', then, is a term that covers a wide range of stories occurring in sequence, from more loosely connected stories to those with multiple close connections. While more loosely connected second stories require more careful linking work from narrators, more closely connected stories require careful inferencing and matching work from listeners. In other words, in all cases the telling of a second story is a collaborative achievement on the part of co-participants.

'My Mind Is With You': Second Stories and the Construction of Male Solidarity

In the all-male conversations I've collected, over a third (35 per cent) of the narratives told by men to their friends occurred as part of a sequence. In other words, in a significant proportion of cases, men choose to follow a story with another story, a choice which carries a strong collaborative message.

This is interesting, given current understanding of masculinity and of male friendship. Contemporary accounts of male friendship suggest that men's friendships are characterized by sociability rather than intimacy, with a focus on activity rather than talk.[13] Social theorists link these characteristics of male friendship to emotional inexpressivity: 'masculinity is an essentially negative identity learnt through defining itself against emotionality and connectedness'.[14] Vic Seidler goes so far as to claim that men's lives are structured by a particular relationship to language whereby 'language comes to be used as a weapon for the defence of masculine identity, rather than a mode of expressing connectedness with others, or honesty about emotional life'.[15]

The conversational data analysed in previous chapters lends support to the view of men as emotionally inexpressive. But while male speakers have been shown to avoid personal topics and mutual self-disclosure, there is no doubt that male speakers express solidarity with each other through the use of linguistic strategies such as swearing, ritual insults, sexist and homophobic remarks, and competitive banter.[16] It is notable that these strategies simultaneously accomplish hegemonic masculinity. What is interesting about the finding that male speakers will often choose to tell a second story is that this is a very different kind of way of accomplishing solidarity. Telling stories in sequence functions, among other things, to display mutual understanding. The capacity of male friends to tell stories in sequence suggests that male speakers *are* able to use language as a 'mode of expressing connectedness with others'.[17]

Conclusion

In this chapter I have explored the role of story sequences in talk among male friends. I have argued that telling a second story involves co-participants in paying careful attention to what each other is saying. By telling a relevant second story, a co-participant communicates 'My mind is with you'. It could be that this aspect of sequential story-telling is valued by men precisely because it makes possible the display of mutual understanding. Most ways of displaying mutual understanding in all-male groups are taboo because of men's fear of appearing feminine, and the associated fear of appearing 'gay'.

Men who meet as friends need strategies for 'doing' friendship. They need ways of showing mutual respect and understanding. Linguistic strategies such as the use of insults and taboo language may achieve solidarity, but at a cost, since such strategies are also highly face-threatening. The capacity of stories told in sequence to testify to the closeness of participants means that telling second stories can be a powerful way of 'doing' friendship. It is therefore not surprising that we find story sequences in conversations involving men friends: through their careful alignment to each other in their telling of second stories, co-participants at talk can display connectedness with each other, while at the same time telling stories of heroism or laddishness which construct and maintain hegemonic masculinity.

Notes

1 Harvey Sacks, *Lectures on Conversation*, p. 257.
2 B. Kirshenblatt-Gimblett, 'The concept and varieties of narrative performance in East European Jewish culture'; K. Galloway-Young, *Taleworlds and Storyrealms*; Alan Ryave, 'On the achievement of a series of stories'; Sacks, *Lectures on Conversation*; Jennifer Shepherd, 'Storytelling in conversational discourse: a collaborative model'.
3 Sacks, *Lectures on Conversation*, p. 249.
4 This parallels the findings of others working on narrative. Jennifer Shepherd discusses a five-story sequence which is the longest in her data-base (Shepherd, 'Storytelling in conversational discourse'). K. Galloway-Young mentions a series of seven stories, but her data is folkloric, not conversational narrative (Galloway-Young, *Taleworlds and Storyrealms*).
5 Sacks, *Lectures on Conversation*, p. 250.
6 Ibid.; Ryave, 'On the achievement of a series of stories'; Galloway-Young, *Taleworlds and Storyrealms*.
7 Galloway-Young, *Taleworlds and Storyrealms*, p. 82.
8 Shepherd, 'Storytelling in conversational discourse'.
9 Ibid., p. 239.
10 Ryave, 'On the achievement of a series of stories'.
11 This is Charlotte Linde's term (see Linde, *Life Stories: The Creation of Coherence*).
12 Ibid.
13 Fern Johnson and Elizabeth Aries, 'The talk of women friends' and 'Conversational patterns among same-sex pairs of late adolescent close friends'; Stuart Miller, *Men and Friendship*; Pat O'Connor, *Friendships between Women*; Joseph Pleck, 'Man to man: is brotherhood possible?'; Victor Seidler, *Rediscovering Masculinity*; Drury Sherrod, 'The bonds of men'.

105

14   Seidler, *Rediscovering Masculinity*, p. 7.
15   Ibid.
16   Deborah Cameron, 'Performing gender identity'; Brendan Gough and Gareth Edwards, 'The beer talking: four lads, a carry out and the reproduction of masculinities'; Koenraad Kuiper, 'Sporting formulae in New Zealand English: two models of male solidarity'; William Labov, *Language in the Inner City*; Jane Pilkington, ' "Don't try and make out that I'm nice": the different strategies women and men use when gossiping'.
17   Where self-promoting stories occur in sequence, then telling a second story can function as a competitive move. In one story sequence in the corpus, the narrator of the second story begins his story with the words *tell you what, I'll beat all of that*, which explicitly labels his narrative as a competitive speech act. Competitive story-telling only occurred in the younger groups in the data-base, where friendship links were less well developed.

5

'She'd Made Sardines in Aspic': Women's Stories, Men's Stories and the Construction of Gender

Up to this point I have focused on men's stories in all-male talk and I have shown how stories play a significant role in the construction of masculinity. So how far do these stories differ from those told by women in all-female conversation? According to Barbara Johnstone, men and women 'are actively creating different worlds in and through their stories, worlds which are at the same time reflective and constitutive of men's and women's psychological, social, and cultural worlds outside their stories'.[1] Is this true of the narratives told by men and women in my data-base? To find out, let's start by comparing a story told by a man to his men friends with a story told by a woman to her women friends.[2]

(1) The Fight
[Three men in their twenties in a pub, talking about an engineer at work who was an alcoholic]
1 he came in this one time,
2 drunk,
3 and he started ordering me about.
4 With kind of personality I've got
5 I told him to piss off,
6 I wasn't taking any of it.
7 So I was making these um alarm bell boxes, the alarm boxes,
8 you put this bell on and you wire these-
9 can't remember how to do it now anyway but-
10 wiring these up,

11   and he come out,

12   and he sss, sss, sss, <MIMICS NOISE>

13   what he did was he threw this knife at me,

14   this is honest truth,

15   threw a knife at me,

16   and then- and there was this cable,

17   you know um like on the workbenches where you connect the
      cables into these three points,

18   a bare wire,

19   he fucking chased me with it,

20   and I thought 'Fuck this',

21   and he kept like having a go and teasing me,

22   and I just smashed him straight round the face with a bell box in
      front of the boss,

23   crack,

24   got away with it as well,

25   I said 'Look', I said, 'he's thrown knives at me',

26   it sounds like something out of a film but it's honest truth.

27   [. . .]

28   Honestly it was unbelievable.

The second story comes from a conversation involving three women friends in their thirties who have met for a meal and a chat in one of their homes.

(2) Sardines in Aspic

[Context = discussion of narrator's eccentric mother]

1   Actually when I first took Martin up there

2   when Martin and I- <LAUGHS> my husband- [*yes*] ex-husband
      and I were first going out together

3   and it was all new and really embarrassing you know <LAUGHS>
      [*yeah*]

4   he only ever used to like traditional English food like-

5   cos he was steak and kidney pie shepherd's pie and roast dinner
      on Sunday [*yeah*]

6   and that was all he'd eat,

7   give him anything foreign [*yeah*] and he'd have hysterics, [*yeah*]

8   so I phoned my mother up before we went up for our very first
      visit

9   and I said 'He only likes plain food so just don't go mad', [*yeah*]

10   cos she always goes mad, [*yeah*]

11 'Don't go mad,
12 just cook something really ordinary',
13 *she does, makes nice food though, really nice food.*
14 So we got there late at night
15 and she said 'I've made something for you to eat',
16 and she'd made sardines in aspic <LAUGHTER>
17 and beetroot in natural yoghurt, <LAUGHTER>
18 plain food <LAUGHTER>
19 *did she do it on purpose?*
20 I don't know, probably.
21 *what did he say?*
22 he wasn't very impressed <LAUGHTER>
23 he kept hauling me down to the little chip shop in the village
       <LAUGHTER>
24 cos he was so hungry,
25 he wouldn't eat anything she made. <LAUGHTER>

In discussing these two stories, one thing I want to avoid is over-simplification. But I am aware that choosing two stories to represent the categories 'man's story' and 'woman's story' runs the risk – precisely – of over-simplifying the picture. Because the English language – and Western culture in general – works in terms of binary distinctions such as man–woman, male–female, masculine–feminine, it is very easy to slip into presenting findings in a binary way which obscures both the complexity and variety of human talk, and the many overlaps between women's and men's ways of talking. But in order to start making comparisons, I need to select some individual stories for detailed analysis. The two stories above are 'typical' as far as I can judge, but of course they cannot possibly do more than hint at some of the differences to be found between stories arising in all-male talk and stories arising in all-female talk.

So what do these two stories have in common? And in what ways do they differ? To begin with, there are some commonalities: both narrators successfully establish a narrative floor, and both groups of friends collaborate in the sense that they support the narrator in his or her telling with supportive contributions such as *yeah* and with laughter. Both stories are eminently tellable: even out of context, they work as stories, and are culturally recognizable as being a heroic tale, in the case of the first story, and a funny story, in the case of the second. Both stories are constructed according to the patterns discussed in chapter 2, and in both characters are animated through the use of direct speech. Both stories occur as part of a sequence of five stories: 'The Fight' is the fourth in a sequence which focuses on events in the workplace; 'Sardines in Aspic' is the fifth in a sequence about the narrator's eccentric mother.

But what leaps out when we read them is the difference between them. The first story is a typical male first-person narrative: the narrator presents himself as a lone protagonist, in conflict with an unnamed (male) other, who he overcomes through an act of violence after being attacked by him. His act is witnessed by 'the boss' (also unnamed), but the narrator boasts that he *got away with it*, thus presenting the fight as a double achievement in that he outfaces the drunk engineer and gets away with this behaviour in front of the boss. All the characters in the storyworld are male. The narrator evaluates the events he recounts as *unbelievable*, an adjective which claims tellability in no uncertain terms. He immodestly compares what had happened to *something out of a film*, but is at pains to assert that the story is *honest truth* (lines 14 and 26) – presumably because the narrator of an 'unbelievable' story runs the risk of not being believed. The narrator grounds the story in reality through the use of detail about the alarm bell boxes and the cable used as a weapon, a key characteristic of men's stories. And linguistically the story performs dominant masculinity through use of taboo words (*piss off, fucking*), through the absence of hedging, and through the making of noises to mimic the throwing of a knife and the *crack* of making contact with someone's face.[3]

The second story, 'Sardines in Aspic', is also a first-person narrative, but a first-person narrative where the narrator/protagonist's actions are not the focus of the story. What the story is about is the first meeting between the narrator's mother and Martin, the narrator's then boyfriend, later her husband, now her ex-husband. These two characters are just as important as the narrator herself, and they are named and fleshed out as characters in a way which contrasts with the thinness of characterization typical of many men's stories. The narrative does not focus on achievement; on the contrary, it could be argued that one theme of this story is failure. The narrator takes her boyfriend up to Liverpool to meet her mother; the quality of the meeting is succinctly conveyed through this anecdote on the subject of food. Martin is characterized as a *steak and kidney pie shepherd's pie and roast dinner on Sunday* person, while the narrator's mother is described as someone who is adventurous in her cooking, someone who likes to *go mad* with food. The narrative recounts the inevitable clash that ensues when the two meet.

The man's story focuses on action, while the woman's story focuses on people. The man, through his story, presents himself as a winner, someone who will not be pushed around, someone who stands up for himself, and also as someone who gets away with things. The events he describes take place in the workplace, and the storyworld he creates is populated entirely by men. The story, 'The Fight', is a performance of hegemonic masculinity. Self-presentation, in the case of the woman's story, is much more subtle: the woman presents herself as someone involved in heterosexual relationships, who is in close contact with her family (represented by her mother), who sees food and meals as a salient arena for the acting out of key issues, and who is sensitive to the complexity and difficulty of human relationships. Her story is set in the private world of the home, and the storyworld she creates includes both men and women. So, in its very different way, this story is a performance of ideal femininity.[4]

At this point, in an attempt to achieve some balance, I would like to examine some less typical stories: two narratives of achievement from the all-female conversations and two stories touching on relationships from the all-male conversations. The first narrative of achievement from the women's conversations describes stripping and re-varnishing the kitchen table. The narrator is Pat, talking in her kitchen to her friend Karen (both women are in their thirties).

(3) *Extract from* **Kitchen Table**
1 Look what I've done to this table
2 [. . .]
3 I've been putting it off for years
4 and the other day Ray put-
5 he must have been going to wash up or something
6 and he put down . a wet frying pan
7 and it absolutely gouged that thick
8 and totally round a huge-
9 and I said 'That's it',
10 and I just scraped it down with bleach
11 and I didn't use paint stripper or anything
12 I put two coats of varnish
13 and it's quite pretty isn't it? [*yes*]
14 [. . .]
15 it's nice isn't it, I'm ever so pleased with it.

Success in this story involves an inanimate object rather than contest with another human being; achievement is firmly located within the domestic sphere. The second narrative I want to quote here recounts a daughter's success in a pub quiz, where her achievement was to draw with one of her school teachers. This short narrative is given in (4) below:

(4) Quiz
[Six friends aged 40+ at J's house; narrator = Janet]
1   ooh I must tell you
2   Vicky- you know the quiz Vicky goes to on Wednesday? *[mhm]*
3   she drew with Robin Lee *[oh <LAUGHS>]*
4   last night <LAUGHS>
5   she got two fifty
6   *in a- in a pub?*
7   it's a- it's a pub *<LAUGHTER>*
8   they have this little quiz
9   and apparently Mr Lee goes now
10   and Vicky was absolutely deLIGHTed *[<LAUGHTER>]*
11   she BEAT him
12   well she didn't beat him
13   she came- she drew.

In 'Quiz', while the story does involve contest with another person, the protagonist is not the narrator, so the main message of the story is that the narrator is proud of her daughter, a highly feminine virtue. And it is notable that while the narrator tries to make her story fit a classic achievement trajectory, her desire to be accurate (and not to 'show off' about her daughter) means that the ending *she drew* (line 13) undermines her triumphant claim *she BEAT him* in line 11.

It was difficult to find narratives of achievement in the all-female conversations, and it was equally difficult to find a man's story that focused on family and/or relationships. Men's stories are only rarely situated in the home, and even more rarely focus on relationships. One apparent example is the story 'A Double-Glazing Jehovah's Witness', a third-person narrative which involves a friend of the narrator, his wife, and a man trying to sell double-glazing (see chapter 4, p. 97). However, the focus is not on the relationships among the characters, but on the theme of coincidence.

The first example to be looked at here is a funny story about a gay man and a lesbian woman, told by Brian to two friends in the pub.

(5) Steve and Vicky

1   Steve was a very close friend of mine
2   I got on very well with him
3   I also got on with (.) this woman (.) Vicky
4   that was- used to work in- in computing
5   now Steve was gay
6   and so was Vicky
7   and pure- you know purely (.) sort of separately
8   I had social dealings with both of them [*oh*]
9   and then you know
10 at one point ((I- this- this- this)) absolutely lovely conversation
        with them
11 ((which er)) <LAUGHS>
12 not with them
13 but with them separately
14 er I'd gone out for a drink with Vicky
15 and I'd gone out for a drink with Steve
16 and I said 'oh what you doing . for the . holidays'
17 and er Vicky had said
18 'oh I'm going to this island'
19 ((it was)) fairly obscure Greek island
20 ((xxxx)) <MUMBLED, CROAKY VOICE>
21 cos I know most of the Greek islands
22 but I didn't know this one
23 so I asked her to describe it,
24 said 'ahh sounds lovely',
25 and just (.) couple of days later
26 I'd gone out for a drink with Steve
27 and er (.) I said er 'oh what you doing for the summer',
28 and he said 'oh I'm going to this-'
29 and same bloody island.
30 I said 'look (.) hang on, <LAUGHTER>
31 something's going on here'. <LAUGHS>
32 I said (.) 'you- you g- (.) you're gay,
33 so <LAUGHING> so is Vick,
34 cos she's told me
35 she'd never ever marry a man again
36 and- and she'll- (.) doesn't want to touch them,
37 she's lesbian,
38 and you're both going to be on the same island together
39 well presumably together-'

40   ah well you've got it,
41   well anyway the twins came the next year
42   er <LAUGHS> [*ah*]
43   <u>so ((it was a little bit))-</u> <LAUGHING>
44   talk about yeah conjunction,
45   ·<u>it was absolutely wonderful.</u> <LAUGHING VOICE> [*mhm*]

This story has its effect because it presents unconventional characters (a lesbian and a gay man) but plots a canonical story (man and woman meet, man and woman fall in love, man and woman have babies). The unexpected denouement makes this a funny story, a fable where everything works out in the end. But although the narrator portrays a storyworld inhabited by women as well as men, and although the narrative has a conventional romantic trajectory, we learn little about the characters and even less about their feelings. We are left to infer from the climactic line *well anyway the twins came the next year* that Vicky and Steve fell in love and moved in together. This doesn't detract from the story: it is a good story, concisely told, involving a clear breach of the canonical script (gay men and women are not supposed to have heterosexual relationships with each other). But it is not a story about relationships in the same way that example (2), 'Sardines in Aspic', is.

Another example comes in a sequence of stories about the 1960s and the significance of certain sorts of clothes and shoes. This story involves a father and son relationship. Example (6) gives a brief extract:

(6) *Extract from* Suedehead
[Three friends in their forties talking after work in the pub]
  1   I went home in these Ivy brogues you know
  2   and they cost- . god knows what it was at the time
  3   fifteen pounds which was astronomical <LAUGHTER>
  4   and my father discovered these brogues
  5   and he was absolutely furious [*mhm*]
  6   that I'd spent all this money on these things
  7   say- he- I'll never forget he grabbed hold of ((1 syll))-
  8   and flung them across the room at me you know
  9   and they sort of- not- not- and because they were so heavy
10   <u>they were really good and heavy with great big .hh ((xx)) quarters in the heels</u> <LAUGHING>

11 I ducked and they . took a bit of plaster out of the wall you know
        behind me
12 all because I decided I wanted to be part of the you know the
        swinging things.

This story involves a father–son relationship, but the narrator (the
son in the story) maintains the ongoing theme of the 1960s and
fashion. He pays attention to detail about the shoes (how much they
cost, how heavy they were), and about other aspects of the dress code
of the 'suedehead', as some earlier lines of the story testify: *yeah I
was- I was- I was a Suedehead, that's right a Suedehead <LAUGHTER> cos
I wasn't- I couldn't be a Skinhead cos I wasn't prepared to- to take all my
hair off [. . .] but you did at least have to have the kind of Ben Sherman shirts,
the Levi Stapress, and the Ivy brogues you know or plaincaps*. While this is
fascinating from a socio-historical perspective, none of what the narrator says tells us about his feelings, apart from his comment that he
wanted to be part of the you know the swinging things. We do not know
whether he experienced fear or anger during this clash with his
father, or whether violent reactions were typical of his father. But the
evidence of my data is that men do not exploit narrative to reflect on
their lives and relationships.

All these stories support the claim that 'women and men . . . are
actively creating different worlds in and through their stories'.[5] I want
to look now at the linguistic means by which women and men create
these different worlds, drawing on the entire narrative corpus.[6]

'Different Worlds': Gender Differences in Narrative

One interesting background statistic is that the women in the conversations I've collected tell more stories than the men do: the all-female
conversations contain on average 17 stories per hour compared with 11
stories per hour in the men's conversations.[7] Moreover, every all-female
conversation in the corpus contains narrative, whereas one of the all-
male conversations contains no stories at all and three contain only
one story each. The all-male conversation which contains no narrative
involves two friends who engage in very focused discussion on impersonal topics for forty-five minutes. Given that most conversations
consist of a mix of discussion and narrative,[8] the absence of any story-
telling in this particular conversation is striking, and can be seen as an
extreme example of men's tendency to avoid talk about personal matters.

Another more structural reason for the frequency of narrative in all-female conversation may be women's propensity to tell stories in sequence. Story sequences are a common phenomenon in conversations of all kind. Structurally there is no difference in women's and men's practice: a story can always be followed by another story and will be perceived as being in sequence as long as it is contiguous and has a topical link. Sixty-two per cent of stories in the all-female conversations were part of a story sequence, compared with 35 per cent of stories in the all-male conversations. This means that stories in women's friendly talk are more likely to be part of a sequence than to stand alone (something which is not true of all-male stories). Story sequences are characteristic of relaxed talk between friends because producing a sequence of stories functions as a display of mutual understanding and demonstrates how well the participants are in tune with each other, as we saw in the previous chapter. It could be that this aspect of serial story-telling is highly valued by women precisely because it makes possible the display of mutual understanding, and that female speakers will therefore be disposed to respond to the telling of a story with another story.

It is possible for the same narrator to tell a sequence of stories, but this happens more frequently in all-male than in all-female conversation.[9] As the last chapter illustrated, in my data-base there are two instances of a male speaker telling five stories in sequence. The evidence of the conversations is that this was completely acceptable to the men concerned, which fits the general observation that men are happy to hold the floor for extended turns. In friendly conversation, by contrast, women tend to take shorter turns and to share the floor.[10]

Another notable difference is that story sequences in women's friendly talk are never competitive, unlike some found in all-male conversation. In other words, the 'I Can Beat That' approach to serial story-telling is absent from the all-female conversations. This is because competition is not part of dominant versions of femininity, whereas it is an important aspect of dominant versions of masculinity. While it would be wrong to over-emphasize the competitive–co-operative contrast between men's and women's talk, given that men's stories often demonstrate considerable collaborative effort, it is certainly the case that men's stories are often about competition and individual achievement and that women's are not. Nearly half (46 per cent) of narratives told by men to their friends focus on individual achievement, whether this takes the form of heroic action, exemplary skill or just a clever prank (and in this respect, 'The Fight' is a typical male narrative).[11]

This focus on achievement is not found in the narratives told by women (only 6 per cent of women's stories were about achievement or skill). Barbara Johnstone, investigating narrative use in the USA, compared men's focus on achievement with the theme of embarrass-ment or fear in women's stories.[12] While stories of embarrassment or fear constitute a smaller proportion of women's stories than achieve-ment stories do for men, there was a clear gender difference in relation to this measure (19 per cent of women's stories expressed embarrass-ment or fear compared with only 2 per cent of men's).

The emotional tone of a story is obviously related to its topic. So what are women's stories about? While stereotypical topics are found, with women telling stories about clothes, periods, children, mothers, or shopping, for example, many stories involve less gendered topics such as going to the optician, courses for school governors, or damaging a fire extinguisher. The majority of women's stories (53 per cent) are set in the home, while the majority of men's stories (54 per cent) are set in the outside world (pubs, sports fields, colleges, etc.). For men, the home is the least favoured setting, with stories set in the workplace (26 per cent) outnumbering those set in the home (20 per cent). For women the workplace is the least favoured setting for stories (15 per cent).[13] Most women work outside the home, but the small number of workplace stories suggests that paid work is less relevant to women's sense of who they are than it is to men's.[14] As David Morgan com-ments: 'workplaces seem to be the crucibles out of which male identities are forged and through which they are given shape and meaning'.[15] Male narrators' preference for settings *outside* the home suggests that men's sense of who they are has strong links with the public sphere.

The domestic setting of many women's stories is inevitably linked to the kinds of themes women choose to talk about and supports the claim that the private sphere is a feminine space, while the public sphere is masculine.[16] Women tell stories as a way of keeping in touch with each other's lives. The fact that so many of these stories are set in the home demonstrates the priority that women give to home life and the relationships that go with it, relationships both with friends and with family (as the story 'Sardines in Aspic' illustrates).

One surprising dimension of difference is that of temporal fram-ing. Narrative analysts distinguish between three time-frames: today stories, stories of the recent past (last week/the other day/yesterday) and stories of the distant past.[17] While the majority of women's stories (54 per cent) are set in the recent past (and 69 per cent involve today or the recent past), the majority of men's stories (almost two-thirds

– 65 per cent) are set in the distant past.[18] This again accords with the differing function of story-telling in men's and women's friendships. While women are concerned to keep in touch with each other's daily lives – which means recounting and listening to stories of today and the recent past – men are more concerned to present themselves as certain sorts of persons, persons who engage in contest and win, persons who laugh at the foolish behaviour of others, and with this goal any relevant story can be told, whatever its time-frame. In Shoshana Blum-Kulka's view, the interactional goal of friendly talk is social harmony.[19] But she argues that where the focus is on today, as it was in the Jewish American families she studied, then something more intense than social harmony is achieved which can be called 'affective convergence'.[20] In other words, where conversational participants choose temporal framing closer to the now of speaking, then they achieve emotional closeness of a kind not achieved where temporal framing is more remote from the now of speaking. It could be argued that the unexpected difference between the temporal framing preferred by female narrators and that preferred by male narrators can be directly correlated with the relative intimacy of the relationships between participants in the friendship groups in my data-base. The personal nature of the stories told by women combined with their setting in the recent past means that they function to maintain very strong interpersonal relationships and to effect mutual understanding and empathy. Such outcomes seem to be less important for male speakers.

'It Was so Embarrassing': Self-disclosure

Self-disclosure is largely absent from men's narratives, but is a significant feature of the stories told by women to their friends. A third (33 per cent) of the first-person stories told by women reveal sensitive personal information, compared with only 9 per cent of men's first-person narratives. In the two stories discussed at the beginning of this chapter, the male narrator of the first, 'The Fight', tells us little about his feelings: he does not say whether he was frightened or angry when attacked by the drunk engineer, just that he *wasn't taking any of it*. The woman narrator of 'Sardines in Aspic', by contrast, discloses that one of her feelings about her relationship with Martin at the time of the story was that it was *all new and really embarrassing*. Her feelings arising from the meeting of these two significant people are not spelled out but are implied by her sarcastic comment *plain food*, and by her description of Martin in line 22, *he wasn't very impressed*: in other words, by telling the story at all, she exposes herself in that the event she recounts was self-evidently difficult for her, since she is caught between her mother and her prospective husband. This difference in self-disclosure is not surprising: women's predilection for self-disclosure and men's avoidance of it are well documented in the social psychological literature.[21]

The following two short stories provide examples of self-disclosure in women's narrative. Both recount an experience when the first-person narrator experienced uncomfortable feelings. The first comes from a conversation between four teenage girls; the second from a conversation among five middle-aged women.

(7) **My Mum**

1   my mum
2   it was so embarrassing
3   she was going- she was saying-
4   we were- we were- we were at Andrew's house
5   and everyone was in the room except my dad
6   and she goes 'I can't see you at all'
7   and this is cos I was lying on the bench
8   cos they have a bench round the front
9   cos they're a bit weird you know
10   *what she say?*
11   'All I can see of you is a p- a large portion of breast'.
12   <LAUGHTER>
13   *how embarrassing!*

(8) **Walking Home Alone**

1   I went to the- for a drink the other night on my own,
2   and met Janet and Paul,
3   and . when I was coming out through the Talbot to that back way,
4   a bloke in the car park sh- shouted across to me,
5   and he said, 'Have you got a car?',
6   and I said, 'er what?',
7   and he said- he said, 'Have you got- Can you give me a lift up there?',
8   and I said, 'I haven't got a car',
9   and I nipped up that back lane up the- the bo- up Talbot Road,
10   and all the way up I thought he was going to come,

11 cos he went the other way up- up Rose Mount,
12 and I thought he was going to cut along . whatever that road's
      called,
13 and . my heart was in my mouth all the way up Poplar Road,
14 and what I did was I walked right next to the houses,
15 normally I walk on the other side of the road,
16 but I thought, 'If e- anyone comes near I'm just leap in this house
17 and batter on one of these doors,
18 "Let me in!"', <LAUGHTER>
19 but at the very top of the road there was a little kind of gap with-
20 where you have to cross over,
21 and I thought I'd had it. <LAUGHTER>

By choosing to tell these stories, the female narrators make themselves vulnerable: they reveal that they felt embarrassment ('My Mum') or fear ('Walking Home Alone') and thus present themselves not as heroes or as people acting confidently in the world, but as people who go through difficult experiences and who are aware of their own vulnerability. Why do women tell stories like this? One of the rewards speakers get from self-disclosing is that fellow-speakers are likely to self-disclose in return.[22] Reciprocal self-disclosure makes speakers feel supported by others, since the mirroring behaviour involved in reciprocal self-disclosure communicates understanding and empathy. A common pattern in women's conversations is that one woman's self-disclosing story will be matched by a second told by another woman: sequences of self-disclosing stories are common and can be quite long. The story 'My Mum' is the first of a short sequence of two stories: Jessica's story is followed by one from Claire about her mother embarrassing her when they go to buy a bra. The story 'Walking Home Alone' is the last in a sequence of six stories, all on the theme of fear of men, involving three different narrators.

In both these stories, the narrator's friends respond with laughter (line 12 in 'My Mum'; lines 18 and 21 in 'Walking Home Alone'). This laughter is a sign of recognition rather than amusement. Through their laughter, the narrator's friends demonstrate a shared worldview: they are in effect saying that they too have experienced the feelings the narrator describes. Sequences of self-disclosing stories play an important role in constructing and maintaining solidarity in all-female friendship groups. This aspect of women's narratives contrasts markedly with what is found in the vast majority of men's narratives which are characterized by emotional restraint.

Contrasting Storyworlds

One significant finding for men's stories was the virtual exclusion of women from the storyworld: 96 per cent of protagonists and 72 per cent of other characters were male. In other words, only 28 per cent of the men's stories include women. This contrasts with the storyworld typical of female narrators, where men are more often present than not (86 per cent of stories in the all-female conversations involve both men and women).[23] In this section I want to look more closely at the people inhabiting the storyworlds of male and female narrators.

In both women's and men's storyworlds, the most common character is the narrator themselves. In other words, first-person narratives are the preferred form for all speakers. In relaxed circumstances we tend to tell stories about ourselves more than we tell stories about significant others (first-person narratives constitute 72 per cent of women's narratives and 68 per cent of men's). This suggests that women's storyworlds will have a bias to female characters and men's to male characters. But nearly all stories involve other characters beside the protagonist, and third-person stories focus on a character who is not the narrator (even though the narrator may be a participant in the events narrated). In other words, there is plenty of scope even in first-person narratives to portray a world which contains both men and women.

But as we have seen in earlier chapters, men's stories often involve no women. The story 'The Fight', discussed above, illustrates this, as do the two main stories discussed in chapter 2, 'The Area Manager's Call' and 'Jonesy and the Lion'. Women's stories, by contrast, nearly always include both male and female characters. The story 'Sardines in Aspic', discussed at the beginning of this chapter, is a good example of this point, as are examples (7) and (8) above, 'My Mum' and 'Walking Home Alone'. In the two latter cases, the female narrator tells a story where she is the chief protagonist, but in both cases she constructs a world inhabited by men as well as women (*Andrew* and *my dad* as well as *my mum* in the first story; *Paul* and *a bloke in the car park* as well as *Janet* in the second).

This means that women, in their narratives, construct a world that has far more in common with the world they actually inhabit than do men in their stories. It must be a very unusual man who does not come into contact with women in his everyday life, yet this reality is not re-created in the stories. The exclusion of women from the storyworld of men's stories is a disturbing aspect of all-male narrative. These narratives do important ideological work, maintaining a discourse position where men are all-important and women are invisible. I argued in chapter 3 that the denial of the feminine is central to masculine gender identity.[24] Is mysogyny the reason for men's construction of storyworlds that seem to deny the existence of women?

'Whinging Bitch': Men's Portrayal of Women

Misogyny certainly seems to inform men's portrayal of women in some of the stories where women appear. Two examples are given below.

(9) This Girl Called Debbie
[Two male friends, aged 19/20, narrator = Lee]
1   I know this girl called Debbie
2   well I used to know her
3   and er-
4   *why did you stop knowing her?*
5   dickhead <LAUGHTER>
6   anyway first time I met her I was sitting in someone's garden having a joint with this bird with my legs like that
7   having a chat with her
8   and suddenly I just felt this like warmth all over my leg
9   I've looked round and she's-
10 no joke I swear to god she had her fucking tits hanging over my leg
11 I just went 'ooh' like that
12 and this girl's just gone.

(10) The Vibrator
[Seven male friends aged mid-twenties, narrator = Gary]
1   I went to this customer's house the other day with um-
2   I was told to go there basically by um the corporate sales director for the Dixons Stores group [*yeah*]
3   he phoned me up and he said 'You've got to go to this customer
4   cos she's been like trying to write letters to Sidney Smith [*=the managing director*] and stuff like this' [*yeah*]
5   so I get round there and there's like nothing wrong with her computer at all
6   whinging bitch

7   it was quite funny when I was walking out though
8   cos I was walking out-
9   the computer's in her bedroom
10   I was just sort of looking around
11   looked down on the floor under her bedri- bedside cabinet
12   and there was this fucking great vibrator
13   [*LAUGHTER*]
14   I sort of looked at her and she looked at me and she was like 'oh
     fuck'
15   [*LAUGHTER*]
16   *it's not the sort of thing you leave about when you got the engineers
     coming to do the PC is it?*
17   she had kids as well though
18   fucking kids walking around
19   bloody great vibrator with a sucking cap on the end of it
20   *was she very nice looking?*
21   no she's a big fat pig [*oh*].

Both these stories function as boasts and perform hegemonic (hetero-sexual) masculinity. Both stories are first-person narratives, and both storyworlds include a female character. But in both the woman is presented in sexual terms. In 'This Girl Called Debbie', the eponymous Debbie is hardly a rounded character: the point of the story is that the narrator felt her breasts on his leg. For the narrator and his friend, it seems that the recounting of such an event is regarded as tellable: it tells us a lot about the internal world of young men that their sense of their own masculinity depends on their claiming of such encounters. It doesn't seem to matter what the woman Debbie was like as a person, since what matters in Lee's construction of himself as a heterosexual male is this contact with part of a woman's body. The reduction of women to body parts is a well-documented phenomenon which objectifies women and strips them of human status. Note that Lee's use of the verb 'know' in the opening lines of the story (*I know this girl called Debbie, well I used to know her*) exploits the ambiguity of this verb for the teenage peer-group: 'know' can have its conventional meaning of 'recognize, be acquainted with', but it can also mean 'fancy, be sexually attracted to'.[25]

In example (10), 'The Vibrator', the narrator is more sophisticated in his self-presentation. He presents himself as a reliable employee (who carries out promptly the orders of an important senior male) and as a responsible citizen upholding moral standards (*she had kids as well though, fucking kids walking around*). However, he simultaneously presents himself as a patriarchal male who treats women with contempt with his backstage comments *whinging bitch* and *a big fat pig*, and as a sophisticated, sexually experienced man who knows about vibrators. This complex self-presentation performs masculinity on many levels. But yet again, the woman in the story is unimportant as a person: she is presented in stereotypical terms as a technically incompetent complaining customer – *whinging bitch* – and as a sexual being. While the narrator's attitude to her sexuality is one of disapproval, what matters is that he consigns her to this sexual pigeonhole.

When women are not defined in sexual terms, they tend to be peripheral characters in men's stories, appearing most commonly as wives or mothers. A good example appeared in the extract from 'The Good Samaritan', discussed as example (5) in chapter 3.

(11) *Extract from* **The Good Samaritan**
　　we walked round this boulder
　　and there sitting on the top . was a European couple
　　with their backs to us,
　　as they heard us approach they turned round,
→ and lo it was my Vice-Chancellor and his wife.

The point of this sub-section of the story is the unexpected meeting between the narrator and his Vice-Chancellor: the Vice-Chancellor's wife is an incidental character. Another good example comes in the story 'Strap 'Er On':

(12) *Extract from* **Strap 'Er On**
　　this bloke called Phil at work
　　lives in Taunton
　　[. . .]
→ and he calls his Mum our Gladys

The reference to the mother is included because the narrator is building up a picture of his strange colleague, Phil: the mother is not a character in the story in any proper sense. The world depicted by the narrator, where Phil behaves in a crazy way, is peopled by men apart from this fleeting reference.

There are a few exceptions to this pattern. One good example is 'Steve and Vicky' (see example (5), this chapter) which involved a woman, a man and babies. A second, 'Loons and Shopping Trolleys' (analysed as part of a sequence in the previous chapter) is a funny story about two women getting their trouser bottoms locked in their supermarket trolleys. Stories such as these come from the conversations of older, well-educated men who seem to have a greater political awareness of gender issues (one of these men even tells a short story about being in a – now defunct – Men's Group). These stories are unusual not only in their inclusion of women in the storyworld, but in their presentation of these women as fully human characters, with names and lives of their own. (However, it is important to note that 'Loons and Shopping Trolleys', the only story in the sub-corpus with a female protagonist, is a re-telling of a story originally told by a woman. In other words, the fact that it patterns more like a woman's story is because it *is* in fact a woman's story.)

'Sensitive Guy': Men in Women's Stories

So how are men portrayed in women's stories? One thing that comes across strongly in the narratives told by women to each other is that men are a significant presence in women's lives. Their visibility in women's stories contrasts markedly with the invisibility of women in the majority of men's stories. Some stories are overtly critical of men, others are positive or neutral, but the storyworld constructed by female narrators presents men as persons who have an impact on those around them. The following two stories are told by a middle-aged woman and a teenage girl respectively, but despite this disparity in age both show how women's presentation of self involves demonstrating their links to men.

The first of these stories (example (13)) comes from a conversation between two women – Pat and Karen – in their thirties. They are talking in Pat's house about buying Christmas trees.

(13) Christmas Tree
1 I didn't get one with roots this year
2 I'm ever so pleased with it
3 but I did my usual <LAUGHS>
4 *what?*
5 I went out Thursday
6 I went down to Carpenter's Nurseries
7 cos you know I got my trees from there [*yeah*]

8   and he'd got lots of rooted ones
9   and I thought 'No,
10   I'm not gonna bother with roots this year',
11   cos it's always a pain to me,
12   I never- never takes in the garden.
13   I thought 'Sod it,
14   I'm not gonna have any worries' [*yeah*]
15   so I bought beautiful tree,
16   fiver,
17   beautiful tree, [*mhm*]
18   when I got home it was too big to go in the house
19   <*SPLUTTER OF LAUGHTER*>
20   and that's the third year running I've done that,
21   I thought, 'He'll kill me',
22   I thought, 'No he won't,
23   I'll see to it myself'.
24   Here's me six weeks out of hospital
25   I'm sawing away at this tree.
26   But five pounds for a nine foot tree
27   *incredible*
28   and it is the most beautiful shape.

The main point of this story is Karen's achievement in buying a Christmas tree for five pounds and solving the problem of its being too big by cutting it down to size. As an achievement story, it can be compared with men's stories on this theme. Note how Karen does not present the story initially as a story of achievement. The abstract *I did my usual* announces a story about some kind of cock-up, and the climax of the story at line 18, *when I got home it was too big to go in the house*, confirms this. But Karen goes on to show how she resourcefully solved the problem. But what she also does is portray herself as measuring her success or failure against the reactions of her husband. In other words, the excessive size of the tree is presented as problematic because of her husband's fantasized reaction to it: *he'll kill me*. This line is clearly not to be taken literally, but indicates the power Karen accords to her husband. Karen therefore sets to and 'saws away' at the tree, despite her recent operation, to avoid 'being killed'.

The second story I want to discuss here comes from a conversation between four teenage girls at Hannah's house; the narrator is Becky.

(14) Bad Back Pain

1   no but remember that time I had really really bad back pain
2   it was on a Friday [*yeah I know*]
3   and remember I cried after school [*yeah*]
4   I cried in school as well and nobody noticed [*really?*]
5   yeah yeah it was in SPACE [i.e. *Social Personal and Careers Education*]
6   and I was just crying,
7   and I was sitting really upright
8   and I sort of just buried my head
9   and I cried [*mhm*] not for very long [*mhm*]
10 just sort of . a few tears
11 *I hate it when no-one notices*
12 I know and Ja-
13 and I just looked up like this
14 and- and Jason said 'Becky looks like she's about to burst into tears' <LAUGHS> like this
15 and ((xxx)) he's the only person that noticed
16 *oh dear!*

This is a classic female teenage story. It involves self-disclosure (and is the second in a sequence of stories about periods and problems associated with periods); the central event described is the narrator crying in class, an admission which performs conventional femininity, but which would be taboo for a young male, and the story constructs a world where the primacy of heterosocial relations is taken for granted. Becky confides in her friends, but her narrative is also an indirect boast about Jason, who she claims is the only person to notice her distress. (Becky has disclosed earlier in the same conversation that she has had a long-term crush on Jason.)

In both these stories the female narrator's self-presentation relies on her displaying herself in relationship to a male. Both stories imply that such relationships are important, and from this we can infer that relationships with males confer status of some kind on women. Both stories demonstrate that alignment with the idealized norms of femininity involves alignment with a normative hetero-sexual identity.

This is true also of stories which function as complaints about men, as the next two examples demonstrate. The first of these (example (15)) is the fourth in a sequence of stories about the inadequacies of men.

(15)   Kitchen Floor
[Three women talking at Sue's house; narrator = Anna]
1   It's like Henry while I was doing the kitchen floor you see
2   he told me before I started it that I was mad to take on the job
3   that I wouldn't do it
4   and he wasn't going to help me.
5   He says- He said 'I'm not going to help you with this
6   so if you do it you're doing it on your own.'
7   I said 'Yeah okay,
8   there's nothing I like more than a challenge.'
9   ((xx)) saying things like that.
10   And he actually did do that,
11   he stood and leaned against the kitchen s- the sideboard in the
      kitchen telling me he was depressed
12   and- and he was going to take-
13   and he- he felt like- he felt like reaching for the water- nearest
      bottle of sleeping tablets he was going to take.
14   He- he'd been driven to it,
15   that afternoon he was going to end it all.
16   [*LAUGHTER*]
17   And meanwhile I'm humping twenty-five kilos of cement across
      the kitchen.
18   [*LAUGHTER*]

The second story to be quoted here comes from a conversation involving three young women in their early twenties, and is the second in a sequence of two stories: the preceding story was about the death of the racing driver, Ayrton Senna, in a car race.

(16)   Mike's Immortal Comment
1   Mike will be forever remembered for a comment he made soon
     after that [*i.e. after Senna's death*]
2   cos um he was-
3   It must have been the weekend after [*mhm*]
4   he came down to stay [*mhm*] with me in Southampton
5   and he was being really really obnoxious [*mhm*]
6   he was being horrible
7   and he was completely ignoring me [*mhm*]
8   and I was really hacked off
9   so I went storming into my room [*mhm*]
10   and- we were in a friend's room

11   and he didn't notice that I'd even gone
12   and I went bang ((xxx))
13   all my friends noticed that there was something desperately
        desperately wrong with me <LAUGHTER>
14   and he didn't at all
15   he was totally oblivious to the whole thing
16   so I was like tidying my room
17   which was absolutely immaculate anyway [yes]
18   just moving stuff from one place to another just to make a noise
19   and he suddenly sort of walked in
20   realized that I'd gone
21   after about half an hour this was
22   and ((he's like)) 'What's the matter with you'
23   'Nothing' <BETWEEN CLENCHED TEETH> <LAUGHTER>
24   'Nothing wrong',
25   ((xx)) quite obvious that there was ((type of thing)) [mhm]
26   and my Mum had sent me some newspaper cuttings about Senna's
        death [mhm]
27   and also it was about the same time that Nelson Mandela- [mhm]
28   whether it was that he got released or whether it was that he got
        elected as President I'm not quite sure [oh right]
29   one of the two
30   well she sent me newspaper cuttings about that as well
31   and I decided that that was going to be a really good time to sit
        and read them all
32   cos I could completely block out this guy that was really annoy-
        ing me at the time
33   <SYMPATHETIC NOISES>
34   so I sat on my bed
35   I was- I read the ones about Nelson Mandela first
36   and then I read the- read the ones about Senna
37   and Mike was like going 'What's the matter?'
38   and at THIS point I couldn't bottle it up any more [mhm]
39   and I burst into tears
40   and he came out with the immortal line
41   'Is it Senna?'
42   <LAUGHTER>
43   and he thought I was going into a right strop because Ayrton
        Senna had died [oh no]
44   and it was him really <NOISES EXPRESSING RESIGNED
        AMUSEMENT>

45 he shall be forever remembered for that line
46 *sensitive guy* <SARCASTIC>
47 oh he was.
48 I should have known from then on that it was fated really shouldn't I?
49 <LAUGHTER>

While the main point of these stories is the inadequacy of men, men are nonetheless significant figures in these two storyworlds. Anna, in 'Kitchen Floor', presents herself in relation to her brother, while the narrator of 'Mike's Immortal Comment' presents herself in relation to her ex-boyfriend Mike. Like the first-person narrative discussed at the beginning of the chapter ('Sardines in Aspic'), these stories are as much about the male character as about the female narrator/protagonist (in fact, it is hard to categorize 'Mike's Immortal Comment' in terms of first- versus third-person narrative, since the narrator is clearly a key protagonist, but the narrative opening (lines 1–7) focuses exclusively on Mike). And while neither of these stories is a flattering portrayal of manhood, the fact that such stories are told (and there are many others like these in the conversations I've collected) suggests that women are interested in men and concerned to understand what makes them tick. In other words, men matter to women. But it seems that women do not matter to men, if these men's stories tell us anything about cultural values.

The final story I shall quote in this section has been selected to show that women's storyworlds can display a sensitivity to the complexity of the world which is often lacking in men's stories. This story, told by a young woman to her friends at the end of the day, is the first in a sequence of stories about men behaving badly on public transport. However, the story ends with a man behaving well, and the narrator's even-handed stance in relation to men's behaviour suggests an appreciation of variety and difference. Men are not simplistically labelled as good or bad; instead there is a recognition that people have to be judged non-sexistly according to their actions.

(17) Pregnant Woman
[Three women friends in their early twenties; narrator = Bernie]
   1   There was a good one today actually
   2   I was sitting there quite happily . in my seat . in the tube [*yeah*]
   3   and it stopped
   4   and like . most of the seats were taken

5   but there was one spare seat opposite me

6   and you know how the seats are like in between two doors, [*mhm*]

7   one person got in this door,

8   one person got in this door,

9   one of them was like a . typical commuter business-man type [*mhm*] man in his pin-stripe suit,

10 very [*upright*] . holding himself very well,

11 very kind of you know fit and active,

12 the other one was a pregnant woman. [*mhm*]

13 Nike* practically pushed pregnant woman out of the way so that he could sit down.

14 *Really? <SUBDUED LAUGHTER>*

15 *SO WHO GOT THE SEAT THEN?*

16 Well . he did,

17 but then . about twenty people stood up to let this pregnant woman sit down. <SYMPATHETIC NOISES>

18 including myself of course.

19 *yeah, good one, quite bad that that ((xx))*

20 *IT IS AWFUL, ((THE MAN WAS)) SO HORRIBLE*

21 The person whose um- the person whose seat she ended up taking

22 was a sort of . probably a lad about our age

23 *oh right*

24 that was very chivalrous [*yeah*] of him I thought,

25 very chivalrous [*mhm*]

[* 'Nike' is pronounced 'Nikec' by the speaker, and is presumably a reference to the brand of trainers of this name.]

As these examples show, the fact that women include men in their storyworlds does not mean that they put them on a pedestal: on the contrary, many of the stories have as their point the fecklessness and unreliability of men. But at least women acknowledge that men are part of the world, whereas the evidence of men's stories is that women do not matter. This is a significant difference, and one that should give us pause for thought.

Gender Differences in Collaborative Talk

The last example, 'Pregnant Woman', is a good example of the way women friends collaborate in the telling of stories. While Bernie is the undisputed narrator of the story, her friends Eleanor (in italics) and Jo (italic capitals) make contributions to the story, in the form of minor supportive noises (*mhm* and *yeah*), but also in the form of a question which prompts the resolution of the story (line 15) and significant evaluative statements (lines 19 and 20). Many of the examples of women's narrative in this chapter involve collaboration. Collaboration in talk is typical of women's friendly conversations but is less common in all-male talk.[26] This pattern seems to be also true of conversational narrative (though men do collaborate in story-telling, as we saw in chapter 3). The two stories discussed at the beginning of this chapter – 'The Fight' and 'Sardines in Aspic' – illustrate this point well, with co-participants in the group of women friends taking a more active part in the construction of narrative than co-participants in the group of male friends.

The statistics for the narratives I've collected show a significant contrast in this aspect of story-telling: 22 per cent of men's stories involve collaboration of some kind compared with 50 per cent of women's stories.[27] The stories I've called 'collaborative' range from those where two or more participants are significantly involved in the telling of a story to those where there is one main narrator but co-participants make contributions to the story. Contributions from co-participants can involve exclamations of amusement or horror, questions seeking further information, and evaluative comments. Where co-participants' contributions consist simply of minimal responses and laughter, stories were not counted as collaborative narratives, even though such contributions are clearly collaborative and are again more typical of women's narratives than of men's. What these statistics show is that, in the conversations I've collected, women are as likely to tell a story in collaboration with a fellow speaker or speakers as to tell a story on their own. This is not true for male speakers, who collaborate in story-telling in less than a quarter of the stories told in all-male conversation.

The full version of the story 'Kitchen Floor', discussed above, is a good example of collaborative story-telling. The full version given here includes the contributions provided by Anna's two co-participants, which demonstrate their alignment with Anna. (Liz's words are in italics, Sue's in italic capitals.)

(18) Kitchen Floor
1   It's like Henry while I was doing the kitchen floor you see
2   *he's so ((xx))*.
3   he told me before I started it that I was mad to take on the job

4   that I wouldn't do it [*yeah*]
5   and he wasn't going to help me.
6   *leaning on the door while he's saying it.*
7   *YEAH I CAN IMAGINE YEAH*
8   He says- he said 'I'm not going to help you with this, [*yeah*]
9   so if you do it you're doing it on your own'. [*yeah*]
10   I said 'Yeah okay,
11   there's nothing I like more than a challenge.'
12   ((xx)) saying things like that.
13   And he actually did do that
14   he stood and leaned against [*yeah, the door, yeah*] the kitchen
        s- the sideboard in the kitchen telling me he was depressed
        [*yes <LAUGHS>*]
15   and- and he was going to take-
16   *<LAUGHS> and you're sweating away putting the tiles ((xx))*
17   and he- he felt like- he felt like reaching for the water- nearest
        bottle of sleeping tablets he was going to take,
18   he- he'd been driven to it [*yeah <LAUGHS>*]
19   that afternoon he was going to end it all.
20   <LAUGHTER>
21   *And you're going 'Yes Henry it's awful isn't it', yeah*
22   And meanwhile I'm humping twenty-five kilos of cement across
        the kitchen
23   *yeah, 'Could you bring in that cement before you do it?'*
24   yeah
25   <LAUGHTER>

The story is the fourth in a sequence on the theme of male inadequacy and all three participants are concerned to demonstrate their
orientation to this topic. Liz and Sue make substantial contributions
to Anna's narrative. They add utterances to support the general theme
of inadequacy (lines 2, 6 and 16). They attempt to complete Anna's
utterances, for example, line 14: 'he stood and leaned against [*yeah,
the door, yeah*] the kitchen s- the sideboard in the kitchen'. They invent
dialogue for Anna and her brother (lines 21 and 23), dialogue which
makes very clear that they appreciate the contrast between Anna's
hard work and Henry's self-indulgent depressive indolence. Note also
how Sue's supportive utterance in line 7, *yeah I can imagine yeah*, is
made at a point where it supports Liz as much as Anna.

Men's stories are much more likely to be solo narratives, with
one well-defined narrator. Male story recipients also tend to give less

133

feedback. This is a gender difference that women are aware of. A recent survey of mobile phone usage found that women were critical of male recipients' non-responsiveness: 'Men don't get this, they don't understand that you're supposed to go "No! Really?!".' As another informant said, 'for women, gossip is a two-way thing'.[28]

But two stories analysed in chapter 3, 'Carpet Tack Revenge' and 'Strap 'Er On', demonstrated that men do engage in collaborative narration. Both these stories are constructed by more than one speaker and collaboration is accomplished through linguistic strategies which parallel those used in women's collaborative narrative. But these two stories, despite their collaborative structure, still embody many features that enable them to perform hegemonic masculinity. They deal with contest, the action takes place in the public arena, and the world they portray is inhabited exclusively by men. Both stories avoid emotion.

Collaborative story-telling, in other words, is used by men to jointly construct dominant masculinity, just as it is used by women to jointly construct dominant femininity. So collaborative story-telling is another way of 'doing gender': stories will differ depending on the gender of the speakers involved in the co-narration.

Alternative Femininities, Alternative Masculinities

Some stories do not conform to conventional gender norms. As we saw in chapter 3, in some of their narratives, male speakers explore alternative masculinities and challenge the hegemony of competition, achievement and emotional restraint as central values of masculinity. The 'untypical' stories discussed at the beginning of this chapter – women's stories of achievement and men's stories involving people and relationships – also illustrate the point that male and female speakers are not straitjacketed by conventional expectations. Female narrators may also exploit the liberating potential of self-disclosure by telling reciprocal stories about behaving 'badly' or in ways that challenge the norms of feminine 'niceness'.[29]

However, it seems that, even when women and men use narrative to express alternative femininities or masculinities, they simultaneously perform more conventional gendered selves in other ways. In chapter 3 I analysed the story 'The Digger' as an example of a non-typical man's story. But although this story introduced the idea that a man might be frightened by experiencing the potential danger of a large machine, in other ways the story was stereotypically masculine, with its focus on heavy outdoor work and big machines. The same tension between more radical and more conventional masculinities is found in the rare self-disclosing story 'Suicidal', discussed at the end of chapter 3. This story is unusual in that it performs an alternative, more sensitive and self-reflexive masculinity. Here is an extract from the heart of this story:

(19) *Extract from* **Suicidal**
12 I mean about . towards . about the middle of last term
13 I quite seriously- . I went out and I bought a big bottle of pills
14 they were codeine and aspirin mix
15 and a bottle of whisky
16 and I went and sat on Twickenham Green
17 and I was going to kill myself [*mhm*]
18 I was going to eat the pills and drink the whisky
19 well <u>it was only a little bottle of whisky</u> <GREATER SPEED>
20 sitting there y'know TOTALLY just about as depressed as you
        could possibly get
21 and then I just thought 'you stupid sod'
22 so I threw away the pills drank the whisky and went home.

The narrator describes a time of deep depression in his life (*last term*) when he decided to take an overdose. Whenever I listen to this story, I am struck not just by its very personal nature, and the unusualness of this man exposing himself emotionally to his friends, but also by the way he simultaneously performs conventional masculinity through his attention to detail. In particular, line 14 *they were codeine and aspirin mix* always shocks me because it is the last thing I, a female overhearer, expect at that emotional moment. What does it matter what the pills were? The point of the story is that Brian was so distraught that he bought pills and whisky in order to kill himself. But such detail about objects matters to male narrators, even when telling a self-disclosing narrative.

A similar conflict between more conservative and more subversive discourses is found in women's stories, as examples (3) and (4) above illustrated. Women do tell stories which focus on achievement, but these stories differ in many ways from those told by men, where the first-person protagonist engages in lone contest from which he emerges successful. Women's achievement stories are often set in the home (as we saw in 'Kitchen Table') and do not involve competition or physical violence. They are often third-person narratives which celebrate the achievement of someone close to the narrator, such as a daughter (as in 'Quiz') or a mother (as in some of the stories in the sequence which 'Sardines in Aspic' comes from). Women, in other words, do not present themselves as heroes.

More subversive discourses also appear in stories where women explore less conventionally feminine aspects of themselves. In the following narrative the narrator self-discloses an event in her past when she had negative feelings about a friend's child (this is the second in a sequence of two stories on this topic):

(20) Little Star
[Five women friends talking at J's house]
 1   I feel like that about a friend of mine who lives in New York
 2   who's- well she refers to her son as her little star,
 3   and that doesn't help.
 4   and when I arrived at the- at the- at her apartment to stay,
 5   and she and her husband were both out at their exciting jobs in
        publishing,
 6   and this lad of s- of seven or eight let me in,
 7   and asked if he could make me some coffee.
 8   [Sally: *oh he is a little star then*]
 9   You know he IS a little star,
10   and he's so perfect that you just want to jump up and down 'im
11   and see if he'd squish you know,
12   [. . .]
13   and I'm so hoping that something marvellous will happen
14   and he'll run away from home
15   and- or you know something will squelch this . . .

But even though this story performs a subversive femininity, where women are not nice and express non-maternal feelings, in other ways this story is profoundly feminine. It is about a child (only one of the narratives in the entire all-male corpus is about a child), it is about relationships between women (the narrator and her friend in New York), it focuses on feelings (note that the first line of the narrative, the abstract, explicitly announces this focus: *I feel [emphasis added] like that about a friend of mine who lives in New York*). The verb *feel* does not appear in the all-male conversations except in contexts like the one illustrated in the story 'This Girl Called Debbie' (example (9)), where it is used to refer to physical sensation (*and suddenly I just felt [emphasis*

*added] this like warmth all over my leg, I've looked round and she's- no joke
I swear to god she had her fucking tits hanging over my leg).*

Narratives of Contest versus Narratives of Community

Despite my intention to avoid binary comparisons, the data has
forced me to recognize that there are some stark differences
between the stories told by men and those told by women. The differences I have found parallel those found by Barbara Johnstone for
North American speakers.[30] Women's conversational narratives
focus on people and relationships, while men's focus on action. So
although all stories have characters and all stories relate a series of
events, a significant difference between women's and men's stories is
the weight given to these two components. Johnstone's distinction
between male narratives of contest and female narratives of community[31] seems very apt: men's stories depict a world where solitary
men pit themselves against the other (this may be another man or
it may be a machine or circumstances generally), while women's
stories depict a world where people are enmeshed in relationships
and are part of a wider community. This difference ties in with
men's tendency to depict a world populated entirely by men, which
contrasts with the mixed world of women's stories. Finally, men's
stories are characterized by emotional restraint, whereas personal
self-disclosure is typical of women's stories, which suggests that
women and men have different goals in telling their stories to their
same-sex peers.

I shall return to discussion of these differences, and the reasons
behind them, in the final chapter. But it is important to note that
not all stories fit this pattern of sharp gender difference. As we
have seen, there are stories where women and men as narrators
subvert gender norms and use the story form to explore alternative
femininities and masculinities. All the same, after listening over
and over again to the conversations I've collected, and after analysing
the transcripts of selected narratives in detail, my sense is that
any competent member of contemporary English-speaking society
would be able to make a good guess at the gender of the narrator.[32]
That is in fact what we should expect, given the theoretical claims
made about the importance of narrative in the construction and
maintenance of the self discussed in the opening chapter. Since the
self is inevitably gendered, then a key function of narrative is the

construction of gender, and this is what we find in the stories I've collected.

But the stories I have looked at so far in this book have all come from conversations among male friends, that is, from all-male talk (just as the women's stories in this chapter come from all-female conversation). Could it be the case that the all-male peer group is the context for talk which differs from that found elsewhere, for talk where male speakers are particularly concerned to orient to hegemonic masculinity? Is it plausible to suggest that, in the company of other men, male narrators tend to exaggerate the masculine and deny the feminine? To see whether men's narratives differ when their co-participants are women as well as men, we need to look at stories occurring in mixed talk. This is the topic of the next chapter.

Notes

1 Barbara Johnstone, 'Community and contest: Midwestern men and women creating their worlds in conversational storytelling', pp. 67–8.

2 For this chapter I have drawn on a data-base of 22 all-female conversations involving women friends: these conversations contained 257 narratives, of which 68 were selected for a narrative sub-corpus designed to parallel the all-male sub-corpus (see note 3, chapter 3). I would like once again to express my gratitude to all the women and girls who participated in this research and who have allowed their talk to be used in this book. All names have been changed.

3 Such 'sound effects' are typical of the talk of male children: see Adelaide Haas, 'Sex-associated features of spoken language by four-, eight- and twelve-year-old boys and girls'.

4 The sociologist R. W. Connell uses the term 'emphasized femininity' to describe the exaggerated ideal of femininity which corresponds to hegemonic masculinity, and which can be described as 'oriented to accommodating the interests and desires of men' (R. W. Connell, *Gender and Power*, p. 183).

5 Johnstone, 'Community and contest', pp. 67–8.

6 Quantitative analysis was carried out on the entire corpus for more general measures, and on the two parallel sub-corpuses (68 stories from the all-male corpus; 68 stories from the all-female corpus) where more detail was required.

7 The raw statistics are as follows: the men's conversations totalled 18 hours 23 minutes and contained 203 narratives; the women's conversations totalled 15 hours 5 minutes and contained 257 narratives. Table 5.1 gives further details.

Table 5.1 The narrative corpus

	Men	Women
Total number of stories	203	257
Average per hour	11.04	17.04
Range (stories per conversation)	0–16	3–22

8 Christine Cheepen, *The Predictability of Informal Conversation*; Jennifer Coates, *Women Talk.*

9 Occasionally, individual women *do* tell several stories in sequence – there is an example of a woman telling a sequence of five in my corpus (Anna's stories about her eccentric mother). But because these stories tend to be short and because co-participants make significant contributions to them, there is not the same feeling of one speaker dominating the floor as when a man tells several stories in sequence.

10 See Jennifer Coates, 'One-at-a-time: the organisation of men's talk'; Carole Edelsky, 'Who's got the floor?'

11 This finding parallels that of Barbara Johnstone for white, middle-class speakers in Indiana, USA (see Barbara Johnstone, *Stories, Community, and Place*; 'Community and contest').

12 Johnstone, 'Community and contest'.

13 Table 5.2 summarizes the statistics for narrative setting.

Table 5.2 Settings for narratives

Setting	Men's stories (n = 61)[a]	Women's stories (n = 61)[a]
Home	12 (19.7%)	32 (52.5%)
Workplace	16 (26.2%)	9 (14.8%)
Outside world (pub, shop, sports ground, etc.)	33 (54.1%)	20 (32.8%)

[a] Stories with a school setting told by younger participants have been excluded from these calculations.

14 The women whose conversations were used in this research all worked, either full-time or part-time, or else were engaged in full-time education.

15 David Morgan, *Discovering Men*, p. 77.

16 Sally Alexander, 'Women, class and sexual differences in the 1830s and 1840s'; Catherine Hall, 'Private persons versus public someones: class, gender and politics in England, 1780–1850'; Victor Seidler, *Rediscovering Masculinity*.
17 See Shoshana Blum-Kulka, *Dinner Talk: Cultural Patterns of Sociability and Socialisation in Family Discourse*.
18 Full details of temporal framing are given in table 5.3.

Table 5.3 Gender differences in temporal framing

Temporal frame	Men's stories (n = 68)	Women's stories (n = 68)
Today	6 (8.8%)	10 (14.7%)
Recent past	18 (26.5%)	37 (54.4%)
Distant past	44 (64.7)	21 (30.9%)

19 Blum-Kulka, *Dinner Talk*, p. 120. Blum-Kulka's research focuses on family talk.
20 G. Aston, quoted in Blum-Kulka, *Dinner Talk*, p. 120.
21 Charles Berger and James Bradac, *Language and Social Knowledge*; V. J. Derlega and J. Berg (eds), *Self-disclosure: Theory, Research and Therapy*; John M. Gottman and Robert W. Levenson, 'The social psychophysiology of marriage'; C. T. Hill and D. E. Stull, 'Gender and self-disclosure'; Helen Reid and Gary Fine, 'Self-disclosure in men's friendships'.
22 Berger and Bradac, *Language and Social Knowledge*.
23 The gender of the protagonist in the stories is given in table 5.4. The gender of other characters in the stories is given in table 5.5.

Table 5.4 Gender of protagonist in men's and women's stories

Gender of protagonist	Men's stories (n = 67)	Women's stories (n = 67)
Male	64 (95.5%)	9 (13.4%)
Female	3 (4.5%)	58 (86.6%)

Table 5.5 Gender of other characters in men's and women's stories

Gender of other characters	Men's stories (n = 67)	Women's stories (n = 66)
All male	48 (71.6%)	18 (27.3%)
All female	1 (1.5%)	9 (13.6%)
Mixed	18 (26.9%)	39 (59.1%)

24 R. W. Connell, *Masculinities*; Adam Jukes, *Why Men Hate Women*; Michael Roper and John Tosh, 'Introduction' to *Manful Assertions: Masculinities in Britain since 1800*; Lynne Segal, *Slow Motion: Changing Masculinities, Changing Men*; Andrew Tolson, *The Limits of Masculinity*.

25 Anthea Irwin, 'The construction of identity in adolescent talk'.

26 Jennifer Coates, 'One-at-a-time: the organisation of men's talk'; 'The construction of a collaborative floor in women's friendly talk'.

27 The statistics for collaboration are given in table 5.6.

Table 5.6 Collaboration in male and female narrative

	Men's stories (n = 203)	Women's stories (n = 257)
Collaborative narration	45 (22.2%)	128 (49.8%)

28 Social Issues Research Centre, 'Evolution, alienation and gossip – the role of mobile telecommunications in the 21st century', p. 18.

29 See Jennifer Coates, 'Women behaving badly: female speakers backstage'; 'Small talk and subversion'.

30 Johnstone, *Stories, Community, and Place*; 'Community and contest'.

31 Johnstone, 'Community and contest', p. 63.

32 I presented uncontextualized narrative transcripts to students on the 'New Zealand English' course at the University of Canterbury, Christchurch, New Zealand, and they had no difficulty identifying the gender of the narrator.

6

'I'm Quite Good at Mexican Food': Men's Narratives in Mixed Conversation

What are men's narratives like when they are talking to women? Is men's self-presentation different when they are in mixed company? Here's Matthew talking to Kate and Amanda (Kate's words are in italics; Amanda's in italic capitals):

(1) *Extract from* Chinese Maggots
 1   I have a maggot anecdote right?
 2   what the Chinese do with maggots right?
 3   and it's a huge delicacy in China [*yeah*]
 4   well what they do right?
 5   they get some dead animal
 6   and they leave it out in the sun for just an hour or so [*yeah*]
 7   and then they put it in a breathable but perfectly sealed capsule
 8   and they bury it
 9   [...]
10   and what happens is
11   the flies in that hour land on this dead animal [*mhm*]
12   and obviously maggots get bred.
13   [...]
14   and after a while they start eating each other [*eugghh!*]
15   and then they eat each other and eat each other and eat each
         other until there's just two left
16   *two maggots*
17   and then it comes down to a battle
18   and in the end there's just one big big maggot left
19   *that is disgusting*
20   and that is a Chinese delicacy

142

21   *THAT IS REALLY RANK*
22   *that is so revolting, I can't believe that*
23   it's lovely
24   it's all about dog eat dog and all of that.

Here we have a young man in his early twenties telling a story to two women friends, also in their early twenties. They have been talking about food and cooking, and Matthew offers to tell an anecdote about maggots which he claims are a Chinese delicacy. The full story is longer, and Matthew takes great delight in going into full detail about the development of these maggots. By contrast, Kate and Amanda shift from supportive listening (with *yeah* and *mhm*) to unequivocal statements of disgust. Matthew's evaluative clause *it's lovely* contrasts markedly with the evaluations made by Amanda and Kate: *that is disgusting; that is really rank; that is so revolting*. What we are witnessing is gender politics acted out over the evaluation of the story. For the male narrator the story has a philosophical point – *it's all about dog eat dog and all that* – while the two women agree in their view of the story as *revolting*. The male narrator displays his scientific detachment while the women perform a version of femininity where even the mention of maggots or any creepy-crawlies produces a negative response (note Kate's *eugghh!* in line 14).

Does this mean that Matthew's story has misfired in terms of his audience? Or has he cleverly designed a story which allows him to perform rational masculinity while allowing his female audience to perform emotional femininity? There is no sign of conflict at the end of the narration, more a sense that they agree to differ. In fact, the story seems to be designed to maintain gender boundaries, to confirm the differences between men and women. As Barrie Thorne puts it, 'although contact [between males and females] sometimes undermines and reduces an active sense of difference, groups may also interact with one another in ways that strengthen their borders'.[1]

'Eugghh!': Recipient Design

We have to assume that Matthew chooses to tell this particular story to Kate and Amanda and that he designs it for them as recipients. Recipient design is a crucial aspect of talk. Although speakers orient to many aspects of social context, 'one – if not the most –

general maxim for talk production in conversation is "speakers should design their talk for recipients"'.[2] One of the things I want to tease out in this chapter is the way men design their talk when recipients are female (or female as well as male), and what the relationship is between different narrative styles and particular recipients.[3]

The narratives told by male speakers in mixed conversation vary far more than those produced in all-male conversation, both in form and in content. A range of masculinities is produced in mixed company, from the most macho, to the more sensitive and expressive. So at one end of the spectrum we find an older male boasting of his wartime exploits to his wife and granddaughter, a middle-aged male boasting of discovering an excellent wine merchant to his wife and close male friend, and a young man boasting of past pranks as a cricket player to a female friend. At the other end of the spectrum we find an older man telling his daughters a funny story about his childhood, a man in his thirties collaborating with his female partner in a story about kittens, and a young man disclosing how he came to suffer from Bell's Palsy (a virus which causes paralysis of the face).

Exactly where a given narrative can be located on the spectrum from most to least macho depends on the specific circumstances in which the narrative was produced. The style of each narrative correlates in a very sensitive way with the gender and status of co-participants and the relationships among them. In the following sections I shall attempt to clarify these correlations by looking in turn at narratives produced in peer group talk and in family talk (couples talk will be the subject of the next chapter).

These categories – 'peer group talk', 'family talk' and 'couples talk' – are far from discrete: heterosexual couples can be involved in both peer group talk and family talk, for example. And other variables, such as age, intersect with gender in complex ways. Peer group conversations and conversations where couples interact with other couples are both contexts which tend to involve speakers of similar ages. Family talk, on the other hand, involves speakers from different generations and is therefore 'mixed' in more than one way. Despite the fuzziness of these categories of mixed talk, I hope to show by examining them separately how male narrators design their stories with great sensitivity to the dynamics of the situation, and to show how all participants, whether male or female, collaborate in the construction of masculinity.[4]

'Have I Told You That Story about Me on Cricket Tour?': Men's Stories in the Mixed Peer Group

The talk of single-sex friendship groups has been widely researched[5] but the talk of mixed groups of friends has received less attention. This is perhaps because sociolinguists and others interested in language have been preoccupied with adolescent speakers, a period characterized by intense same-sex interaction.[6] Older speakers have been more often recorded in contexts where peer relations of friendship are less salient than relations among family members or between couples.[7] Only rarely has analysis aimed to show how mixed conversation can be a resource for 'doing friendship'.[8] In this section I shall show how friendly talk involving men and women constructs and maintains gendered identities.

The next example comes from a conversation involving two friends in their early twenties, Tony and Emily. Their talk functions to maintain their friendship but, as the narrative below demonstrates, it also functions to strengthen gender boundaries. The narrative is told by Tony at a friend's house; it initiates a sequence of stories about sporting prowess and clever pranks.

(2) The Fire Alarm
1   have I told you that story about um . me on cricket tour? [*no*]
2   got no relation to what I've been saying but- [*E LAUGHS*]
3   no, I'll tell you anyway.
4   this must've been when we were about thirteen
5   and we stayed at this really posh school
6   it was in the summer holidays
7   cos it was like the cricket season obviously <LAUGHS>
8   and um- and we're all like in a corridor
9   it was like the Essex team which was like all the ((xx))
10 had to be under-13 yeah
11 and we were on one corridor
12 and on the opposite corridor was like um Lancashire
13 and there was like Somerset
14 and all the different counties in the big building [*yeah*]
15 and um we're like all pissing about
16 must've been about the second night
17 and all the coaches and stuff and managers stayed on the same floor [*E LAUGHS*]
18 it's not that funny yet [*OK*]

19   and um- and we're just like pissing about in the corridor playing
        cricket
20   and it's got like an alarm like probably that one up there . or
        something [*yeah*]
21   and I've bowl- bowled this-
22   we're mucking about
23   I've bowled this ball
24   and it's hit the top of this chair which we used as a wicket
25   and it's gone-
26   it's only a tennis ball
27   and it's hit like . the main alarm [*E LAUGHS oh dear*]
28   and it's evacuated the-
29   I'm not joking
30   must be about a hundred and fifty people in this building
        [*E LAUGHS*]
31   and um . this is like two in the morning [*bloody hell*]
32   before the day of the cricket match or whatever the first
33   I think it must've been before the first day of all the cricket matches
34   like proper like country competition
35   like they were all the . country- all the counties
36   and people have come out like in their t- like in dressing gowns
37   obviously they've known it was us cos they know which fire
        alarm it is anyway
38   <u>cos we were dressed</u> <LAUGHING> [*E LAUGHS*]
39   and we've all come downstairs
40   and we were shitting it
41   they've like they've come upstairs
42   and they've located like which one it was
43   and they've gone 'it's this one, it's Essex boys' [*oh no*]
44   and so we've- they've gone 'Right who's done it, who's done it'
45   and we're going 'Dunno how it happened'
46   it wasn't damaged or anything
47   so we've come up with this story the next day
48   like I've gone 'er . I was- I was putting some deodorant on <u>and it
        must've-</u>' <LAUGHING>
49   and my room was right next to the fire alarm
50   anyway I said 'It must've just set the smoke alarm off' [*E LAUGHS*]
51   all the deodorant fumes [*E LAUGHS*]
52   and they go 'oh really'
53   and they go- they said to me 'What are you doing putting deodor-
        ant on at two o'clock in the morning?' [*E LAUGHS*]

54   and I'm like going- and I've like gone 'Oh I don't really know'
         <LAUGHS> [*E LAUGHS*]
55   shit like this
56   and then . our manager's like gone to us 'Look'
57   this was about two days later
58   cos they said 'If we find out who did it and what the real reason
         was, gonna send you home'
59   and I'd have been like devastated if I'd got sent home
60   and um . we said to our manager 'Oh we were mucking about
         playing cricket and the alarm went off'
61   and he went 'Oh . oh is that all, I'll- well I'll sort it out'
62   and just sorted it out for us
63   that was- I shit my pants if I'd've got sent home
64   *aah your Dad would've spanked your bottom*
65   my Dad- my Dad would've killed me, yeah.

This is a long story but I've reproduced it in full here to make
the point that in mixed talk, male speakers seem to feel free to take
long turns at talk and are encouraged in their story-telling by female
co-participants. I've chosen this narrative to be the first full-length
example because it is similar to narratives we have looked at in earlier
chapters, that is, narratives produced in all-male conversation. First,
this first-person narrative falls into the genre of laddish pranks: it is
similar to the stories 'The Area Manager's Call' (chapter 2, p. 17) and
'The Pornographic Video' (chapter 3, p. 51). Stories like this form a
subset of achievement stories and recount tales not of heroic conquest
but of 'men behaving badly'. They accomplish important gender work
in boasting of 'getting away' with pranks of various kinds. Second,
though the narrator/protagonist is part of a team, at critical points in
the telling of his story he chooses to use the pronoun *I/me*: for example,
the abstract (line 1) promises *that story about me on cricket tour*, and the
climax of the story (lines 22–7) is worded as follows: *we're mucking
about, I've bowled this ball . . . and it's hit like the main alarm*. The switch
from *we* to *I* here positions the narrator as the agent responsible for
the key event (setting the alarm off). This fits the pattern observed in
all-male narrative of achievement being seen in terms of the individual
rather than the group. Third, the story presents an all-male storyworld,
peopled by boy cricketers and their trainers and managers. Fourth,
the narrative topic is stereotypically masculine (sport), and the narrative focuses on events rather than on people and feelings (though
feelings are part of the story, as I shall discuss below).

In many ways, then, this narrative does not seem to differ from those told in an all-male context and constructs a dominant form of masculinity. Yet the narrator is talking here to a female friend. How can the narrative be said to be designed for this particular recipient? The opening of the narrative 'The Fire Alarm' is noteworthy: after making a bid for the narrative floor with the question *have I told you that story about me on cricket tour?* (to which Emily responds *no*, in effect granting him the floor), Tony comments that his story has no topical coherence with what has gone before but asserts confidently *I'll tell you anyway*. His confidence here assumes a willing listener, an assumption which does not always underlie story-telling among young male friends, where speakers are more likely to compete for the floor. In other words, the narrative opening shows an awareness of a particular kind of recipient, one who is a willing listener and who is supportive and co-operative. He then tells this long story about his cricket tour, and his story is received with laughter and with minimal responses such as *yeah* and *oh dear* which function to support his narrative endeavours.

The language of this story differs from stories told by men of this age group in the all-male corpus in that there is little use of taboo language. The narrative does include some taboo words, for example: *and we're just like pissing about in the corridor playing cricket* (line 19), *I shit my pants if I'd've got sent home* (line 63), but they occur less frequently than in parallel stories told by young men to their male friends, and there are no tokens of *fuck* or its derivatives. This suggests careful recipient design by the narrator. He seems to be orienting to the conventional belief that swearing is unfeminine and that men should not swear in front of women. In fact, male and female speakers are both sensitive to the perceived norms of the other gender in their use of taboo language in mixed talk: while the all-male sub-corpus contains much taboo language and the female sub-corpus virtually none (a grand total of ten tokens of *bloody*, no examples at all of *shit* or *piss* or *fuck*), the mixed sub-corpus contains far less taboo language in the narratives produced by male speakers, and far more in the narratives produced by female speakers.[9] This kind of accommodation to the (assumed) norms of other speakers is a good example of recipient design.

The narrator's fear – first, of being found out, and second, of being sent home – is a significant theme in this story. Moreover, the narrative ends with the evaluative line *I shit my pants if I'd've got sent home* (line 63) (which repeats the sentiment expressed earlier in line 59 – *I'd have been like devastated if I'd got sent home*). This line makes clear that the narrator's slant on the story is that he only just avoided being sent home and that being sent home would have been terrible. This is subtly different from parallel laddish tales in the all-male conversations, which tend to end on a note of triumph or bravado. It is plausible to infer that this narrator tells his story as he does because the story recipient is female: he feels able to make his feelings a key theme, thereby orienting to female speakers' expectation that first-person narratives will include emotional information. He also gives the story this slant to elicit sympathy from his female recipient. But at the same time, the main point of his story – that he did something 'bad' and got away with it – is unaffected. If anything, the emphasis on his fantasy that he would be sent home only serves to underline the fact that he was *not* sent home, and *did* get away with it. This is conveyed linguistically by the contrast between the simple past of the verbs in the narrative clauses, which recount what happened (e.g. *said, went, sorted out*), and the complex verb phrases expressing hypothetical meaning (e.g. *would have been devastated, had got sent*).

However, Emily, the story recipient, responds to Tony's closing evaluation with the words *aah your Dad would've spanked your bottom*. These words show her orienting to Tony's fantasy of being sent home in disgrace: they push the fantasy further by introducing Tony's father as a character, the character who would instantiate Tony's parents' anger and disappointment. There is a gentle mocking quality to these words, in their positioning of Tony as a naughty boy; this is reinforced by Emily's initial *aah*, the noise stereotypically produced by women and girls in response to small vulnerable objects such as babies and small animals. So these words demonstrate Emily's careful listening and empathy, but they simultaneously undermine Tony's self-important self-presentation. Tony chooses to respond to the first of these two messages by paraphrasing Emily's words using lexis that has no babyish connotations: *my Dad would've killed me, yeah*. This is a skilful response which repositions Tony as someone who nearly got into major trouble and which rejects Emily's less serious interpretation.

While there is much evidence in this story of the ways speakers orient to each other in talk, there is one point where Tony and Emily miscommunicate:

15   and um we're like all pissing about
16   must've been about the second night

17   and all the coaches and stuff and managers stayed on the same
      floor [E LAUGHS]
18   it's not that funny yet [OK]
19   and um- and we're just like pissing about in the corridor playing
      cricket

Line 18, *it's not that funny yet*, is a most unusual line in that it has
nothing to do with the narrative: Tony breaks away from his narrative to tell Emily that her laughter is inappropriate. He does this by
means of conversational implicature: the utterance 'it's not that funny
yet' implies that laughter is only appropriate once 'it' (the story) is
funny. The fact that he feels obliged to make this non-narrative comment suggests that he is disconcerted by laughter from a recipient
at this point in the story, a point which he considers 'not that funny'.
Equally interesting is Emily's response to this reprimand: she utters
a meek *OK*, in other words, she acknowledges Tony's right to tell
her what is appropriate. (Note that she does not laugh again until
the climactic line *and it's hit like . the main alarm* (line 27).) Does this
hiccup in narration derive from different gender norms? Certainly,
the research evidence is that female interactants give far more
feedback – including laughter – during talk than male interactants,[10]
so Tony could interpret as 'too much' recipient behaviour which would
be unremarkable in all-female talk. Certainly, the evidence of this
brief chunk of talk is that Tony fails at this point to design his narrative
carefully enough for his recipient and has to coerce his story recipient
into responding in the way he desires.

Tony's somewhat cavalier attitude to his story recipient (shown
both in the extract above and in his story introduction) suggests a
power imbalance in male–female relationships at this age. Whereas
young males compete with their male peers to tell stories of individual prowess, young males talking to female peers expect to be
indulged. The conversation between Tony and Emily which 'The Fire
Alarm' comes from contains a total of twenty narratives; of these
fifteen are told by Tony, four by Emily, and one is a joint effort. Not
only does Tony dominate the conversation in terms of narrative, he
uses these narrative opportunities to construct a dominant form of
masculinity and is supported in doing this by Emily.

To assess how common this pattern is, let's look at a story from
a conversation involving a different group of speakers. This narrative
comes from the same conversation as 'Chinese Maggots', and is again
told by Matthew to Kate and Amanda. Matthew seizes the opportunity

presented by one of Kate's questions to Amanda on the subject of culinary disaster to tell the following story. (Kate's words are in italics and Amanda's are in italic capitals.)

(3)   Culinary Disaster

 1   *well you haven't had any culinary disasters in the kitchen yet have you?*

 2   *DISASTERS? . AS IF I WOULD HAVE – IT'S COS I'M NOT ADVEN-TUROUS ENOUGH TO HAVE ANY*

→ 3   I have

 4   I cooked for my housemate

 5   <LAUGHING> *I LIKED MY HOUSEMATE*

 6   I'd only been living there a week

 7   and I thought 'I'll really impress them'

 8   cos I'm actually quite good at some things

 9   so I'll make-

10   *what? toasted sandwiches?*

11   *I WAS GOING TO SAY BEANS ON TOAST*

12   I'm quite good at Mexican food

13   curries and things like that

14   so I thought I'd- I'd make Mexican

15   Mexican chicken

16   so I did it

17   I got all the ingredients

18   but um . I'd mixed up this sauce

19   and put it into . a ketchup bottle

20   and I was going to pour it over [*yeah*]

21   I picked up the wrong bottle out of the um cupboard [LAUGHTER]

22   and it was the bloody vinegar [LAUGHTER]

23   I poured this vinegar in

24   and I didn't- I didn't think . to until it was already on the plate to test it [*oh no*]

25   and er I dunno I just had to pour it all back into- [LAUGHTER]

26   so I poured it all back into the frying pan

27   and chucked in all this other stuff

28   trying to disguise it

29   *trying to take away the-*

30   all this sugar and stuff [LAUGHTER]

31   and it just- it really was dog food that was [LAUGHTER]

32   and I don't know why but I still served it up to her

33   and she's going 'Mmm, this is lovely' [LAUGHTER]
34   *EH, NICELY DONE*
35   so that was a bit of a disaster
36   *well you couldn't waste it could you?*

There are many ways in which this narrative shows careful recipient design. First, Matthew orients to Kate's phrase *culinary disasters*. This phrase, addressed to Amanda, not to Matthew, is gendered in two ways: first, disaster stories are a staple of women friends' conversation, and Kate's question *well you haven't had any culinary disasters in the kitchen yet have you?* potentially invites Amanda to tell a disaster story. Second, in everyday life the culinary is still seen as part of women's domain, not men's. So for Matthew to announce that he has a story to tell on this theme is to accommodate to more feminine norms of what constitutes material for a story. Matthew frames his narrative as a disaster story. He opens the story with the line *I have* (meaning *I have had a culinary disaster*), a line which provides an abstract, while his final line *so that was a bit of a disaster* provides evaluation as well as making his narrative lexically cohesive with Kate's initiating question.

However, Matthew simultaneously tells a classic masculine narrative of making a cock-up and getting away with it. If we ignore the opening and closing lines, the narrative can be seen to have a conventional masculine trajectory. It provides us with background information where Matthew boasts of his culinary prowess, *I'm actually quite good at some things*, and is frank about his goal: *I'll really impress them*. The narrative core recounts how he used vinegar by mistake, how he took steps to disguise his mistake, and how he served up the food to his (female) flatmate, who apparently enjoyed it: *'mmm this is lovely'*. At one level, the narrative is about the gullibility of women, since the narrator contrasts her appreciative comment about the food with his own evaluation of it: *it really was dog food that was*. His female recipients support him in his presentation of himself as getting away with murder, both with laughter and with Amanda's comment *eh, nicely done*.

Kate and Amanda provide support throughout Matthew's story, with frequent laughter once the story reaches its climax (line 21), and with supportive comments (such as *oh no*, line 24) and collaborative rephrasings (*trying to disguise it//trying to take away the-*, lines 28–9). But there is also a teasing element: both women attempt to undermine his boasting at the beginning of the narrative. First, Amanda adds the teasing comment *I liked my housemate* after Matthew's first narrative clause *I cooked for my housemate*, a comment which implies that if you like your housemate you do not cook for them. Second, both Kate and Amanda add anti-climactic completions to Matthew's statement of what he intended to cook, *so I'll make . . .* (line 9). They suggest *toasted sandwiches* (Kate) or *beans on toast* (Amanda), suggestions which convey their low opinion of his culinary skills. He carries on unabashed and provides his own rephrased completion, *so I thought I'd- I'd make Mexican, Mexican chicken.* Interestingly, while Amanda supports his triumphant laddish ending with her *nicely done*, it is Kate, the initiator of the culinary disaster theme, who responds to his final evaluative line *so that was a bit of a disaster* with the words *well you couldn't waste it could you?* These words again have a teasing quality: they perform a (tongue-in-cheek) conventional femininity, where throwing food away is frowned on. But despite their mocking quality, what these words do is justify Matthew's actions and thus query Matthew's claim that this episode can be called 'a disaster'. In other words, like Amanda's final comment, they support Matthew's underlying theme of getting away with it, rather than the overt theme of disaster.

Examples (2) and (3) both show young men enjoying themselves telling stories about themselves to female friends. Example (4) involves older speakers but shows how men also enjoy telling stories about themselves to male friends in mixed company. The following narrative, 'Buying Wine in Cornwall', comes from a conversation involving a middle-aged man (Michael), his female partner (Suzanne) and a close male friend (Bill) during a meal at Michael and Suzanne's house. So unlike the two previous examples, the narrator here has a mixed audience consisting of a woman and a man. The narrative emerges from general conversation about wine and wine-drinking. (Suzanne's words are in italic capitals; Bill's in italics.)

(4) Buying Wine in Cornwall
1   my wine's on the way Suzanne
2   *IT'S BEEN ON THE WAY FOR A LONG TIME*
3   no, no, it's on the way
4   *you've got lots of room to store it here haven't you in the cellar*
→ 5   funnily enough we went to an inn in Cornwall
6   which had a most impressive display of . wine bottles on the
        wall [*mhm, MHM*]
7   um . well you may see Bill after you've finished

8   and um .
9   *these were empty bottles*
10   no no, they were full I mean
11   and they had a- a-
12   and- and . it was recommended as a place to eat by various
        guidebooks
13   so we had a meal there
14   and got chatting to the owner
15   cos I thought his wine was very good
16   and very reasonable- very reasonably priced [*yes*]
17   and so well we have a list
18   so er-
19   [. . .]
20   paradoxically . I- I've ordered um four cases of wine from
        Cornwall
21   which is bizarre
22   but um-
23   *it does seem a little bizarre* [*VERY BIZARRE*]
24   I thought we'd- ((xx))
25   *was- was that when you- was that when you went on your . trip to
        Dartmouth?*
26   yeah, well I thought it'd be interesting to try-
27   *was that your other-* [*NO, NO, NO*]
28   go through the range and see what- see what it's-
29   you know, see what they're like
30   and um-
31   *NO, WE WENT TO DARTMOUTH IN THE SUMMER*
32   *yeah cos I remember you when you were doing that*
33   *AND THEN UM . THIS WAS- WE WENT OFF TO CORNWALL
        BEFORE EASTER*
34   *AND IT RAINED A LOT*
35   *SO . WE HAD TO CONSOLE OURSELVES=*
36   *=drinking* <u>*bottles of wine*</u> *<LAUGHING>*
37   console yourselves with some nice wine
38   *((XX DIDN'T YOU)) Michael*
39   well I thought this man had a very good palate
40   they had a Cote-
41   *so you got cases of what?*
42   well ((I mean))- he had a Cote du Rhone of '93
43   which I think he was selling at five pounds fifty a bottle
44   and it was really good [*mhm mhm*]

45   I thought well at that price you know
46   *it's very reasonable*

While this narrative displays the emotional restraint typical of middle-class middle-aged men, it is still in essence a boast. The narrator/protagonist presents himself as someone who cleverly spots that a Cornish inn-keeper has a good palate and orders four cases of wine from him. This is a narrative of achievement, but achievement in a social context where being a hero is acted out in terms of wine connoisseurship rather than engagement in physical contest with another man (cf. 'The Fight', chapter 5) or getting drunk (cf. 'Quadruple Jack Daniels', chapter 3) or enduring pain (cf. 'Appendicitis', chapter 3).

Bill is positioned as the narrative's chief recipient: note how Michael switches from addressing his remarks to Suzanne (line 1) to addressing Bill (line 7) once the narrative begins. By using the pronoun *we* in the opening line of the story – *funnily enough we went to an inn in Cornwall* – he positions Suzanne as a potential co-narrator and as a protagonist in the narrative, thus making a clear distinction between Suzanne (part of *we*) and Bill (*you*). Side-comments made by Michael during and after his narrative are explicitly directed at Bill: *well you may see Bill after you've finished* (line 7) and *so I was thinking well, if it extends across the range I'll put you on the mailing list* (after the narrative).

Bill seems to accept his role as chief recipient. In lines 44–6, for example, he supports Michael's claim that the wine is a good price both through minimal responses, and through his supportive comment *it's very reasonable*. Michael's partner, however, is less supportive. In the talk preceding the narrative, she is critical of the time it has taken for the wine to be delivered (*it's been on the way for a long time*, line 2). During the narrative itself, she intervenes when she realizes that Bill is confused about when the events recounted took place, since Suzanne and Michael have had two recent trips to the Southwest (lines 31–7). This section of the narrative is fascinating, as it becomes a duet between Suzanne and Bill, with Michael having to wait to re-take the narrative floor:

31   *NO, WE WENT TO DARTMOUTH IN THE SUMMER*
32   *yeah cos I remember you when you were doing that*
33   *AND THEN UM . THIS WAS- WE WENT OFF TO CORNWALL BEFORE EASTER*
34   *AND IT RAINED A LOT*
35   *SO . WE HAD TO CONSOLE OURSELVES=*

36   =drinking *bottles of wine* <LAUGHING>
37   console yourselves with some nice wine

Suzanne and Bill share the narrative floor with ease, alternating their contributions and constructing joint utterances (*so we had to console ourselves//drinking bottles of wine*). Michael makes a bodged attempt to join in this duet by repeating Bill's words (line 37), but his sense of exclusion from the collaborative talk is revealed by his use of the reflexive pronoun *yourselves* instead of *ourselves*, as if the two people who had been drinking in Cornwall were Suzanne and Bill, rather than Suzanne and Michael.

In line 39, Michael regains the narrative floor, though the initial *well* suggests he is experiencing some difficulty.[11] Bill's question in line 41 again interrupts the story, but may have been intended to demonstrate that he has resumed his role of chief recipient. Certainly, Suzanne makes no further contribution to the narrative, whereas Bill, after Michael has finished his narrative, tells a minimal narrative about wine-buying which aligns him very positively with Michael's point of view and performs solidarity between the two men. It also functions to position him as another wine connoisseur.

All three examples analysed in this section constitute performances of hegemonic masculinity. In examples (2) and (3) the story recipients were female. In example (4), 'Buying Wine in Cornwall', the chief recipient, at first glance, is male. But a better analysis of example (4) is to see it as a performance of masculinity by two male friends to a female audience. In other words, the similarities between these three narratives can be seen to result from their all three being designed, ultimately, for a female recipient or recipients.

Example (4) shows how complex recipient design can be, with the primary narrator–recipient duo (Michael and Bill) being attended to in turn by another recipient, Michael's partner. The fact that the primary duo consists of male speakers, while the secondary recipient is female, is highly salient to the narrative's design. Suzanne, apart from helping to clarify a particular point in the story, does not make any contribution to the narrative, but her silent presence is vital to our understanding of what Michael and Bill are doing, which is in essence a form of masculine (heterosexual) display.[12]

This analysis suggests that, all other things being equal, male and female co-participants in talk will co-operate in the maintenance of normative gender roles. But sometimes these norms are challenged, as the next example demonstrates. This brief extract comes from a conversation between four students, Lucy, Hannah, Keith and John. Lucy has raised the topic of Keith's 'little rendezvous with Rebecca' and the conversation continues as follows:

(5) Keith and Rebecca

1	Lucy:	so why did it come to an end Keith?
2	Keith:	because it shouldn't have ever started in the first place
3	Hannah:	what did it consist of, you and Rebecca?
4	Keith:	⌈um-
5	Lucy:	⌊meeting every Friday night and getting off with each other basically
6	Hannah:	<LAUGHS> ((I wonder what he means)) by that
7	Lucy:	that was a very suspicious 'um' there wasn't it?
8	Keith:	<BRIEF LAUGH>
9	Lucy:	what else is there to tell?
10	Keith:	nothing, nothing ((xx bother))
11	Hannah:	no, no, tell us
12	Keith:	no <EMPHATIC>

Lucy and Hannah ask Keith several questions (in lines 1, 3 and 9) which invite him to tell a story. But he rejects these invitations, and in fact gives an emphatic 'no' when the questions mutate into commands with Hannah's 'tell us'. In examples (1), (2) and (3) we have seen how male speakers enjoy taking the floor and telling stories to attentive female listeners, but in this example Keith chooses not to tell a story because the topic set up for him by Lucy would involve him in personal self-disclosure. As analysis of men's narrative has revealed, male speakers tend to avoid self-disclosure. But Keith's failure to take the narrative floor is met with renewed invitations from his two female co-participants, who are either deliberately tormenting him, or failing to see that they are in effect asking him to behave like them, that is, like a woman. This is something Keith cannot do, particularly when one of the potential recipients of his story about his relationship would be his friend John.

In this section, we've looked at stories told by men in mixed company. Examples (2) and (3) suggest that in the peer group setting, when men take the narrative floor and the story recipient or recipients are female, then we can expect performances of dominant masculinity, with the male narrator and the female audience colluding in maintaining gender norms. Example (4) shows how a story told by a male speaker to a male recipient may be embedded in a wider context where the men's telling of and listening to a story is on display to a female audience; in other words, stories may be designed for more than one recipient. Example (5) shows that men will not automatically take the narrative floor when offered it by female peers if to do so would involve them in personal self-disclosure.

There are many similarities between these narratives produced by male speakers in the mixed peer group and the narratives found in all-male talk. At the same time, these stories differ from those found in all-male talk in that they involve a wider range of topics (cooking as well as cricket), storyworlds that often contain women as well as men, the inclusion in some stories of information about emotions, and a linguistic style that relies far less on taboo vocabulary.

'And Me With Egg All Over Me': The Construction of Masculinity in Family Conversation

Just as mixed peer group talk can be seen to construct and maintain male–female relationships, so family talk can be seen to construct and maintain political order within families. In particular, narrative activity within families can be shown to confirm roles and power structures within families.

The following narrative comes from a conversation involving a mother, a father and two daughters aged about 22 and 19. The story is elicited by the mother (whose words are printed in italic capitals). The main narrator is Celia, with her sister Phoebe acting as co-narrator (Phoebe's words are printed in italics).

(6) Whoops!

```
   1   TELL DADDY- COS I'VE NEVER TOLD HIM I DON'T THINK
   2   WHAT HAPPENED AT NANNY'S WHEN YOU DROPPED HER OUT
         THE WINDOW ONTO THE . BAY WINDOW
   3   you knew I dropped her out the window didn't you?
   4   ((see)) he doesn't
→  5   oh well I got in a temper with her= <LAUGHTER>
   6   =threw my shirt out
   7   THIS WAS WHEN THEY WERE STAYING AT NAN AND GRAMPS
   8   threw her shirt- threw her shirt and it went out the window
   9   you know the windows go out like that=
  10   =ONTO THE ASPHALT OF THE BAY
  11   so . I went to get a broom to try and get the shirt in
```

12 and ((like)) I dropped the broom
13 *and a curtain pole*
14 [. . .]
15 well I got a curtain pole
16 a metal curtain pole
17 so I tried to get the broom and the shirt back with that
18 then I dropped that out
19 and I- I thought 'well that's the longest thing
20 Phoebe I'm going to have to dangle you out' <LAUGHTER>
21 *((don't forget)) the curtain pole*
22 <u>so I got her by the ankles</u> <LAUGHING>
23 and then she was going 'just a bit more' <LAUGHTER>
24 and just reaching and reaching
25 and then I said 'Whoops' <LAUGHTER>
26 and then she went tumble tumble tumble <LAUGHTER>
27 and landed on the bay window <LAUGHTER>
28 I- well I- 'what am I going to do now?'
29 'you'll have to climb back up,
30 pass me the curtain pole first' <LAUGHTER>
31 and then Phoebe had to climb up the tiles.
32 all this was going on and Nan and Gramp didn't even hear
     <LAUGHTER>
33 *SAT DOWNSTAIRS WATCHING TV*

This short example shows the systematic work carried out in family narrative production. The father is positioned as the primary recipient of the story: he is referred to as 'Daddy' by his wife, a practice which confirms that his role as father is the key one here. He is also referred to in the third person, even though he is present, because the mother is addressing Celia directly (*Tell Daddy . . . what happened when you . . .*). Phoebe is also referred to in the third person (*when you dropped her out the window*). Celia responds by asking her father directly whether he knows this story (*you knew I dropped her out the window didn't you?*), but comes to the conclusion that he doesn't. This is expressed in a side-comment to her mother and sister: she switches from the 'you' of direct address to third-person reference for her father: *((see)) he doesn't.* Having established that the story is new for her father, she begins her narration, with her sister and her mother involved as co-narrators, as lines 6 and 7 show.

One of the striking aspects of this extract is the father's non-participation. He is positioned as chief recipient by the mother, and the two daughters perform the narrative as requested, with support from their mother. These three female members of the family tell this story for the father's amusement: but it is noticeable that the laughter which accompanies the second part of the story (as the events get more and more hilarious) comes from the three women, not from the father. The narrative performs important family work in other ways, as it recounts an event which took place at Celia and Phoebe's grandparents when they were young, and so constructs a sense of family which is wider than the basic nuclear family. The ease with which the three women collaborate in telling the story suggests that these events have been recounted before and are part of family history. The story testifies to Celia's temper, to the sisters' joint efforts to get the shirt back, to their success in not being discovered by their grandparents. Stories like this affirm the significance of the family and of family relations. The evidence is that it is mothers who act as family historians, who remember family stories and elicit them at key moments when the family is gathered.[13]

In their analysis of family conversation, Elinor Ochs and Carolyn Taylor have identified a range of 'narrative roles' and have demonstrated that these roles are systematically linked with particular family members.[14] For example, they found that mothers tend to introduce narratives, fathers tend to be the main recipients of stories, and fathers also have the role of chief problematizer, that is, fathers get to comment on and evaluate the actions of other family members as revealed in narrative.

Ochs and Taylor's data consisted of white middle-class two-parent American families with young children. My family conversations involve no young children, and often span three generations. But as we shall see, women, in their roles as adult daughter, mother and grandmother, tend to orchestrate narrative activity in the family, while older males (fathers and grandfathers) are either positioned as the main recipients of stories told by other family members, or are encouraged to take the narrative floor as narrators/protagonists. Family members co-operate in this activity which distributes power differentially: older women have control over topic and over who tells stories to whom, while older men perform dominance (through taking the narrative floor and through telling stories which build a strong identity) and exert control over story evaluation.

Not surprisingly, since the 'children' in the family conversations I've collected are all adults, the pattern of mothers inviting their children to tell a story to their fathers is not so prominent. Where small children are concerned, the invitation to 'tell Daddy what you've done today' 'tends to ratify children as topical *objects* of narration but not as *active agents* of narrative activity'.[15] But such invitations can still be found in conversations involving adult children, though adult offspring can be active agents of narrative activity as well as topical objects, as the story 'Whoops!' illustrates.

Sometimes the roles are reversed and the mother elicits a narrative from the father who is required to perform for his daughters. The next example is taken from a conversation involving the same family; this time all three daughters are present. (The mother's words are in italic capitals; contributions from the daughters are given in italics.)

(7) Harold the Babysitter

TELL THEM ABOUT . WHEN HAROLD USED TO BABYSIT

→ 1   well Harold used to babysit for me when I was in Malta [*mhm*]
  2   and he used to have his mates round
  3   and they used to get on my Dad's drink
  4   *GET THE BEERS IN*
  5   and I was about seven months old sort of thing
  6   and he used to say 'are you 'ungry lads' <NORTHERN ACCENT>
  7   they'd say 'OK'
  8   and he'd be cooking them egg and bacon and all the rest of it
  9   and chips
10   so he'd think oh he'd feed me that as well you know <MAKES BABY NOISES>
11   <M, C AND P LAUGH> *NOTHING CHANGES*
12   and then he said 'we'll- we'll have a drink'
13   and he'd get my Dad's whiskey out
14   and then he'd say 'd'you wanna cigar?'
15   and he'd pass all the cigars around
16   *CAN'T YOU JUST SEE HIM*
17   and they're all sat there
18   you can see Harold doing it can't you? [*MHM*]
19   and they're all sat there
20   feet on the table
21   cigar
22   whiskey
23   he'd got my Dad's gun out
24   and he's shooting the pictures on the wall <LAUGHTER>

25   *COS THEY'RE STONE WALLS*
26   and who walks in?
27   *your Dad*
28   my Dad
29   and they're all sat there
30   big cigar
31   you know glass of whiskey
32   gun *<LAUGHTER>*
33   and me with egg all over me *<LAUGHTER>*
34   chips- chips all down me *<LAUGHTER>*
35   going 'ah agag' <BABY IMPRESSION>
36   *<LAUGHTER>*

This narrative achieves a great deal. In terms of masculinity, it creates a storyworld peopled entirely by men, men who like to drink and smoke and who fool around with guns. The context of the story is Malta, where the father's family was stationed (we know from other stories that this is a family with links to the armed forces). This context strengthens the construction of hegemonic masculinity, but this version of masculinity is in tension with more feminine elements in the narrative: Harold and his friends are in charge of a baby (the narrator), and they get hungry and cook themselves egg and chips. Babies and food are not archetypally masculine topics. The narrative succeeds as a funny story precisely because of the incongruity of these hard army men with their whiskey and cigars and the domestic details of the baby covered in egg and chips. Besides doing important gender work, the narrative also reinforces family power structures through the distribution of narrative roles: the father is constructed as powerful, as narrator and protagonist, the mother displays her organizing power through her setting up of this story, the daughters accept their role as appreciative audience. Family cohesion is performed through collaboration: the mother acts as a co-narrator in support of the father, the daughters provide occasional minimal responses and a great deal of laughter, and Helen (the eldest daughter) provides the climactic line on cue (*your Dad*).

In the family conversations in my corpus there are other examples of fathers and grandfathers telling stories about themselves as children. It appears that certain family members – those who are older and male – have privileged access to the narrative floor. The following example is a story told by a grandfather to his wife, his granddaughter and the granddaughter's boyfriend. The granddaughter elicits the story after the grandfather mentions setting the heath on fire when he was a little boy. (The granddaughter's words are in italics, the grand-mother's in italic capitals.)

(8) Heath on Fire

1 I think the- apart from when I set the heath on fire when I was a little boy that's the biggest fire I've seen
2 *ha you set the heath on fire*
3 yeah the heath it yeah <LAUGHS>
4 oh yes me and my- me and my brother did actually
5 we were- we were schoolboys at the time
6 and um at summertime we used to- we used to like to go up on the heath you know
7 kick a football around and sort of sit down and have a fag
8 as all boys did at that time
9 and that was a very very-
10 we always used to have long hot dry summers in those days [*yeah*]
11 when we're on holidays always
12 and of course heathland and gorse bushes they-
13 you know they get- you know they're-
14 it doesn't take much to start them off [*no*] if they're allowed
15 and er one of us I don't know which one it wa- was
16 either dropped a match or a cigarette end down there
17 and all of a sudden wooof! [*oh*]
18 went up
19 and we were- we went- we cycled there actually
20 and we cycled
21 we- we panicked
22 we got on our bikes and we- we rode the wrong way
23 we <LAUGHS> finished up in Martlesham actually
24 [. . .]
25 the sky was full of black smoke that night [*ahhh*]
26 *I EXPECT IT WAS*
27 I've never told anybody that that was us but I knew
28 for several days afterwards every time there was a knock on the door
29 or look at those [*look there*] sh- shaking in our- in our shoes [*yeah*]
30 and we- we- week or two later we went up there and cor!
31 acres and acres and acres there was all black

32   all these black charred bushes and these- [*ha*] [*HA*]
33   that we'd set fire to.

Not only does the granddaughter elicit this story, she is also its chief recipient: note her frequent supportive responses. This is one of many stories told by this grandfather about events in his past – about accidents such as falling downstairs or cutting his hand on a rusty drainpipe, about adventures and mishaps such as being poisoned by a fish while fishing on Southwold beach. All the stories are embedded in the East Anglian countryside that the grandfather has lived in all his life. This story constructs the narrator as a normal boy, someone who liked to *kick a football around and . . . have a fag*. But it also recounts how scary it was when the fire they start gets out of control: *we panicked we got on our bikes and we- we rode the wrong way*. These are not heroic actions, but they vividly demonstrate the impact of the fire. The narrator skilfully emphasizes the magnitude of the fire by various descriptive comments: *the sky was full of black smoke that night; acres and acres and acres there was all black*. The magnitude of the fire is contrasted with the boys and their sense of guilt. This story is a youthful version of the laddish tales we have looked at in earlier chapters, tales where male narrators describe getting into scrapes. A key theme in such stories is 'getting away with it'. In the talk following the telling of 'Heath on Fire', the granddaughter comments *and you got away with it*, to which the grandfather responds in a triumphant tone *we got away with it yeah*.

Fathers and grandfathers are not restricted to childhood in their narratives: they also tell stories about their exploits as young men and about the exploits of significant (male) others. The following story comes from a different family group involving a grandfather, grandmother and granddaughter. Their conversation revolves around the grandfather's stories about his early comic experiences as a city boy working on a farm (where he met the grandmother) and about his wartime experiences. The following story is a good example of his wartime stories (the granddaughter's words are in italics).

(9)   Shite-Hawks
1   Remember when I was telling you about that- birds . the=
2   *like shite-hawks*
3   yeah shite-hawks
4   we used to have-
5   they're like eagles

6   and as you walk from the tent, like the mess tent
7   and you're going to find some place to sit down to eat it
8   and these big birds used to sweep down
9   and if you got a billy-can just a billy-can you know like bit of
     a handle on it
10 they used to sweep down
11 pinch everything out of the can with their big talons
12 and their claws
13 even ((with your)) bit of an army knife like you know you had
     like
14 swoop that and all you lose that and all
15 and all your dinner's gone
16 and your can's gone sometimes
17 so you go and ge- scrounge and ge- borrow somebody else's
18 anyway one day there thc- we got fed up with this every day
19 these shite-hawks flying down
20 and they hit you with the wing
21 it don't half hurt
22 you know cos the wing span's about three or four feet like you
     know
23 and then what happened one day
24 they- one of the blokes got fed up with it so they caught one
25 they said 'I'll learn him a lesson'
26 so they sewed its backside up <LAUGHTER> yeah
27 and give it a dose of castor oil <LAUGHTER>
28 and let it go
29 *did it die? must've died*
30 must have done yeah
31 *what cos it couldn't- . oh no*
32 we just ((xx)) and let it go
33 course we was all laughing
34 well course I mean you have your dinner pinched every day
35 you've just about had enough you know.

This is a powerful performance of masculinity. The narrator constructs
a tough all-male storyworld where the central contest is between a
group of soldiers and huge eagle-like birds. The narrator presents the
episode where the men *sewed its backside up* as a decisive triumph over
their opponents (something which clearly overstates the case). Note
that in this story the male protagonists are presented as operating
as a group, not as individuals. While the grandfather is granted the

narrative floor by his female relatives, and while he doubtless impresses them with his performance of hegemonic masculinity, there is some evidence that he does not design this story carefully enough for this particular audience: his granddaughter intervenes at the climax of the story to clarify whether the hawk would have died, and is audibly upset when the consequences of the men's actions dawn on her – *what cos it couldn't- . oh no.* The closing lines suggest that the narrator has oriented to his granddaughter's dismay: in these lines he declares that they all laughed after they had let the hawk go (he may be hinting that laughter is more appropriate than dismay) and justifies their actions and their laughter by reiterating that they had *had enough* (earlier he had used the phrase *fed up,* lines 18 and 24). This justification frames the narrative core. But even though the grandfather shows some awareness of his granddaughter's dismay, it is still noticeable that his emotional commentary on the events recounted extends no further than the anger and frustration conveyed by the phrase *fed up.* He does not mention fear, though the description of the hawks with their talons and their four-foot wing span would justify fearful reactions. The men's laughter after they had had their revenge on one of the hawks also conveys emotional distance: unlike the granddaughter (whose reaction suggests empathy with the bird) the grandfather and his mates feel no pity for their tormentor.

In this example, the grandfather's masculine theme of men triumphing over nature comes into conflict with the granddaughter's orientation to the bird's suffering. But despite occasional clashes like this, fathers and grandfathers are supported in their reminiscing by their wives and by other female family members. I have found no examples of mothers (or grandmothers) telling stories about their childhood in the family context; it seems that women's stories may be reserved for all-female conversation. These stories of men's childhood construct the older males in the family as important: other family members, in listening to these stories, ratify the older male's status.

Younger men may also be chosen by mothers as chief protagonists and narrators. The following example comes from a family conversation involving a mother, a father, a daughter and the daughter's boyfriend, Nick. (Nick's words are in italics.)

(10) The Talbot Samba
1 Nick was making me laugh the other day
2 what did you think you were in? <TO NICK>

3   and Celie was asleep
4   what did you-
5   *thought I was in my XR2*
6   and he was in my ⎡Talbot Samba
                    ⎣*Talbot Samba*
7   and he tried to overtake
8   'what am I doing?
9   I'm trying to overtake in a Talbot Samba!'
10 Celie said she woke up and said 'What's going on?' <LAUGHTER>
11 *up Bath hill*
12 big mistake
13 you don't overtake in a Talbot Samba.

The mother introduces the narrative with a statement about Nick – *Nick was making me laugh the other day* – followed by a question which invites Nick to take the floor or at least to become a co-narrator – *what did you think you were in?* Nick takes up the latter option, and he and Celie's mother co-narrate the story about him driving the mother's Talbot Samba and trying to overtake on a hill. This is a brief narrative but it does important work in the construction of family relationships. The mother's narrative implicitly brings Nick into the family group. She demonstrates her familiarity with his life (and with her daughter's) through the story she tells, in particular, her animation of him as a character in the story through direct speech. Nick's collaboration in this act of story-telling symbolizes his growing connection to the family: he responds to the mother's question with a key line *thought I was in my XR2* (line 5), he co-constructs line 6, and he adds the information *up Bath hill* in line 11.

In telling this story, the mother privileges the father as audience, by using third-person pronouns to talk about Nick and Celie (except when she draws Nick into the story-telling by checking details with him) thereby leaving 'you' free to be the person who the story is directed at. The father, then, is positioned as the chief recipient of this narrative. But telling and re-telling stories which encapsulate key events in family history is also done for the amusement of all participants.

It is notable that this story is about a car: this is a common topic in all-male conversation, but there are no examples in my all-female conversations. By choosing this topic for her narrative, the mother accommodates to masculine norms and makes it more likely that Nick will feel comfortable as a co-narrator. (Compare this with Lucy and

167

Hannah's failed attempt to get Keith to tell a personal story in example (5) above.)

In these stories told in a family context we see men performing a variety of roles and a range of masculinities. We see how male and female speakers in families collude in the construction and maintenance of normative family relationships and normative gender roles. In the stories I have collected which involve families with adult children, the narrative role of elicitor/introducer tends to be the preserve of mothers, while the roles of chief recipient and narrator/protagonist tend to be assigned to fathers. These are the most empowering roles, and construct parents as the key players in the family. But while mothers tend to be stage managers, it is fathers (and sometimes grandfathers) who are the stars in these performances.

'Who's George?': Female Subversion of Men's Stories

As we have seen, men and women co-operate in story-telling in the family to maintain family roles and power structures. However, there is some evidence that female family members sometimes co-operate in a way that gently undermines the father's authority.

The following example is the opening section of a story told by a father to his wife and daughter, a story to which his wife and daughter make many contributions. But it is not clear that this should be seen as an example of collaborative narration, since the father, while tolerating their interventions, tries to maintain his role as solo narrator. It could be argued that some of the contributions from the female speakers, especially the daughter, have a teasing quality and are not designed solely as collaborative contributions. (The wife's words are in italics; the daughter's words are in italic capitals. Arrows indicate points where the narrator seems to be experiencing difficulty of some kind.)

(11) The Army Girls
   1   now then I want to tell-
   2   I want you to tell me what you make of this
   3   and what the answer is
   4   cos I don't know what the answer is OK.
   5   I'm driving along the other day
   6   [. . .]
   7   and I called at that lay-by from Headington

8   you know, where the toilets are

9   for a bacon sandwich and a wee

10   *what- with Hugh's- where Hugh's um girlie is?*

11   yeah, yeah [*yes*]

12   'I'D LIKE A BACON SANDWICH AND A WEE PLEASE'
       <LAUGHTER>

→ 13   and er I pull in there

14   and there's a police motorcycle parked up [*uh huh*]

15   and he is talking to three dolly birds [*mhm*] dressed in army
       fatigues

16   they'd got you know the army camouflage overalls on

17   *what do you mean dolly birds? [M AND E]*

→ 18   well I mean they were dolly birds

19   *glammy*

20   they were really glammy

21   *what make-up and everything?*

22   *STRIPOGRAMS?*

→ 23   yeah, yeah, you know glammy, yeah

24   I don't know

25   they'd got all the army combat gear on

26   boots you know and all the rest of it

27   and I'm thinking-

28   *so they weren't like all legs showing?*

→ 29   no, so I said to-

→ 30   no, no, they'd got- they'd got like-

31   *combat bikini?*

32   *PERHAPS THEY WERE DOING A MARILYN MONROE*

33   they'd got like army overalls on

34   *berets?*

35   but they'd got all the hair-

→ 36   no, no berets [*mhm*]

37   got the hair and the make-up and everything

38   and I mean you know they're all five foot ten

39   real model sorts

40   *and were they- were they all going 'aha ha ha'?*

41   *or was it all a bit serious?*

42   I wasn't close enough

→ 43   but they were stood there

44   and two of them had files in their arm

45   *mhm, with your earwigging powers I would have thought you'd have
       heard them*

46   well I said to George
47   I said, 'what's going on here then George?'
48   *WHO'S GEORGE?*
49   he's the bloke you know that owns the snack bar [*OH RIGHT*]
50   he said, 'I dunno, it's a funny job' he said . . .

This extract from the narrative 'The Army Girls' is co-constructed in the sense that all three conversational participants make contributions to the story. But if we examine the father's narrative, we can see that the contributions made by his wife and daughter often lead to disfluency or force him into extra detail which, left to himself, he would omit. For example, the daughter's first jokey contribution *'I'd like a bacon sandwich and a wee please'* (line 12), which fantasizes that these were her father's words to George at the snack bar in the lay-by, results in the first filled pause – *er* – in the father's next line: *and er I pull in there*. The distribution in talk of such hesitation phenomena is non-random. They occur where a speaker is planning a new utterance or, as here, where a speaker is experiencing some difficulty in holding the floor. The next co-participant contribution of any substance comes in line 17 and is produced simultaneously by mother and daughter: *what do you mean dolly birds?* The father's response – *well I mean they were dolly birds* – begins with the adverbial *well*, which signals a dispreferred move,[16] that is, in this case the father's answer is insufficient (he just repeats the phrase *dolly birds*), which in turn signals his unwillingness to be diverted from his narrative theme. *Well*, like hesitation phenomena, can be interpreted as 'one of a set of strategies available to speakers for communicating "difficulty"'.[17]

At this point (line 19) his wife interjects the word *glammy*, a move which can be seen as an attempt to help the father to define 'dolly bird'. The father accepts this contribution and incorporates it into his narrative – *they were really glammy* – only to be questioned further by his wife: *what make-up and everything?* and by his daughter: *stripograms?* The father's response, *yeah, yeah, you know glammy, yeah, I don't know*, with its repetition of *yeah* and its use of the phrase *you know* which makes an appeal to shared knowledge, suggests frustration at this continued demand for detail. But his attempt to recapture his narrative thread, *and I'm thinking* (line 27), despite its attention-grabbing use of the historic present, is interrupted by his wife with the question *so they weren't like all legs showing?* Questions and comments asking for more detail continue, and it isn't until line 46 that the father regains control of the narrative: *well I said to George, I said, 'what's going on here then George?'*, only to be asked by his daughter *who's George?*

This narrative comes from a series of family conversations which involve a great deal of collaborative narration (see the stories 'Whoops!' and 'The Talbot Samba'), but it is noticeable that collaboration is initiated by and primarily involves the female members of the family (mother and daughters). Narrators are never granted a solo floor in these conversations, and the father's stories always include contributions from female members of the family. But in the extract above, from the narrative 'The Army Girls', the contributions have a teasing quality that is not always present, and there seems to be a conflict between the father's wish to tell a solo narrative and his wife and daughter's wish for greater detail. This may result from their interpretation of his opening lines. He initiates the story by saying *now then I want to tell-*, an utterance which he doesn't complete, rephrasing it as follows: *I want you to tell me what you make of this*. These two utterances set up the basic tension between the father telling his first-person account (that is, *I want to tell-*) and the two women wanting more detail (responding to the invitation: *I want you to tell me what you make of this*). There is also some evidence from the way the mother and daughter coordinate their contributions that, like female speakers in general, they are just enjoying themselves, with collaborative construction of talk being seen as a kind of play.[18]

Conclusions: The Construction of Masculinity in Mixed Talk

We have seen in this chapter how the presence of women can affect men in a variety of ways. In some cases, men perform hegemonic masculinity, seeming to construe the presence of female interactants as an opportunity for display. But in the presence of women men also explore topics such as cooking which do not appear in the all-male conversations, and construct storyworlds which include women. Where female interactants are family members, men's story-telling also functions to maintain dominance in family roles such as husband or father or grandfather. The linguistic behaviour of male speakers in mixed company depends in a very delicate way on the men's relationships with the women present.

The presence of other men also affects men's linguistic behaviour in mixed company. Men may co-operate with each other in performing hegemonic masculinity, positioning female co-participants as the ultimate recipients of their talk; or they may refuse invitations to take the narrative floor where to do so would upset dominant norms and would expose them to the censure of co-present males.

Many of the stories in this chapter show men constructing and maintaining male dominance with the active collusion of women. However, a subset of stories suggests that women will sometimes gently subvert male dominance. This seems to happen when two or more women can collaborate in subversive activity. For example, as we saw in 'Culinary Disaster', Kate and Amanda both added unhelpful collaborative completions to Matthew's opening boastful remarks:

Matthew: and I thought 'I'll really impress them' cos I'm actually quite good at some things so I'll make-
Kate: *what? toasted sandwiches?*
Amanda: *I WAS GOING TO SAY BEANS ON TOAST*
Matthew: I'm quite good at Mexican food.

Their suggestions about what he might cook imply a low estimate of his cooking ability, but their comments are affectionately teasing rather than hostile. Similarly, the mother and daughter collaborate to undermine the father's story in 'The Army Girls', but their contributions are produced in a spirit of fun, not of malice.

In this chapter we have looked at men's narratives in the context of the peer group and in the context of the family. The next chapter will focus on men and story-telling in the context of the heterosexual couple.

Notes

1 Barrie Thorne *Gender Play: Girls and Boys in School*, p. 65.
2 Harvey Sacks, *Lectures on Conversation*, p. 445. The term 'recipient design' was coined by Sacks.
3 Allan Bell (1997) explores the phenomenon of recipient design under the term 'audience design'. He claims 'speakers design their style primarily for and in response to their audience' ('Language style as audience design', p. 244). But 'audience' is an unsatisfactory term when discussing linguistic variation in talk, and particularly when discussing conversational narrative, since conversation is an essentially interactive phenomenon.

The term 'audience' implies a silent body of people who attend to what is said but have no rights to talk themselves. But in conversational interaction, talk can be seen as an achievement which involves the collective activity of all participants.

4   The mixed corpus consists of 20 conversations, containing a total of 248 narratives. This material was collected in the same way as the other data discussed in this book. I am grateful to all those who participated in the recordings for allowing their words to be used; I am particularly grateful to students on my Conversational Narrative course who allowed me to have access to their data.

5   See, for example, Deborah Cameron, 'Performing gender identity: young men's talk and the construction of heterosexual masculinity'; Jenny Cheshire, *Variation in an English Dialect*; Jennifer Coates, *Women Talk*; Penelope Eckert, 'Cooperative competition in adolescent "girl talk"'; Donna Eder, '"Go get ya a french": romantic and sexual teasing among adolescent girls'; Marjorie Goodwin, *He-Said-She-Said: Talk as Social Organisation among Black Children*; William Labov, *Language in the Inner City*; Ben Rampton, *Crossing*.

6   Ben Rampton says of the 11- to 16-year-olds he studied, 'there was a general tendency to associate with peers who were of the same sex and ethnic background' (*Crossing*, p. 27).

7   The dinner-table conversation has been the focus of many of these studies, and analysis has aimed to show how conversation is drawn on as a resource for maintaining family structures (e.g. Shoshana Blum-Kulka, *Dinner Talk*; Elinor Ochs and Carolyn Taylor, 'The "father knows best" dynamic in dinnertime narratives') or for maintaining or challenging husband and wife roles (e.g. Mary Talbot, '"I wish you'd stop interrupting me": interruptions and asymmetries in speaker-rights in equal encounters').

8   But see Deborah Tannen, *Conversational Style: Analysing Talk among Friends*.

9   Table 6.1 gives details of taboo words in the narratives in the all-male and the mixed sub-corpuses.

Table 6.1   Taboo words in conversational narrative

	fuck	*shit*	*piss*	*bloody*	*Other*	*Euphemisms*
All-male (n = 68)	74	14	32[a]	7	46	2
Mixed (n = 63)	12 (5M; 7F)	9 (5M; 4F)	14 (7M; 7F)	11 (8M; 3F)	9 (7M; 2F)	6 (3M; 3F)

[a] 30 out of 32 examples come from an adolescent story sequence [ME01-11] about getting drunk ('pissed').

10 For a summary see Jennifer Coates, *Women, Men and Language*, pp. 116 and 192.
11 Marion Owen, 'Conversational units and the use of "well"'.
12 See Robin Dunbar, *Grooming, Gossip and the Evolution of Language*.
13 See Deanna Hall and Kristin Langellier, 'Storytelling strategies in mother–daughter communication'.
14 Elinor Ochs and Carolyn Taylor, 'Family narrative as political activity'.
15 Ibid., p. 337; italics in original.
16 Anita Pomerantz, 'Agreeing and disagreeing with assessments: some features of preferred/dispreferred turn shapes'.
17 Owen, 'Conversational units and the use of "well"', p. 111.
18 Coates, *Women Talk*, p. 151.

7

'Still in Shock Weren't You Darling': Masculinity and the Heterosexual Couple

We've looked at men in the (mixed) peer group and men in the family. I now want to look at men in couples. Do male speakers design their talk differently when they present themselves as part of a heterosexual couple? In particular, are men more likely to produce collaborative narratives when they tell stories with a female partner?

Here is a narrative told by an older married couple, Arthur and Marian, to their daughter Kim and their grandson William. (Arthur's words are in normal typeface; Marian's words are in italics; Kim's are in italic capitals.)

(1)   They Lost a Child
1   *THEY LOST A CHILD DIDN'T THEY?*
2   they lost one son
3   *they lost er- their son in his twenties*
4   *he dashed across the road to get . um-*
5   ((there's a)) big dual carriageway=
6   *=dual carriageway . um*
7   and he leapt over the=
8   *=leapt over the centre barrier=*
9   =that's right=
10 *=and was killed=*
11 =couldn't stop
12 cos a car came up as he- as he sort of landed from that=
13 *=yeah=*
14 *=CAR HIT HIM =*
15 =mhm=
16 *=yeah, he was in his twenties wasn't he*

17 she was distraught wasn't she
18 *yeah, when they came over here he was er- it w- it hadn't long happened*
19 *and they were still . very much in grief and- with it*
20 mhm
21 *MHM, SHOCK*

This is a relatively short narrative but it is a good example of the collaborative style adopted by male narrators when they co-narrate a story with a partner. In this example, there is also collaboration with a third speaker, the daughter, whose utterance *they lost a child didn't they?* initiates the story.

So what are the main features of collaborative narrative? First, collaborative narration involves two narrators making contributions to the story which join together seamlessly (note the frequency of the latching symbol in the transcript (=) which indicates that turns follow each other without any gap). Second, collaborative narration involves frequent repetition. This can involve phrases – for example, *dual carriageway*, lines 5 and 6, or whole clauses – for example, *they lost one son//they lost their son in his twenties*, lines 2–3. Speakers also rephrase each other's ideas using different words (for example, *they were very much in grief*, line 19, rephrases *she was distraught*, line 17). Another significant feature of collaborative narration is the shared construction of utterances. For example, Arthur says *and he leapt over the=* (line 7) and Marian completes the utterance: *=leapt over the centre barrier* (line 8). There is also frequent use of back-channel support to signal acceptance of the other speaker's contributions (*that's right*, line 9; *yeah*, lines 13, 16, 18; *mhm*, lines 15 and 20). A collaborative narrative constitutes a powerful display of 'togetherness'. In this example, Arthur and Marian display their shared knowledge of events to their daughter and their grandson.

'That's Nothing Compared to Our Little Horror Story': Stories Told by Couples

The ability of speakers to share the narrative floor is symbolic of intimacy. Collaborative narration requires very careful syntactic, semantic and prosodic monitoring on the part of both speakers, and is characteristic of people who know each other well. Of course, in one sense all talk involves co-operation[1] and increasingly conversation is seen as an achievement which involves 'the collective activity of individual

176

social actors whose final product . . . is qualitatively different from the sum of its parts'.[2] But what Arthur and Marian achieve in telling the story 'They Lost a Child' is only possible where conversational participants know each other very well, have shared knowledge of the topic, and are prepared to do the work of co-narration.

The joint telling of a story is sometimes described as a 'duet'. This term was coined to describe examples like (1) above, where the two co-narrators function as a single speaker.[3] 'Duetting' is characteristic of friendly talk among women but is far less common in all-male talk, as previous chapters have demonstrated.[4] While male speakers do produce collaborative narratives, as we saw in chapter 3, they seem to prefer solo narration.

Yet the evidence of the mixed conversations I have collected is that men quite often engage in collaborative story-telling when the co-narrator is a woman, specifically a woman partner. The co-construction of stories is now recognized as a key way for couples to 'do' their relationship in public.[5] The chapter began with Arthur and Marian's story of their friend's son's death in a road accident. Let's look at two more examples of collaborative narrative where the narrators are a heterosexual couple.

The first of these examples comes from a conversation involving two couples. It is an extract from a very long narrative told by Ian, a man in his thirties, about his experiences delivering parcels for a major delivery firm. The extract comes from the opening section of the narrative. (Ian's partner Diane's words are in italics.)

(2) *Extract from* **Parcel Delivery**
1   he said- he just said to me 'Do you know the Old Kent Road?'
2   I said 'Yeah',
3   he said 'You'll be all right then',
4   he sent me to Rotherhithe with a hundred and two parcels,
5   *on Ian's first day <LAUGHS>*
6   my first day
7   a hundred and two drops
8   blocks of flats, shops, doctors' surgeries,
9   ⎡there were drugs-
10 ⎣*and you couldn't deliver half of them could you?*
11 [. . .]
12 I had no lunch break
13 I just went flat out
14 I did seventy drops

15 I m- I came back and ⌈((xxx))
16   ⌊<LAUGHS>
17 ⌈((xx)) I've got thirty parcels
18 ⌊*Ian didn't speak for twenty minutes ((xx))*
19 ⌈I got- I got thirty parcels ((xx))
20 ⌊*still in shock weren't you darling*
21 [. . .]
22 *the supervisor said 'blah blah blah how many did you have?'*
23 I said 'I dunno'
24 he said 'Where's your sheet mate?'
25 I said 'I dunno mate' [. . .]
26 and he went 'Jesus mate what've they done to you?'
27 I was like '((xxxx))'
28 ⌈he went 'oh blimey'
29 ⌊*((xxx)) first day ((xxx))*
30 so he- I went through it all
31 and he went and got this sheet
32 and he said 'Fucking hell mate,
33 hundred and two drops' he said.
34 *'you should only have fifty'*
35 ⌈'you should've only have fifty to start with'
36 ⌊*'it was only your first day'*
37 [. . .]
38 and I'd done   ⌈twenty more than I should've
39   ⌊*yeah it was just like*
40 *'oh here comes the **wanker of the week*
41 *let's see** if we can pull a fast one', yeah*
42 **ooh I couldn't believe it**

Ian is the chief narrator of the story 'Parcel Delivery'. He tells a very long story about the trials and tribulations of delivering parcels in the Rotherhithe area of London on a hot summer's day. His story fits the classic pattern observed in previous chapters where the lone protagonist engages in contest with something or someone – here, with the impossible demands of the job. Ian's super-human efforts mean he triumphs over these demands, but at enormous cost.

Ian's story makes several points: one is that delivery firms are incredibly inefficient; another is that Rotherhithe is a dangerous place; but most importantly, that he was set an impossible task by the parcel delivery firm. The main theme of the story is his heroism: Ian constructs himself as a hero, but he emphasizes rather than conceals the physical cost of his triumph. The final evaluative line of the full story is *it was just incredible*, a line which recapitulates *ooh I couldn't believe it* (line 42). Such statements emphasize the extraordinariness of what he experienced and make a strong claim for tellability. To claim that the events narrated were 'not ordinary, plain, humdrum, everyday or run-of-the-mill'[6] is an important task for a narrator, particularly a male narrator. We can compare these two lines with the final line of 'The Fight', *honestly it was unbelievable* (see chapter 5, page 108). Male narrators, in both single-sex and mixed contexts, are concerned to communicate to story recipients that they have experienced something which deserves special attention.

So in many ways this story performs a conventional version of masculinity. But at the same time the story is a performance of coupledom. Ian is supported in his narration by his partner, Diane, and many parts of the story are told as a duet. As the extract illustrates, Diane adds significant information to the story (lines 5, 10, 18, 20, 29, 36) as well as making contributions which move the story along (for example, *the supervisor said 'blah blah blah how many did you have?'*, line 22; *'you should only have fifty'*, line 34). There is a great deal of repetition, including whole lines such as *you should only have fifty* (lines 34 and 35); the phrase *first day* recurs throughout the narrative. Diane's contributions often overlap with Ian's (lines 10, 18, 20, 29, 36, 39, 40), a feature of the story which is highly collaborative and symbolizes connection between the two speakers. Sometimes overlap results from Diane adding a comment to Ian's narrative: *still in shock weren't you darling*, line 20; *first day*, line 29. Sometimes it results from polyphonic talk, where co-narrators make parallel points simultaneously (lines 17–20, 38–42).

It is not just Diane who contributes to Ian's narrative: the other participants, Jean and Martin, do too (though this aspect of the narrative is not illustrated by the extract given here). They comment on the inefficiency of the delivery firm (for example, Jean says *they need to organize themselves* and *that's a ridiculous waste of money*) and ask questions about what happened (for example, Martin asks *what did they say then when you said you had thirty?*). They also provide collaborative completions (for example, Ian describes putting a parcel on one side, then losing track of it, with the words *when you come to the end you think=* and Martin provides his imagined thought: *=there it is*). So Ian's narrative is multi-functional: it performs a dominant version of masculinity, which re-affirms his gender identity in front of his partner and friends; it displays coupledom in that Diane makes significant collaborative contributions which demonstrate their shared knowledge of the events recounted; and it also performs friendship in that all four conversational participants feel free to contribute to the telling. Ian's story is carefully designed to achieve all these functions.

Sometimes the couples context allows male speakers to explore less conventional versions of masculinity. The following story[7] is initiated by Gemma, who invites Sam to co-narrate it with her. Sam takes some time to warm up but by the end of the story he is the main narrator. The story is told to their friend Adam. (Gemma's words are in normal typeface; Sam's in italics.)

(3) Interesting Weekend
  1 you remember when we were going shopping a few weekends ago in the West End?
  2 we st- we were trying to park the car in Berner Street near Middlesex Hospital about 2 o'clock in the afternoon
  3 and Sam was making a second attempt to get it into the parking space
  4 when the taxi just drove up behind him
  5 and they have a collision
  6 and um go on Sam what happened?
  7 well the taxi driver says to the passengers
  8 *yeah hit me from behind*
  9 'Well do you believe this? can you believe this?'
10 Sam gets out of his car
11 and starts ranting and raving about who was right
12 *yes I was calling him everything under the bloody sun, yes*
13 and the taxi driver's saying you know 'me, I was stationary,
14 and you- and you reversed into me,
15 I thought you were-
16 I thought you were leaving, not parking'
17 *and I said 'How on earth was I leaving if I was indicating that I was getting in- into this parking space?'*
18 [. . .]
19 *and then I went and lost my credit cards*
20 that wasn't that day was it?
21 *the same day, yes, yes [. . .]*
22 *I went to um to Oxford Street to Bookstock [. . .]*
23 *and I bought a few books*
24 *and I left my cards behind [. . .]*
25 ahh but you didn't discover until Sunday

26 you didn't realize your credit cards were missing
27 *yes I didn't realize until next Sunday*
28 *that I didn't have my- my- my wallet with me*
29 *so I lost my cheques my address my credit cards*
30 *everything in there*
31 ***my store cards***
32 **but he thought** because he'd been to Earl's Court to buy
      some newspapers
33 that he had dropped them **in the newsagents in Earls Court**
34 ***in the sto- in the newsagent in Earls Court***
35 [. . .]
36 *so that was a **beautiful weekend shopping in the West End*
37 *my car being hit from behind***
38 **so this is all- this is the outcome
39 this is all from you know because of the taxi**
40 *and I'm- I've **lost my credit cards***
41 **the taxi you know** all the incident happened from that
42 *so you know that was a very interesting weekend*

This is a classic disaster story of the kind frequently found in women's friendly talk. In fact it is two disaster stories: first, Sam reverses into a taxi which mistakenly thinks he is leaving the parking space; second, Sam leaves his wallet in a bookshop because he is in such a state after the collision with the taxi. There is no way that Sam can be seen as a hero in this story: the story is told to entertain his friend Adam with its unremitting theme of things going wrong.

So this story does not construct dominant masculinity in the normal sense. What it does do, though, is construct coupledom. Through co-telling a story, Gemma and Sam 'achieve the appearance of being together in interaction'.[8] Gemma initiates the story, a story which revolves around Sam, and she invites Sam to tell it with her (*go on Sam what happened?* line 6). Sam eventually accepts this invitation, though he allows Gemma to act as the main narrator in the first part of the story. Once the story moves on to the loss of his wallet, however, Sam narrates the story jointly with Gemma. This narrative exhibits many features of duetting: the two co-narrators say the same thing in different words (*they have a collision//yeah hit me from behind*, lines 5 and 8; *he starts ranting and raving//I was calling him everything under the bloody sun*, lines 11 and 12), they repeat each other's words (*still no sign of any police//any police* from omitted portion; *in the newsagents in Earls Court//in the newsagent in Earls Court*, lines 33–4), and

181

they complete each other's utterances (*he thought he'd dropped them//in the sto- in the newsagents*, lines 32–4). There is also increasing use of overlapping narration as the story comes towards the end, with Sam and Gemma summing up simultaneously (lines 38–42). Sam ends the story with the (ironic) evaluative line *so that was a very interesting weekend*.

This story functions as a powerful display of 'togetherness'. Sam and Gemma display their shared knowledge of events to their friend, and their collaboration symbolizes the closeness of their relationship. Note how Gemma tells us what Sam 'thought' in line 32 (*he thought . . . that he had dropped them in the newsagents in Earls Court*). This is a strong way of indicating how close they are: 'To suggest that one has knowledge of someone else's thoughts . . . implicitly claims intimacy with them.'[9] Sam and Gemma choose to present themselves as a couple, rather than one of them telling a solo story. The topic of the story – a bad weekend – is more in the tradition of women's disaster stories than of men's more achievement-focused narratives.

The next example again involves a man collaborating in story-telling with a woman partner in order to explore a theme untypical of classic masculine stories. This story, 'Bats', comes from a conversation involving three friends, Paul, Becky and Roger. The story is initiated by Paul but is then jointly told by Paul and his partner Becky; it follows on from talk about cockroaches. (Becky's words are in italics; Roger's in italic capitals.)

(4) Bats
1   but I mean you know that's nothing [. . .] compared to our little horror story
2   we never expected that thing remember in Italy
3   *you um do you mean Viareggio? <LAUGHS>*
4   *oh god never again*
5   *WHAT? YOU DIDN'T TELL ME ABOUT THIS*
6   *well yes in a- in a- on a holiday in Italy and um I think a few summer- a few summers ago*
7   *well you know when it's when it's very hot*
8   *I mean you just close **the shutters and leave the windows open you see in old buildings***
9   **here when you go out you leave your windows open for the room to get cooler**
10 *and it was you heard all this flipping and flapping around* [MHM]
11 *and put the light on*

12 *and lo and behold the room is full of bats* [*LAUGHTER*]

13 *of all things* [*OH MY GOD*]

14 *so we're trying to get these bats out of the* <LAUGHING> *window with sheets and goodness knows what you know*

15 *and I nearly had a heart attack* [*OH NO*]

16 *and the next morning we went down to breakfast*

17 *and set about trying to explain to the front desk you know about this*

18 *and he says 'ah si si pipistrello pipistrell- pipistrella'* <MIMICS ITALIAN VOICE>

19 bloody pipistrello

20 [*LAUGHTER*]

21 *I said 'oh that's what it's called in Italian is it?'*

22 *I said 'yeah well it's not very nice you know'*

23 you know sleeping there

24 *having those-* <LAUGHING> *those flying around in your room*

25 *WHAT DID THEY SAY?*

26 *they just said 'well um you know-'*

27 *'we'll get somebody to you know- we'll send somebody'*

28 *they just shrugged their shoulders you know*

29 yeah but it's the shock isn't it you know?

30 I mean you are there, you are in- in a- in a dark room

31 and then-

32 *yeah it's the shock*

33 *I mean the- the- the flapping of a- a- of wings*

34 *it sounded like it was a little bit too- too loud for just a mosquito* [*MHM*]

35 **I thought it was a ghost

36 I mean you know I thought a bloody ghost

37 I mean you know somebody was there you know**

38 **first of all I thought it was birds*

39 *birds you know*

40 *a bird, birds,** a bird in the room*

41 *and switched on the light*

42 *and oh my god what a shock*

43 *can you imagine all these bats flying around you know*

44 yeah she thought they were going to come to suck her

45 and you know she thought they were bloody- you know

46 she has seen too many films of Dracula you know

47 **she thought it was Count Dracula was coming for her you know**

48 **I was go- I was screaming**

49 screaming there

50   **'*get out!*' *<LAUGHING>***
51   **you know jumping on top of the bed** with a pillow hitting
       them you know
52   *getting the sheets <LAUGHS> and slapping them <LAUGHS>*
53   *aw dear it was a nightmare wasn't it?*
54   *and then it's all in the morning as though oh you know pipistrello*
55   *it's like it's a- you know a regular thing you know*
56   *you have it in your hotel room in Italy*
57   *pipistrellos flying- flying around*
58   ***bats in your- <LAUGHING>***
59   **yeah very shocking you know**
60   it was very shocking really you know
61   being woken you know by flapping you know
62   *wings ugh it's something- I'll never forget that*
63   *never never never*
64   yeah you can take it the- the- the you know the funny side of it
65   Dracula you know a real adventure but-
66   *ugh yes one of your worst nightmares come true.*

This is a story whose central theme is fear, a theme more typical of
women's stories than of men's. Paul introduces it as *our little horror
story*, a framing device which allows for the telling of frightening
events. By using the pronouns *we* and *our* and by appealing to Becky's
memory *we never expected that thing remember in Italy*, Paul invites her
to co-narrate the story with him. This both displays their relationship,
but also creates a space for him to collaborate in the expression of
fear. The two co-narrators collaborate in maintaining the theme of
fear throughout the story. Paul uses the word *shock* in line 29 and this
is echoed by Becky in line 32 and again later in line 42. Paul repeats
the phrase *very shocking* (lines 59 and 60) as part of the closing evaluation; he also confesses to having thought the bats were *a bloody ghost*.
But it is Becky who presents herself, in stereotypical feminine style,
as nearly having *a heart attack* (line 15) and as screaming (line 48),
while Paul describes her as fantasizing that *Count Dracula was coming
for her* (line 47). (Paul's claim *she thought it was Count Dracula was
coming for her* again involves one partner in a couple claiming to know
the other's thoughts.) Becky's final line, *ugh yes one of your worst nightmares come true*, underlines the scariness of their experience and nicely
mirrors Paul's opening (with *nightmare* balancing *horror story*).

   Although each narrator gets extended turns at telling the story,
there is also a great deal of overlapping talk where the co-narrators

make the same point in different words (for example, lines 8 and 9, where both narrators explain the Italian practice of closing the shutters in daytime in summer; lines 35–40, where both narrators recount their first response to the bats). There are also collaborative completions (for example, *screaming there//'get out'*, lines 49–50) and repetition of words and phrases (*screaming*, lines 48 and 49; *it's the shock*, lines 29 and 32).

Paul and Becky put a great deal of effort into convincing Roger that what they experienced was extremely frightening. The first half of the story concentrates on the events, the second half on their reactions. They only move on to the exploration of their reactions once Roger has shown that he is fully in sympathy with their story. His initial minimal responses develop into stronger response forms such as *oh my god* and *oh no*. He also laughs loudly when the protagonists' English horror is contrasted with Italian nonchalance (lines 18–20).

The narrative 'Bats' shows a young man reminiscing about a frightening experience and proving capable of owning feelings of vulnerability. It is significant that he manages to do this when telling a story collaboratively with a female speaker, a woman who he feels very comfortable with. This example provides a strong contrast with the narrative 'Buying Wine in Cornwall', discussed in the last chapter (p. 153). In both, a first-person narrative about an event involving a heterosexual couple is told to a third participant, a male friend. But whereas the narrative 'Bats' is co-narrated by the couple to their friend, the narrative 'Buying Wine in Cornwall' is a solo performance by a male speaker. This shows that it is not possible to make general claims about the behaviour of couples in conversation. Michael, on the evidence of the story 'Buying Wine in Cornwall', uses storytelling to construct himself as an independent, achievement-oriented male rather than as a partner in a heterosexual couple, and his performance of hegemonic masculinity is produced in negotiation with his friend Bill and his partner Suzanne. By contrast, Paul uses collaborative story-telling to construct himself as someone in relationship with a woman and as someone who is not afraid to talk about frightening experiences.

'This Thing Just Could Not Survive': New Men?

It seems that when men are talking to other men they prefer to tell solo narratives rather than to co-construct stories. But in mixed company, men will often choose to tell a story in collaboration with a female partner. In this chapter we have looked at several examples which illustrate this phenomenon. The story 'They Lost a Child' (example (1)) is told by an elderly couple (Arthur and Marian) to their daughter and grandson. The story 'Parcel Delivery' (example (2)) is told by Ian with significant collaborative support from his female partner to their friends, another couple in their thirties. The story 'Interesting Weekend' (example (3)) is told by a young couple in their twenties to a male friend. The story 'Bats' (example (4)) is told by another young couple to a male friend.

As these examples show, collaboratively constructed narratives arise in a variety of settings and are told to a range of recipients. But all these examples exhibit the key features of collaborative talk: repetition, joint construction of utterances and overlapping speech. In all of them, the narrative floor is shared by two people. And in all of them, this sharing of the floor symbolizes the connection between the two speakers.

Dominant discourses of masculinity assert independence and downplay connection, as we saw in chapter 3. In all-male contexts, men have to affirm their separateness from each other in order to avoid the accusation of homosexuality. But in mixed contexts, it seems that men have more latitude to explore a wider range of masculinities and to display more feminine aspects of themselves. Does this mean that the men who co-construct narratives with female partners are exemplars of the 'new man'?

To answer this question, I want to focus on two examples which occur in sequence. They come from the same conversation as 'Parcel Delivery' and involve the same two couples, Diane and Ian and Jean and Martin. What is remarkable about this sequence of two stories about kittens is that both stories are collaboratively constructed, with Jean and Martin telling the first and Diane and Ian telling the second. (Jean's words are in normal typeface, Martin's in italic.)

(5) Kittens 1
1   we looked out of our window today
2   we saw two little kittens didn't we?
3   ⌈I thought 'what the hell is that doing out there'
4   ⌊*dashing past the window yeah, tiny*
5   **cos I thought i- it was too young to be out
6   one of them was like that

7   just chucked in the garden**
8   **only one of them that big and one was just a little bit bigger there*
9   *it just- they had the- ***
10 I thought   ⌈'((xxxxxxxxxxx))'
11   ⌊*chasing each other round the garden*
12 I knocked next door,
13 I said 'have you got two new kittens?',
14 and he said 'yeah',
15 and I said 'Have they escaped or something or what?',
16 'They're alright as long as they don't go that way',
17 like pointing to the road,
18 I thought well can't really guarantee that really can you?
19 *no the road is a- it's a busy road.*

This narrative is co-constructed by Jean and Martin, and recounts a shared experience. They describe an incident when their neighbour's new kittens were allowed to wander unchecked in the garden; they both express concern for the kittens and emphasize how small they were. Jean initiates the story with two narrative clauses, then Martin joins in so that the orienting details about the kittens is jointly produced in simultaneous speech (staves 2–10). This is a very good example of the way two speakers can hold the floor simultaneously for an extended period, in defiance of theoretical claims – and common-sense assumptions – that only one speaker should speak at a time.[10] Recipients have no trouble processing this kind of polyphonic talk.[11]

Jean provides the narrative core of the story, with Martin providing a final line which extends Jean's previous line. These two last lines are essentially evaluative, expressing in different ways their anxiety over the kittens. Both the evaluative stance and the topic of the story can be seen as feminine rather than masculine, and it is only in narratives in mixed conversation that I have found men adopting such values and choosing such topics.

Jean and Martin's story is followed directly by another one, told by Ian and Diane, again on the subject of kittens. The story is initiated by Ian, who makes the topical link with the first story, but Diane provides the second line, and from then on they construct the story collaboratively, with occasional contributions from Jean and Martin. Example (6) gives an extract from this (longer) story. ('Jazz' is Ian and Diane's cat. Ian's contributions are in normal typeface; Diane's in italics; Jean's in italic capitals.)

(6)   Kittens 2

1   it's like that stupid bat who lived next door to me in . Allen Close
2   *she had a cat that could* ⌈*never have been more than five weeks old*
3   ⌊she- she had a . ((little)) cat that big
4   *no way maybe even four weeks old*
5   like that
6   *NOT WITH THE MOTHER? [no] OH THAT'S AWFUL*
7   ((there)) there and sh- she put it out for the day
8   ⌈((xxxxxxxxxxxxxxxxx))
9   ⌊*((put it out there))*
10 *and Jazz used to bring it home*
11 ⌈she just put it out
12 ⌊*and it is so tiny*
13 *it couldn't even get through the catflap*
14 it couldn't ⌈reach up into the catflap
15   ⌊*that's how . tiny he was*
16 [. . .]
17 *he was completely black and just absolutely . adorable wasn't he?*
18 and on one day 'bug doosh' <SOUND EFFECT>
19 through there ⌈in the catflap ((2 words))
20   ⌊*and one day he actually got through*
21 *and i- he was- he was hanging through the catflap with his little paws*
        dangling
22 ⌈he was like <RUNNING NOISE>
23 ⌊*but . he couldn't get the rest of his body through*
24 and he got through the catflap
25 and that was it
26 he used to come ⌈in and out and then out
27   ⌊*they went up and down the stairs*
28 ⌈they w- it didn't want to go
29 ⌊*we used to feed him and everything*
30 and she used to put it out all day like
31 I mean this thing was like . just could not survive
32 *I used to get in from work and ((take it from)) the door and feed him and*
        everything

'Kittens 2' is a classic example of collaborative narration. The story is co-narrated by two speakers who share the floor to give an account of a shared experience, using repetition of words and phrases and simultaneous speech to tie their contributions together. The narrative falls into three sections. The first (lines 1–15) provides orientation (details about who, where and when) and an abstract: *it couldn't even get through the catflap*. The second section (omitted from this extract) consists of a habitual narrative, describing the relationship between the kitten and their own cat Jazz and finishing with the evaluative line *it was so funny*. The final section (lines 17–32) describes the kitten finally managing to get through the catflap. The narrative ends with evaluative lines which re-state the opening theme of the neighbour's irresponsibility, thus framing the narrative and simultaneously aligning it with the previous narrative.

This example, like the previous one, shows that male speakers can perform alternative versions of masculinity in certain contexts. Ian and Martin both choose to collaborate in narratives where the topic is kittens and where key themes are care and concern about vulnerable creatures. Such themes are not characteristic of narratives produced in all-male talk. What seems to be crucial about the circumstances of this conversation is that both men (Ian and Martin) are in stable partnerships with women, and the four speakers are also friends with each other.

So does this mean that Ian and Martin and the other men whose stories have appeared in this chapter are 'new men'? It is certainly the case that, when co-constructing stories with female partners, men engage with topics which are rare in (or absent from) all-male talk, topics such as death ('They Lost a Child'), fear ('Bats'), concern for small animals ('Kittens 1' and 'Kittens 2'). Moreover, in co-constructing a narrative with another speaker, male narrators display human connection, something they tend to avoid in all-male contexts. So in some ways it is true to say that collaborative narration involving a man and a female partner performs a different kind of masculinity and displays more feminine aspects of manhood.

But if we examine Ian and Diane's contributions to 'Kittens 2' carefully, we can see that as co-narrators they still take up conventional gender positions relative to each other.[17] Diane's contributions draw on a nurturing or maternal discourse; examples are *Jazz used to bring it home* (line 10), *we used to feed him and everything* (line 29), *I used to get in from work and ((take it from)) the door and feed him and everything* (line 32). They also pay attention to the kitten's adorability and smallness: *he was [. . .] just absolutely adorable wasn't he?* (line 17), *that's how tiny he was* (line 15), *with his little paws dangling* (line 21). Ian contributes more narrative clauses than Diane (compare lines 11 and 12 where Ian's narrative clause *she just put it out* is said at the same time as Diane's evaluative line *and it is so tiny*). Ian's contributions focus

189

more on the kitten achieving its goals: *and within the week he learned how to get there* (from the omitted central section); *and he got through the catflap and that was it* (lines 24–5). So Ian and Diane simultaneously perform coupledom through collaborating in story-telling and also maintain gender distinctions through subtle differences in the perspectives they adopt as co-narrators.

Another question which needs asking is: why is it that men *only* co-construct stories with female speakers in mixed talk? The mixed conversations are full of collaborative narration, involving heterosexual couples, fathers and daughters, mothers and male family members, as well as mothers and daughters, sisters, female friends. But there are no examples in the mixed conversations of men collaborating with other men to tell a narrative. Why should men avoid collaborative talk in the company of male peers and in mixed company? Is it the case that, given the homophobia which informs hegemonic masculinity, men avoid ways of talking which display closeness with men for fear of being accused of being gay? And in mixed talk do men choose to co-construct talk with a female partner to display their non-gayness? Heterosexuality is at the heart of dominant versions of masculinity, so when male speakers perform the heterosexual couple through co-narration with a female partner, they are by definition also performing hegemonic masculinity.

In other words, far from being 'new men', the male speakers who collaborate in story-telling with female partners are very much 'old men'. They may exploit the potential of co-narration with a woman to tell stories on less macho topics, but through displaying their connection to a woman they are performing heterosexuality and therefore (hegemonic) masculinity.

Conclusions

As the examples in this chapter demonstrate, the collaborative construction of talk, specifically of narrative, is not confined to female speakers. But male speakers, in the conversations I've collected, are more likely to construct talk collaboratively in mixed company rather than in all-male company. Perhaps the most significant finding to come out of my analysis of mixed talk is that male speakers share the construction of narrative only with female speakers: there are no examples in the mixed conversations of collaboratively constructed narratives involving two male speakers. This suggests that collaborative modes of talk may be avoided by male speakers in contexts where the closeness symbolized by co-construction threatens hegemonic masculinity, and, by contrast, may be chosen in contexts where the closeness symbolized by co-construction functions as a display of heterosexuality.

Notes

1 H. P. Grice, 'Logic and conversation'.
2 Alessandro Duranti, 'The audience as co-author: an introduction', p. 239.
3 Jane Falk, 'The conversational duet'.
4 See Jennifer Coates, *Women Talk*; 'One-at-a-time: the organisation of men's talk'; and 'The construction of a collaborative floor in women's friendly talk'.
5 See Jennifer Mandelbaum, 'Couples sharing stories'.
6 William Labov, *Language in the Inner City*, p. 371.
7 This story has been edited for reasons of space. Omissions are marked by the symbol [. . .].
8 Mandelbaum, 'Couples sharing stories', p. 147.
9 Ibid., p. 163.
10 The classic exposition of the one-at-a-time theory of conversational turn-taking is found in Harvey Sacks, Emanuel Schegloff and Gail Jefferson's article 'A simplest systematics for the organisation of turn-taking in conversation'. Sacks, however, was well aware that overlapping speech is a regular feature of relaxed conversation among equals (see his *Lectures on Conversation*). For further discussion of this issue, see Coates, 'No gap, lots of overlap: turn-taking patterns in the talk of women friends'; 'One-at-a-time: the organisation of men's talk'; 'The construction of a collaborative floor in women's friendly talk'.
11 Wallace Chafe, 'Polyphonic topic development'.
12 I am grateful to Julia Stevens for this insight.

8

'There Are Problems': Men's Talk and Contemporary Masculinities

So what do the conversations we've looked at in this book tell us about men today? What do men's narratives tell us about men's lives and men's identities at the turn of the twenty-first century?

In order to answer these questions, I want to begin with a story. It comes from a discussion about the 1960s and whether or not things are better today than they were then. (The story 'Suicidal' came earlier in the same discussion.) Pete has made the claim that 'things have got better'. Tony disagrees, and this extract is his response to being asked for his reasons why.

(1) Captain Cook
1   I've got a number of rather . painful reasons why this can't be
      the case
2   um . Captain Cook
3   [*Brian: <LAUGHS> that's a <u>non sequitur isn't it</u> <LAUGHING>*]
4   [*Pete: well . it's a lovely non-sequitur though isn't it*]
5   [*Brian: yes . ((it's)) really enjoyable <LAUGHS>*]
6   you see- i- it was reported
7   that when Cook's vessel of exploration first arrived . in this . bay
      . in Australia
8   the . indigenous population
9   some of whom happened to be present on the beach
10 pursuing their . immemorial lives and so on
11 actually were not capable . of perceiving the presence . of Cook's ship
12 and it wasn't until . the . er rowing boats were lowered
13 that is until something happened on a kind of scale that they
      could grasp

14   that they were actually . erm . able to respond to the situation
15   I'm afraid . the problems that civilization faces at the moment
16   are on the scale of Captain Cook's ship as it were
17   There are problems with which we're- er it seems to me . er . we
        ignore them
18   we have to ignore them
19   because we don't know what the fuck to do with the bastards
20   ah- but then- I mean nobody's going to lower any boats on these
        problems

The narrative core of this story is anomalous, since it does not contain the usual narrative clauses with simple past tense verbs. But it definitely tells a story, and could be paraphrased as follows: *Captain Cook's ship arrived off the coast of Australia, and the indigenous people didn't see it because it was on a scale that was outside their experience, then Cook lowered little boats, and the people saw them.* The lines that surround this narrative core provide us with a (deliberately opaque) abstract at the beginning, and a final section that makes clear what the point of the story is, ending with the evaluative clause *nobody's going to lower any boats on these problems.* This forcibly makes the point that contemporary society is in a mess and, even worse, nothing is going to make us aware that we are in a mess.

One aspect of contemporary society that many commentators think is in a mess is masculinity. In this chapter I want to explore the idea that contemporary masculinity has problems and that it is only very recently that we have begun to be aware of the problems. In other words, it is only very recently that we have begun to have an inkling that there is a ship moored out there. Tony is pessimistic about the future: *nobody's going to lower any boats on these problems.* But in terms of the problems associated with masculinity, I want to suggest that boats are being lowered and we are able to see them.

Masculinity in Crisis?

The idea that we are witnessing some kind of crisis of masculinity is a popular one, and the phrase 'masculinity in crisis' turns up frequently in media commentary. Anthony Clare, well known for the radio series 'In the Psychiatrist's Chair', recently published a book entitled *On Men* which has the phrase *Masculinity in Crisis* as its subtitle. In the book he argues that 'the roles that make men secure in their maleness – provider, protector, controller, father – are all under assault'.[1] He points out that male suicide rates are growing and that 'when it comes to aggression, delinquent behaviour, risk taking and social mayhem, men win gold'.[2] Michael Kimmel, in a recent summary of work on gender, asks the following question: 'what gender comes to mind when I invoke the following current American problems: "teen violence", "gang violence", "suburban violence", "drug violence", "violence in the schools"?'[3] Certainly, daily news items about conflict around the globe, about race riots in British cities, about football hooliganism, underline the fact that men, in particular young men, seem to be angry and out of control. 'And yet', as Anthony Clare says, 'for all their behaving badly, they do not seem any happier.'[4]

All this suggests that there is a problem. At the heart of the problem seems to be the fact that 'the old certainties about the male role' are disappearing[5] and that traditional assumptions about gender identity are being challenged. Much of this challenge has come from feminism and from the social changes resulting from women's struggle for equal rights. Although popular commentators use the phrase 'crisis of masculinity', it is clear that this is short-hand for a phenomenon that involves women as well as men, femininity as well as masculinity. The sociologist Bob Connell argues that it is more accurate to talk about a crisis in 'the modern gender order', because what is under threat is the entire system of gender relations.[6] This is a better way of thinking about the changes that are going on in women's and men's lives, and the impact these changes are having on cultural notions of masculinity and femininity.

One of the reasons it is sometimes hard to grasp what is going on, to *perceive the presence of Cook's ship*, as it were, is that there have not been cataclysmic changes in everyday life. Things *are* changing, in terms of patterns of employment, of educational achievement, of marriage and child-rearing, but the more significant changes are not in the daily patterns of women's and men's lives but in the values we attach to those patterns. In the past, the following traits were associated with men and seen as good: *logical, disciplined, controlled, rational, aggressive.* By contrast, women were associated with the following traits, which were seen as weak and as in some way justifying the inferior position of women: *emotional, spontaneous, intuitive, expressive, compassionate, empathic.* Today, however, these values are being reversed: the traits associated with men are now seen as markers of deviance, while the traits associated with women are now seen as markers of maturity and health.[7]

The other reason it has been so difficult to see the problem arises from the unmarked nature of maleness and masculinity. As I said in chapter 1, until recently 'man' and 'person' were often indistinguishable, while 'woman' was a marked term. Being unmarked is a privilege conferred by power. A hundred years ago, Georg Simmel wrote: 'Man's *position of power* does not only assure his relative superiority over the woman, but it assures that his standards become generalised as generically human standards that are to govern the behaviour of men and women alike.'[8] Powerful groups like men have enjoyed 'the privilege of invisibility'.[9] But as long as men are invisible – as long as we speak of hooligans, delinquents, child abusers, without specifying that these are not just any people but (usually) male people – then it is difficult for society to address the problems of hooliganism, delinquency, child abuse, domestic violence, etc. As Michael Kimmel warns: 'If we ignore masculinity – if we let it remain invisible – we will never completely understand these problems, let alone resolve them.'[10]

The men whose talk has been examined in this book provide us with a kind of snapshot of masculinity at the turn of the century. Can this snapshot help us to understand the problems of contemporary men? What light does the analysis of the talk of these men throw on the debate about masculinity? The men whose conversations were recorded for this book represent a wide range of current masculinities, old and young, working-class and middle-class, but there are obviously limits to the representativeness of the sample. To begin with, everyone who took part in the research belongs to a friendship group or a family group, and gets on with them well enough to agree to have their talk recorded. This means that certain men, for example, loners and those estranged from their families, are not represented. Moreover, those whose talk was recorded agreed to co-operate in a research project for no obvious reward, while others refused to participate. Inevitably, then, the sample has a bias to those with more co-operative personalities.

But despite these caveats, it has been possible to establish a picture of contemporary men from these conversations. This picture gives an impression of order and stability and is, in many ways, surprisingly traditional. Men friends meet in the pub for a drink after work and have a laugh or mull over what's going on in the world. Young men in mixed company put on a display to impress women friends, while in heterosexual couples, men collaborate in story-telling as a way of displaying coupledom. Close inspection of talk in these contexts reveals that gender demarcations are carefully maintained, with women colluding in constructing male dominance. In family talk, men are positioned as significant members, with the power to evaluate other members' contributions, and fathers and grandfathers are given space to tell stories of the past, unlike women. The only obvious symptom of perturbation in the gender order is in the gentle teasing that occurs when women friends or wives or daughters make subversive contributions to men's stories.

In many ways, the phrase 'the crisis of masculinity' is unhelpful: it suggests something dramatic, something startling. But in order to understand why the modern gender order is in trouble, we need to bring men and masculinity into focus. In other words, by looking closely at the conversations men have with their friends, with their partners and with their families as part of their everyday lives, I hope to contribute to making men more visible.

'The Constraining Hand of Hegemonic Masculinity'

One of the most striking features of the men's talk discussed in this book is its orientation to the hegemonic norms of masculinity. In most of the conversations most of the time, it is evident that male speakers are acting in a way that aligns them with these dominant norms, norms which prescribe 'acceptable' maleness. This dominant mode of 'being a man' is typically associated with 'heterosexuality, toughness, power and authority, competitiveness and the subordination of gay men'.[11] It seems to me imperative that we understand the influence that these norms exert on men. It can be argued that men suffer from the narrowness of these norms: they restrict men in terms of what they feel they can do and say and how they are with other people. It is not an exaggeration to speak of the 'distortions' produced by 'the constraining hand of hegemonic masculinity'.[12]

The talk I have analysed certainly demonstrates that most men in most groups are constrained by the hegemonic norms. As we have seen, many narratives emphasize men's toughness, whether in winning a fight with a drunken workmate ('The Fight', chapter 5) or in enduring pain ('Appendicitis', chapter 3, 'Tablets and Drink', chapter 3). Men's use of taboo language in telling their stories also performs toughness. The theme of winning or of 'getting away with it' is common to many of the stories, and male protagonists tend to be portrayed as lone heroes pitted against the odds. The theme of competitiveness is also widespread, and covers stories about sporting achievement (such as 'Amazing Left', chapter 3) and violent conflict ('The Paint Dispute', chapter 3) as well as stories of more middle-class achievements such as finding a good wine merchant or being knowledgeable about mobile phones. The emphasis on achievement and on getting the better of those in authority (such as the police) suggests a strong awareness of power and authority. Power is also an important theme in the more sexist stories in the data-base (for example, 'The Vibrator', chapter 5), as well as in homophobic ones (e.g. 'Queerie', chapter 3), with women and gay men being constructed as 'other' and as inferior. Claiming heterosexuality is central to men's self-presentation. It may be done through talking about pornography ('The Pornographic Video', chapter 3) or in expressing horror at cross-dressing ('Queerie'). In mixed talk, as we saw in chapter 7, men collaborate in story-telling with women in an explicit performance of the heterosexual couple.

So the evidence of the conversations I've discussed is that men's self-presentation is strongly constrained by the norms of hegemonic masculinity. But 'the constraining hand of hegemonic masculinity' is even more apparent in conversations collected by *male* researchers for a variety of research projects. These research projects involved men talking in the 'locker room' before and after sporting events, boys talking about sex, men meeting for a drink and a chat, and men talking about drink and violence.[13] Much of this material is more sexist and homophobic than anything I have collected. For example, the men's talk in my data-base does not involve explicit talk about male genitalia,[14] sustained talk about women in terms of body parts,[15] or fantasies about rape.[16] Does this mean that male speakers censor themselves unconsciously when the researcher is female? Alternatively, it could suggest that men are more constrained by the hegemonic norms when designing their talk for the ears of a male researcher. Certainly, the more 'macho' elements of hegemonic masculinity are more in evidence in data collected by male researchers, just as they are more in evidence in my data in the all-male conversations than in the mixed conversations.

'Concealing Our Vulnerability': Men and the Expression of Emotion

The absence of talk about feelings is perhaps the most notable consequence of 'the constraining hand of hegemonic masculinity' in the conversations I've collected. The imperative to avoid vulnerability means that men have to put a lot of effort into keeping up a front (or wearing a mask). Victor Seidler writes: 'In concealing our vulnerability to ourselves and others, we learn to present a certain image of ourselves. We become strangers to aspects of ourselves. This reflects itself in our relationship to language as we distance and disown parts of ourselves. We refuse to experience parts of ourselves that would bring us into contact with our hurt, need, pain and vulnerability since these threaten our inherited sense of masculinity.'[17] It is Seidler's view that men's historic association with reason and with the rational (in contrast to women's association with the emotional) has led to serious problems. Masculinity comes to be 'an essentially negative identity learnt through defining itself against emotionality and connectedness'.[18]

The stories discussed in this book tend to support Seidler's view that men avoid the emotional when they talk with each other. But as we have seen, men find indirect ways of expressing connectedness: for example, they tell stories collaboratively (chapter 3) or tell stories in sequence (chapter 4). They also 'have a laugh' with stories about things nearly going wrong – such stories have the additional function of allowing participants to be in touch with the anxiety associated with what might have been.

More significantly, in some groups individual men take the risk of challenging the hegemonic norms. Brian, in his story 'Suicidal' (chapter 3), takes the risk of self-disclosing to his friends. Pete and Tony, in a conversation following Brian's self-disclosure, take the risk of reflecting on the costs of keeping up a front and make the claim that admitting to vulnerability might have benefits as well as costs. Alan, in conversation with fellow carpenters, introduces the notion that powerful machines can be dangerous ('The Digger', chapter 3), while in the very different environment of a public school, Julian and Henry reflect on the rumour that they are 'closet fags'.

These examples range from well-educated middle-class professionals to skilled manual workers and privileged boys. In other words, evidence that male speakers are sometimes prepared to challenge the hegemonic norms is not restricted to one particular group. More importantly, two of the examples referred to above come from conversations involving only two speakers. This seems to be highly salient for men friends: in groups of more than two speakers, men are anxious not to be seen to be displaying characteristics which could be labelled 'feminine' and therefore 'gay'.

The significance of talk involving just two speakers is confirmed by a contemporary survey of boys in London schools. Teachers were sceptical about the boys co-operating in the research as well as about their ability to talk at length, but the boys confounded their expectations by vying to take part in the research interviews. Even more poignant was the willingness of boys individually to open up to a sympathetic male interviewer.[19] As the researchers say: 'Boys struggle to find a forum in which they can try out masculine identities which can be differentiated from the "hegemonic" codes of macho masculinity.'[20] Both boys and men seem more likely to do this in the presence of just one close friend (or a single trusted adult).

Another factor which has meant that men have avoided emotional talk with each other is that they have historically preferred to do this kind of talk with women. A recent survey of mobile phone use claims that men now gossip more than women, but reveals that women's 'gossip partners' tend to be women friends and family, while men's 'gossip partners' tend to be women partners, female friends and work colleagues.[21] As the examples in chapters 6 and 7 show, in mixed talk male narrators deal with a wider range of topics (such as cooking and kittens) and involve women as well as men in their storyworlds. In joint story-telling with a female partner, men even co-construct narratives which are not all about heroism and success and which deal explicitly with emotions such as fear or frustration.

However, as women become impatient with doing this emotional work, men will need to develop more 'connectedness' with other men. But men have a history of friendships which stress sociability rather than intimacy, which could be described as 'side-by-side' rather than 'face-to-face'.[22] So although it is acknowledged that men and boys have a lot of fun together, at the same time there is a sense 'of something missing emotionally'.[23]

This sense of something missing in men's talk is the strongest evidence of some kind of crisis in contemporary masculinity. Men's concern with the referential function of language at the expense of the affective function[24] has served them well in the public arena, where information is highly valued. But it is crucial that speakers, both male and female, understand the role of talk as a means of relating to other people and expressing feelings as well as a means of exchanging information. Some older educated men in my sample clearly do understand this, as we saw in the conversational extract 'Englishness' (chapter 3, p. 76). And those involved in the research on boys in London schools are hopeful that things can be changed: 'By encouraging boys to talk about themselves and their relationships in single-sex groups, close and supportive relations with other boys can be forged.'[25] As Anthony Clare puts it: 'What I want as a man, and what I want for men, is that we become more capable of expressing the vulnerability and the tenderness and the affection we feel, that we place greater value on love, family and personal relationships and less on power, possessions and achievement . . .'[26]

Lowering the Boats

What I have tried to do in this book is to lower a boat into the water – that is, my aim has been to make men and masculinity more visible. When we tell stories in the course of everyday conversation with friends and family, we make choices about how to present ourselves. Men, as I have shown, normally choose to present themselves in alignment with the norms of hegemonic masculinity.

I have tried to bring into focus men's inexpressivity and their seeming preference for friendships with other men which stress sociability rather than intimacy. Men enjoy having a laugh with each other and mulling things over, but they avoid self-disclosure and any behaviour that could be construed as feminine. The stories we have looked at also show that men's relationships with women are complex and betray contradictions. On one hand, men's fear of the feminine results in misogyny at one extreme or in the exclusion of women from the storyworld at the other. On the other hand, men's propensity for constructing stories jointly with a female partner functions as a display of intimacy and togetherness. But, as I have pointed out, it also functions as a powerful display of heterosexuality, and so performs hegemonic masculinity.

While the majority of men whose stories I have discussed seem content to align themselves with hegemonic masculinity, research exploring men's attitudes suggests that men are constantly renegotiating their relationship with current masculinities.[27] Perhaps we can take heart from the evidence of the talk presented in this book that some men are struggling to reflect on masculinity and to challenge traditional norms. In his conversation with Pete ('Englishness', chapter 3) Tony says *life would be improved by people being more open with each other*, and makes the brave claim that *all the masks and so on are supposed to keep vulnerability at bay but . . . they only do this at a very high cost.* As men and masculinity lose their old privileged, unmarked position and become increasingly visible, hopefully more men will, like Tony, begin to reflect on the high costs of the masks. It is important to remember that 'we are both constrained and enabled by language'.[28] In other words, while men are constrained by prevailing hegemonic discourses, they are simultaneously enabled by other, competing discourses which potentially allow them to construct alternative, counter-hegemonic identities for themselves.

According to Michael Kimmel, it is only in the last few decades that we have become aware that 'gender is one of the central organising principles around which social life revolves'.[29] This awareness of the centrality of gender in our lives is part of the growing visibility of gender. With this new visibility comes an understanding that men, as well as women, are gendered. It is only through problematizing men and through denying masculinity the privilege of unmarked status that we can begin to bring men and masculinity into focus. This study of the everyday talk of ordinary men with friends and family is a small contribution to making men more visible and to improving our understanding of the conflicting masculinities available to men today.

Notes

1   Anthony Clare, *On Men*, back cover.
2   Ibid., p. 3.
3   Michael Kimmel, *The Gendered Society*, p. 8.
4   Clare, *On Men*, p. 3.
5   Vivian de Klerk, 'The role of expletives in the construction of masculinity', p. 156.
6   R. W. Connell, *Masculinities*, p. 84.
7   Clare, *On Men*, p. 68.
8   Georg Simmel, quoted in Kimmel, *The Gendered Society*, p. 8.
9   Ibid., p. 7.
10 Ibid., p. 10.
11 Stephen Frosh, Ann Phoenix and Rob Pattman, *Young Masculinities*, pp. 75–6.
12 Ibid., p. 261.
13 Timothy Curry, 'Fraternal bonding in the locker room'; Brendan Gough and Gareth Edwards, 'The beer talking'; Stephen Tomsen, 'A top night: social protest, masculinity and the culture of drinking violence'; Julian Wood, 'Groping towards sexism: boys' sex talk'.
14 Gough and Edwards, 'The beer talking'.
15 Ibid.; Wood, 'Groping towards sexism'.

16   Curry, 'Fraternal bonding in the locker room'; Wood, 'Groping towards sexism'.
17   Victor Seidler, *Rediscovering Masculinity*, p. 153.
18   Ibid., p. 7.
19   Frosh, Phoenix and Pattman, *Young Masculinities*.
20   Ibid., p. 259.
21   Social Issues Research Centre, 'Evolution, alienation and gossip – the role of mobile telecommunications in the 21st century'.
22   Joseph Pleck, 'Man to man: is brotherhood possible?'
23   Frosh, Phoenix and Pattman, *Young Masculinities*, pp. 259–60.
24   See, for example, Janet Holmes, *Women, Men and Politeness*.
25   Frosh, Phoenix and Pattman, *Young Masculinities*, p. 263.
26   Clare, *On Men*, p. 221.
27   Nigel Edley and Margaret Wetherell, 'Jockeying for position: the construction of masculine identities'; Frosh, Phoenix and Pattman, *Young Masculinities*.
28   Edley and Wetherell, 'Jockeying for position', p. 206.
29   Kimmel, *The Gendered Society*, p. 5.

Bibliography

Abrahams, Roger (1983) *The Man-of-Words in the West Indies: Performance and the Emergence of Creole Culture*. Baltimore: Johns Hopkins University Press.

Alexander, Sally (1990) 'Women, class and sexual differences in the 1830s and 1840s: some reflections on the writing of a feminist history', pp. 28–50 in Terry Lovell (ed.) *British Feminist Thought*. Oxford: Blackwell.

Alexander, Sally and Taylor, Barbara (1981) 'In defence of "patriarchy"', pp. 370–3 in R. Samuel (ed.) *People's History and Socialist Theory*. London: Routledge.

Baldwin, Karen (1984) '"Woof!" A word on women's roles in family storytelling', pp. 149–62 in Rosen Jordan and Susan Kalcik (eds) *Women's Folklore, Women's Culture*. Philadelphia: University of Pennsylvania Press.

Bauman, Richard (1986) *Story, Performance, and Event*. Cambridge: Cambridge University Press.

Bell, Allan (1984) 'Language style as audience design', *Language in Society* 13(2), 145–204.

Bell, Allan (1997) 'Language style as audience design', pp. 240–50 in Nikolas Coupland and Adam Jaworski (eds) *Sociolinguistics*. Basingstoke. Hants: Macmillan.

Benjamin, Jessica (1990) *The Bonds of Love*. London: Virago.

Berger, Charles and Bradac, James (1982) *Language and Social Knowledge*. London: Edward Arnold.

Bettelheim, Bruno (1976) *The Uses of Enchantment*. New York: Knopf.

Blum-Kulka, Shoshana (1993) '"You gotta know how to tell a story": telling, tales, and tellers in American and Israeli narrative events at dinner', *Language in Society* 22(3), 361–402.

Blum-Kulka, Shoshana (1997) *Dinner Talk: Cultural Patterns of Sociability and Socialisation in Family Discourse*. London: Lawrence Erlbaum Associates.

Bohan, Janis S. (1993) 'Regarding gender. Essentialism, constructionism, and feminist psychology', *Psychology of Women Quarterly* 17, 5–21.

Brod, Harry (1987) 'A case for Men's Studies', pp. 263–77 in Michael Kimmel (ed.) *Changing Men: New Directions in Research on Men and Masculinity*. London: Sage.

Bibliography

Brown, Penelope (1998) 'How and why are women more polite', pp. 81–99 in Jennifer Coates (ed.) *Language and Gender: A Reader*. Oxford: Blackwell.

Bruner, Jerome (1987) 'Life as narrative', *Social Research* 54(1), 11–32.

Bruner, Jerome (1990) 'Autobiography as self', pp. 33–66 of J. Bruner *Acts of Meaning*. Cambridge, MA: Harvard University Press.

Bruner, Jerome (1991) 'The narrative construction of reality', *Critical Inquiry* 18(1), 1–21.

Cameron, Deborah (1997) 'Performing gender identity: young men's talk and the construction of heterosexual masculinity', pp. 47–64 in Sally Johnson and Ulrike Hanna Meinhof (eds) *Language and Masculinity*. Oxford: Blackwell.

Carter, Ron and Simpson, Paul (1982) 'The sociolinguistic analysis of narrative', *Belfast Working Papers in Linguistics* 6, 123–52.

Chafe, Wallace (1980) 'The deployment of consciousness in the production of narrative', pp. 9–50 in Wallace Chafe (ed.) *The Pear Stories: Cognitive, Cultural and Linguistic Aspects of Narrative Production*. Norwood, NJ: Ablex.

Chafe, Wallace (1994) *Discourse, Consciousness and Time: The Flow and Displacement of Conscious Experience in Speaking and Writing*. Chicago: University of Chicago Press.

Chafe, Wallace (1997) 'Polyphonic topic development', pp. 41–54 in T. Givón (ed.) *Conversation: Cognitive, Communicative and Social Perspectives*. Philadelphia: John Benjamins.

Cheepen, Christine (1988) *The Predictability of Informal Conversation*. London: Pinter Publishers.

Cheshire, Jenny (1982) *Variation in an English Dialect*. Cambridge: Cambridge University Press.

Clare, Anthony (2001) *On Men: Masculinity in Crisis*. London: Arrow Books.

Coates, Jennifer (1993) *Women, Men and Language*, 2nd edn. London: Longman.

Coates, Jennifer (1994) 'No gap, lots of overlap: turn-taking patterns in the talk of women friends', pp. 177–92 in David Graddol, Janet Maybin and Barry Stierer (eds) *Researching Language and Literacy in Social Context*. Clevedon: Multilingual Matters.

Coates, Jennifer (1996) *Women Talk: Conversation Between Women Friends*. Oxford: Blackwell.

Coates, Jennifer (1997a) 'One-at-a-time: the organisation of men's talk', pp. 107–29 in Sally Johnson and Ulrike Hanna Meinhof (eds) *Language and Masculinity*. Oxford: Blackwell.

Coates, Jennifer (1997b) 'The construction of a collaborative floor in women's friendly talk', pp. 55–89 in T. Givón (ed.) *Conversation: Cognitive, Communicative and Social Perspectives*. Philadelphia: John Benjamins.

Coates, Jennifer (1999) 'Women behaving badly: female speakers backstage', *Journal of Sociolinguistics* 3(1), 67–82.

Coates, Jennifer (2000a) 'Small talk and subversion: female speakers backstage', pp. 241–63 in Justine Coupland (ed.) *Small Talk*. London: Longman.

Coates, Jennifer (2000b) ' "So I thought 'Bollocks to it' ": men, stories and masculinities', pp. 11–38 in Janet Holmes (ed.) *Gendered Speech in Social Context*. Wellington: Victoria University Press.

Connell, R. W. (1987) *Gender and Power*. Stanford, CA: Stanford University Press.

Connell, R. W. (1995) *Masculinities*. Cambridge: Polity Press.

Cronon, W. (1992) 'A place for stories: nature, history and narrative', *Journal of American History* 78(4), 1347–76.

Curry, Timothy (1991) 'Fraternal bonding in the locker room: a pro-feminist analysis of talk about competition and women', *Sociology of Sport Journal* 8, 119–35.

Davidoff, Leonora and Hall, Catherine (1982) *Family Fortunes: Men and Women of the English Middle Classes 1780–1850*. London: Hutchinson.

DeFrancisco, Victoria L. (1991) 'The sounds of silence: how men silence women in marital relations', *Discourse & Society* 2(4), 413–24.

De Klerk, Vivian (1997) 'The role of expletives in the construction of masculinity', pp.144–58 in Sally Johnson and Ulrike Hanna Meinhof (eds) *Language and Masculinity*. Oxford: Blackwell.

Derlega, V. J. and Berg, J. (eds) (1987) *Self-disclosure: Theory, Research and Therapy*. New York: Plenum.

Dunbar, Robin (1996) *Grooming, Gossip and the Evolution of Language*. London: Faber & Faber.

Duranti, Alessandro (1986) 'The audience as co-author: an introduction', *Text* 6(3), 239–47.

Eckert, Penelope (1993) 'Cooperative competition in adolescent "girl talk" ', pp. 32–61 in Deborah Tannen (ed.) *Gender and Conversational Interaction*. New York: Oxford University Press.

Eckert, Penelope and McConnell-Ginet, Sally (1992) 'Think practically and look locally: language and gender as community-based practice', *Annual Review of Anthropology* 21, 461–90.

Eder, Donna (1993) ' "Go get ya a french": romantic and sexual teasing among adolescent girls', pp. 17–31 in Deborah Tannen (ed.) *Gender and Conversational Interaction*. New York: Oxford University Press.

Edelsky, Carole (1993) 'Who's got the floor?', pp. 189–227 in Deborah Tannen (ed.) *Gender and Conversational Interaction*. New York: Oxford University Press.

Edley, Nigel and Wetherell, Margaret (1997) 'Jockeying for position: the construction of masculine identities', *Discourse & Society* 8(2), 203–17.

Falk, Jane (1980) 'The conversational duet', *Proceedings of the 6th Annual Meeting of the Berkeley Linguistics Society*, vol. 6, 507–14.

Frosh, Stephen, Phoenix, Ann and Pattman, Rob (2002) *Young Masculinities*. London: Palgrave.

Fuss, Diana (1989) *Essentially Speaking*. London: Routledge.

Galloway-Young, K. (1978) *Taleworlds and Storyrealms*. Lancaster: Kluwer Academic Publishers.

Bibliography

Georgakopoulou, Alexandra (1995) 'Women, men and conversational narrative performances: aspects of gender in Greek storytelling', *Anthropological Linguistics* 37(4), 460–86.

Gergen, Kenneth J. and Gergen, Mary M. (1988) 'Narrative and the self as relationship', *Advances in Experimental Social Psychology* 21, 17–56.

Giles, Howard and Smith, Philip (1979) 'Accommodation theory: optimal levels of convergence', pp. 45–65 in Howard Giles and Robert StClair (eds) *Language and Social Psychology*. Oxford: Blackwell.

Goffman, Erving (1971) *The Presentation of Self in Everyday Life*. Harmondsworth: Penguin.

Goodwin, Charles (1986) 'Audience diversity, participation and interpretation', *Text* 6(3), 283–316.

Goodwin, Marjorie Harness (1990) *He-Said-She-Said: Talk as Social Organisation among Black Children*. Bloomington: Indiana University Press.

Gottman, John M. and Levenson, Robert W. (1988) 'The social psychophysiology of marriage', pp. 182–200 in P. Noller and M. A. Fitzpatrick (eds) *Perspectives on Marital Interaction*. Clevedon: Multilingual Matters.

Gough, Brendan (1998) 'Men and the discursive reproduction of sexism: repertoires of difference and equality', *Feminism & Psychology* 8(1), 25–49.

Gough, Brendan and Edwards, Gareth (1998) 'The beer talking: four lads, a carry out and the reproduction of masculinities', *The Sociological Review*, August 1998, 409–35.

Grice, H. P. (1975) 'Logic and conversation', pp. 41–58 in P. Cole and J. Morgan (eds) *Speech Acts* (*Syntax and Semantics*, vol. 3). New York: Academic Press.

Haas, Adelaide (1978) 'Sex-associated features of spoken language by four-, eight- and twelve-year-old boys and girls'. Paper given at the 9th World Congress of Sociology, Uppsala, Sweden, 14–19 August.

Hall, Catherine (1990) 'Private persons versus public someones: class, gender and politics in England, 1780–1850', pp. 51–67 in T. Lovell (ed.) *British Feminist Thought*. Oxford: Blackwell.

Hall, Deanna and Langellier, Kristin (1988) 'Storytelling strategies in mother–daughter communication', pp. 107–26 in Barbara Bate and Anita Taylor (eds) *Women Communicating: Studies of Women's Talk*. Norwood, NJ: Ablex.

Hamilton, Jane (1999) *The Short History of a Prince*. Harmondsworth: Penguin.

Herek, G. M. (1987) 'On heterosexual masculinity: some psychical consequences of the social construction of gender and sexuality', pp. 68–82 in Michael S. Kimmel (ed.) *Changing Men: New Directions in Research on Men and Masculinity*. London: Sage.

Hill, C. T. and Stull, D. E. (1987) 'Gender and self-disclosure', pp. 81–100 in V. J. Derlega and J. Berg (eds) *Self-disclosure: Theory, Research and Therapy*. New York: Plenum.

Hollway, Wendy (1983) 'Heterosexual sex: power and desire for the other', pp. 124–40 in Sue Cartledge and Joanna Ryan (eds) *Sex and Love: New Thoughts on Old Contradictions*. London: Women's Press.

Holmes, Janet (1995) *Women, Men and Politeness*. London: Longman.

Holmes, Janet (1998) 'Why tell stories? Contrasting themes and identities in the narratives of Maori and Pakeha women and men', *Journal of Asian Pacific Communication* 8(1), 1–29.

Holmes, Janet (1999) 'Story-telling in New Zealand: women's and men's talk', pp. 263–93 in Ruth Wodak (ed.) *Gender and Discourse*. London: Sage.

Irwin, Anthea (2002) 'The construction of identity in adolescent talk'. Unpublished PhD thesis, University of Surrey, Roehampton.

Jackson, David (1990) *Unmasking Masculinity*. London: Unwin Hyman.

Jefferson, Gail (1978) 'Sequential aspects of storytelling in conversation', pp. 219–48 in J. Schenkein (ed.) *Studies in the Organisation of Conversational Interaction*. New York: Academic Press.

Johnson, Fern and Aries, Elizabeth (1983a) 'The talk of women friends', *Women's Studies International Forum* 6, 353–61.

Johnson, Fern and Aries, Elizabeth (1983b) 'Conversational patterns among same-sex pairs of late adolescent close friends', *Journal of Genetic Psychology* 142, 225–38.

Johnstone, Barbara (1990) *Stories, Community, and Place*. Bloomington: Indiana University Press.

Johnstone, Barbara (1993) 'Community and contest: Midwestern men and women creating their worlds in conversational storytelling', pp. 62–80 in Deborah Tannen (ed.) *Gender and Conversational Interaction*. Oxford: Oxford University Press.

Jukes, Adam (1993) *Why Men Hate Women*. London: Free Association Books.

Kaminer, Debra and Dixon, John (1995) 'The reproduction of masculinity: a discourse analysis of men's drinking talk', *South African Journal of Psychology* 25(3), 168–74.

Kemper, Theodore (1990) *Social Structure and Testosterone: Explorations of the Socio-bio-social Chain*. New Brunswick, NJ: Rutgers University Press.

Kerby, Anthony (1991) *Narrative and the Self*. Bloomington: Indiana University Press.

Kiesling, Scott Fabius (1998) 'Men's identities and sociolinguistic variation: the case of fraternity men', *Journal of Sociolinguistics* 2(1), 69–99.

Kimmel, Michael S. (1987) 'Rethinking "masculinity"', pp. 9–24 in Michael S. Kimmel (ed.) *Changing Men: New Directions in Research on Men and Masculinity*. London: Sage.

Kimmel, Michael S. (2000) *The Gendered Society*. Oxford: Oxford University Press.

Kirshenblatt-Gimblett, B. (1974) 'The concept and varieties of narrative performance in East European Jewish culture', pp. 283–308 in R. Bauman and J. Scherzer (eds) *Explorations in the Ethnography of Speaking*. New York: Cambridge University Press.

Kuiper, Koenraad (1991) 'Sporting formulae in New Zealand English: two models of male solidarity', pp. 200–9 in J. Cheshire (ed.) *English around the World*. Cambridge: Cambridge University Press.

Bibliography

Labov, William (1972a) *Language in the Inner City*. Philadelphia: University of Pennsylvania Press.

Labov, William (1972b) 'The transformation of experience in narrative syntax', pp. 354–96 of *Language in the Inner City*. Philadelphia: University of Pennsylvania Press.

Langellier, Kristin (1989) 'Personal narratives: perspectives on theory and research', *Text and Performance Quarterly* 9(4), 243–76.

Langellier, Kristin and Peterson, Eric (1992) 'Spinstorying: an analysis of women storytelling', pp. 157–80 in Elizabeth Fine and Jean Haskell Speer (eds) *Performance, Culture and Identity*. London: Praeger.

Laqueur, Thomas (1990) *Making Sex: Body and Gender from the Greeks to Freud*. Cambridge, MA: Harvard University Press.

Lieblich, Amia and Josselson, Ruthellen (eds) (1994) *Exploring Identity and Gender: The Narrative Study of Lives*, vol. 2. London: Sage.

Linde, Charlotte (1993) *Life Stories: The Creation of Coherence*. New York: Oxford University Press.

Linde, Charlotte (1996) 'Whose story is this? Point of view variation and group identity in oral narrative', pp. 333–45 in J. Arnold *et al.* (eds) *Sociolinguistic Variation: Data, Theory and Analysis* (Selected Papers from NWAV 23 at Stanford). Stanford, CA: CSLI Publications.

Livia, Anna and Hall, Kira (eds) (1997) *Queerly Phrased: Language, Gender and Sexuality*. New York: Oxford University Press.

Looser, Diana (1997) 'Bonds and barriers: language in a New Zealand prison', *The New Zealand English Journal* 11. Christchurch: Canterbury University Press.

Mandelbaum, Jennifer (1987) 'Couples sharing stories', *Communication Quarterly* 35(2), 144–70.

Maybin, Janet (1996) 'Story voices: the use of reported speech in 10–12 year olds' spontaneous narratives', *Current Issues in Language & Society* 3(1), 36–48.

Messner, Michael (1997) *Politics of Masculinities: Men in Movements*. London: Sage.

Miller, Peggy, Potts, Randolph, Fung, Heidi, Hoogstra, Lisa and Mintz, Judy (1990) 'Narrative practices and the social construction of self in childhood', *American Ethnologist* 17(2), 292–311.

Miller, Stuart (1983) *Men and Friendship*. San Leandro, CA: Gateway Books.

Milroy, Lesley (1987) *Observing and Analysing Natural Language*. Oxford: Blackwell.

Moore, Bruce (1993) *A Lexicon of Cadet Language*. Canberra: Australian National Dictionary Centre.

Morgan, David H. J. (1992) *Discovering Men*. London: Routledge.

Nelson, Marie Wilson (1998) 'Women's ways: interactive patterns in predominantly female research teams', pp. 354–72 in Jennifer Coates (ed.) *Language and Gender: A Reader*. Oxford: Blackwell.

O'Connor, Pat (1992) *Friendships between Women: A Critical Review*. London: Harvester Wheatsheaf.

Ochs, Elinor and Taylor, Carolyn (1992) 'Family narrative as political activity', *Discourse & Society* 3(3), 301–40.

Ochs, Elinor and Taylor, Carolyn (1995) 'The "father knows best" dynamic in dinnertime narratives', pp. 97–120 in Kira Hall and Mary Bucholtz (eds) *Gender Articulated*. London: Routledge.

Owen, Marion (1981) 'Conversational units and the use of "well"', pp. 99–116 in Paul Werth (ed.) *Conversation and Discourse*. London: Croom Helm.

Phillips, Jock (1996) *A Man's Country? The Image of the Pakeha Male – a History.* Auckland: Penguin.

Pilkington, Jane (1998) '"Don't try and make out that I'm nice": the different strategies women and men use when gossiping', pp. 254–69 in Jennifer Coates (ed.) *Language and Gender: A Reader.* Oxford: Blackwell.

Pleck, Joseph (1975) 'Man to man: is brotherhood possible?', in N. Glazer-Malbin (ed.) *Old Family, New Family.* New York: Van Nostrand.

Pleck, Joseph (1995) 'Men's power with women, other men, and society: a men's movement analysis', pp. 5–12 in M. S. Kimmel and M. A. Messner (eds) *Men's Lives* (3rd edn). Boston: Allyn & Bacon.

Polanyi, Livia (1979) 'So what's the point?', *Semiotica* 25(3/4), 207–41.

Polanyi, Livia (1982a) 'Literary complexity in everyday storytelling', pp. 155–70 in D. Tannen (ed.) *Spoken and Written Language: Exploring Orality and Literacy.* Norwood, NJ: Ablex.

Polanyi, Livia (1982b) 'The nature of meaning of stories in conversation', *Studies in 20th Century Literature* 6(1–2), 51–65.

Polanyi, Livia (1985) *Telling the American Story: A Structural and Cultural Analysis of Conversational Storytelling.* Norwood, NJ: Ablex.

Pomerantz, Anita (1984) 'Agreeing and disagreeing with assessments: some features of preferred/dispreferred turn shapes', pp. 57–101 in J. Atkinson and J. Heritage (eds) *Structures of Social Action: Studies in Conversation Analysis.* Cambridge: Cambridge University Press.

Pujolar i Cos, Joan (1997) 'Masculinities in a multilingual setting', pp. 86–106 in Sally Johnson and Ulrike Hanna Meinhof (eds) *Language and Masculinity.* Oxford: Blackwell.

Rampton, Ben (1995) *Crossing: Language and Ethnicity among Adolescents.* London: Longman.

Reid, Helen and Fine, Gary (1992) 'Self-disclosure in men's friendships', pp. 132–52 in Peter Nardi (ed.) *Men's Friendships.* London: Sage.

Rich, Adrienne (1980) 'Compulsory heterosexuality and lesbian existence', *Signs* 5, 631–60.

Riessman, Catherine K. (1993) *Narrative Analysis.* London: Sage.

Rogers, Annie G., Brown, Lyn Mikel and Tappan, Mark B. (1994) 'Interpreting ego loss in ego development in girls: regression or resistance?', pp. 1–36 in Amia Lieblich and Ruthellen Josselson (eds) *Exploring Identity and Gender: The Narrative Study of Lives.* London: Sage.

Bibliography

Roper, Michael and Tosh, John (1991) 'Introduction', pp. 1–19 in Michael Roper and John Tosh (eds) *Manful Assertions: Masculinities in Britain since 1800*. London: Routledge.

Ryave, Alan (1978) 'On the achievement of a series of stories', pp. 113–32 in J. Schenkein (ed.) *Studies in the Organisation of Conversational Interaction*. New York: Academic Press.

Sacks, Harvey (1995) *Lectures on Conversation* (vols 1 and 2). Edited by Gail Jefferson. Oxford: Blackwell.

Sacks, Harvey, Schegloff, Emanuel A. and Jefferson, Gail (1974) 'A simplest systematics for the organisation of turn-taking in conversation', *Language* 50, 696–735.

Sarbin, Theodore (ed.) (1986) *Narrative Psychology: The Storied Nature of Human Conduct*. New York: Praeger.

Schiffrin, Deborah (1996) 'Narrative as self-portrait: sociolinguistic constructions of identity', *Language in Society* 25(2), 167–204.

Segal, Lynne (1990) *Slow Motion: Changing Masculinities, Changing Men*. London: Virago.

Seidler, Victor (1989) *Rediscovering Masculinity: Reason, Language and Sexuality*. London: Routledge.

Sheldon, Amy (1992) 'Conflict talk: sociolinguistic challenges to self-assertion and how young girls meet them', *Merrill-Palmer Quarterly* 38(1), 95–117.

Shepherd, Jennifer (1997) 'Storytelling in conversational discourse: a collaborative model'. Unpublished PhD thesis, University of Birmingham.

Sherrod, Drury (1987) 'The bonds of men: problems and possibilities in close male relationships', pp. 213–39 in Harry Brod (ed.) *The Making of Masculinities*. Boston: Allen & Unwin.

Social Issues Research Centre (2001) 'Evolution, alienation and gossip – the role of mobile telecommunications in the 21st century'. BT Cellnet.

Talbot, Mary (1992) ' "I wish you'd stop interrupting me": interruptions and asymmetries in speaker-rights in equal encounters', *Journal of Pragmatics* 18, 451–66.

Tannen, Deborah (1984) *Conversational Style: Analysing Talk among Friends*. Norwood, NJ: Ablex.

Tannen, Deborah (1989) *Talking Voices: Repetition, Dialogue and Imagery in Conversational Discourse*. Cambridge: Cambridge University Press.

Thornborrow, Joanna (2000) 'Principal, plausibility and the historic present: the construction of conflicting accounts in public participation TV', *Language in Society* 29(3), 357–77.

Thorne, Barrie (1993) *Gender Play: Girls and Boys in School*. Buckingham: Open University Press.

Tolson, Andrew (1977) *The Limits of Masculinity*. London: Tavistock Publications.

Tomsen, Stephen (1997) 'A top night: social protest, masculinity and the culture of drinking violence', *British Journal of Criminology* 37(1), 90–102.

Toolan, Michael J. (1988) *Narrative: A Critical Linguistic Introduction*. London: Routledge.

Weedon, Chris (1987) *Feminist Practice and Poststructuralist Theory*. Oxford: Blackwell.

Wetherell, Margaret and Edley, Nigel (1999) 'Negotiating hegemonic masculinity: imaginary positions and psycho-discursive practices', *Feminism & Psychology* 9(3), 335–56.

Willott, Sara and Griffin, Christine (1997) '"Wham bam, am I a man?": unemployed men talk about masculinities', *Feminism & Psychology* 7(1), 107–28.

Wilson, John (1987) 'The sociolinguistic paradox: data as a methodological product', *Language and Communication* 7, 161–77.

Wilson, John (1989) *On the Boundaries of Conversation*. Oxford: Pergamon Press.

Winter, Michael F. and Robert, Ellen R. (1980) 'Male dominance, late capitalism, and the growth of instrumental reason', *Berkeley Journal of Sociology* 249–80.

Wolfson, Nessa (1981) 'Tense-switching in narrative', *Language and Style* 14(3), 226–31.

Wood, Julian (1984) 'Groping towards sexism: boys' sex talk', pp. 54–84 in Angela McRobbie and Mica Nava (eds) *Gender and Generation*. London: Macmillan.

Wood, Kathleen (1999) 'Coherent identities and heterosexist ideologies: deaf and hearing lesbian coming out stories', pp. 46–63 in Mary Bucholtz, A. C. Liang and Laurel Sutton (eds) *Reinventing Identities: The Gendered Self in Discourse*. New York: Oxford University Press.

Zimmerman, Don and West, Candace (1975) 'Sex roles, interruptions and silences in conversation', pp. 105–29 in Barrie Thorne and Nancy Henley (eds) *Language and Sex: Difference and Dominance*. Rowley, MA: Newbury House.

Index